Working With Families

Working With Families

Guidelines and Techniques

Second Edition

John T. Edwards, PhD

WILEY

John Wiley & Sons, Inc.

Published by John Wiley & Sons, Inc., Hoboken, New Jersey.
Published simultaneously in Canada.

For general information on our other products and services please contact our Customer Care Department within the U.S. at (800) 762-2974, outside the United States at (317) 572-3993 or fax (317) 572-4002.

Wiley also publishes its books in a variety of electronic formats. Some content that appears in print may not be available in electronic books. For more information about Wiley products, visit our website at www.wiley.com.

Library of Congress Cataloging-in-Publication Data:
Edwards, John T.
  Working with families : guidelines and techniques / John Edwards. — 2nd ed.
    p. cm.
  Includes bibliographical references and index.
  ISBN 978-0-470-89047-9 (pbk. : acid-free paper)
  ISBN 978-1-118-13880-9 (ebk)
  ISBN 978-1-118-13881-6 (ebk)
  ISBN 978-1-118-13879-3 (ebk)
  1. Family psychotherapy. 2. Counseling. 3. Marital psychotherapy. I. Title.
  RC488.5.E27 2012
  616.89′1562—dc23
                                                    2011016590

Printed in the United States of America
10 9 8 7 6 5 4

To Vishvamitra (Sid Jordan, PhD)

I honor the life you've led and your many gifts to me and others. Most of all, I honor you.

CONTENTS

Preface xi
Acknowledgments xiii

Chapter 1: Foundation Ideas 1
    Introduction 2
    Part 1: Concepts 3
        Learning Family Counseling 3
        Why Family Work? 4
        Assumptions of a Family Systems Model 5
        The Systems Orientation in Theory 6
        The Systems Orientation in Practice 7
        The Systems Orientation in Concepts 8
        Levels of Systems Interventions 9
        Cause and Effect in Systems 11
        The Systems-Oriented Program Assessment 12
        Code of Ethics 13
        Cultural Sensitivity 14
        Uses of Family Counseling 16
        Forms of Family Work 17
        Family Work in Different Settings 18
        Suggestions for Family Work in Different Settings 20
        Rationales for This Approach 22
        Bedrock Beliefs About Families 23
        A Theory of Change 24
        Children Raise Adults 25
        Neglected Relationships in Family Counseling 26
        Getting a Grip on the Obvious 27
        Experience Is Primary 28
        Too Many Variables 29
        Too-Brief Family Counseling 30
        Traveling Pairs of Concepts 31
        Research on Marital and Family Therapy 32
    Part 2: Procedures and Processes 37
        Recruiting Families for Counseling 37
        Conducting the Initial Family Interview 40
        Initial Interview Summary 42
        Tips for the First Family Interview 43
        Four Basic Tools for Family Counseling 44
        General Guidelines 46
        If the Presenting Problem Is a Child or Young Person 49
        If the Presenting Problem Is a Marital or Couples Issue 51
        General Clinical Suggestions 53
        Session-by-Session Guidelines 56
        Session Checklist for Family Counseling 57

Chapter 2: Special Situations 58
    Introduction 59
    Therapeutic Themes by Family Type (Child Identified Patient) 60
    Blended and Single-Parent Families 62
    Blended Families: Tips for Two Common Scenarios 64
    The Powerless Parent 65
    The Parental Mind-Set 66
    Parent-Child Enmeshment 67

''Split'' Parenting   68
Parental Denial   69
Difficult Parents   70
Child Diagnosis in Plain English   71
The Three Worlds of the Adolescent   73
Managing Adolescents in Family Sessions   74
Couples Work   75
Couples Counseling: Additional Tips   77
Closed Families   78
Friends as Family   79
Family Resistance   80

CHAPTER 3: COUNSELOR IDEAS   83
Introduction   84
Fear of Family Work   85
Inexperienced vs. Experienced Family Counselors   86
A Novice's First Family Interview   87
Counseling Style   89
Counselor Mistakes   92
Counselor Successes   93
Counselor Self-Disclosure   94
Induction Worksheet   95
Whose Family Stuff Is It?   96
Use of Self   97
Counselor Centrality   98
Colleague Consultation   99
Supervising Family Work 100
Review Lists for Family Counselors 101
Questions and Answers 105

CHAPTER 4: TECHNIQUES 106
Introduction 107
Alter Ego 108
Brief Network Intervention (BNI) 109
Chair Work 111
Circular Questions 112
Colleague Teamwork 113
Drawings 115
Family Mapping 117
Family Questions in Individual Counseling 119
Guardrail 120
The MIGS Sheet 121
New Talk 126
Paradox 127
Parent's Childhood 128
Reflecting Team 129
Reframing 130
Relabeling 133
Safe Rebellion 134
Sculpting and Movement 135
Sibling Talk 137
Strategic Child Assessment 138
Strategic Predictions 139
Toybox 140
Worried Child 141
Summary of Systemic Techniques 142

CHAPTER 5: MULTIPLE FAMILY GROUPS   143
    Introduction.   144
    Suggested Procedures for Multiple Family Groups.   145
    Family Recruitment for Multiple Family Groups   145
    Clinical Tips   146
    Therapeutic Activities   147

CHAPTER 6: WORKING WITH CHEMICAL DEPENDENCY IN FAMILIES   149
    Introduction.   150
    A Working Definition of Chemical Dependency   151
    Drugs of Abuse   152
    Chemical Dependency   153
    The Disease Concept   154
    Indirect Signs of Chemical Dependency   155
    Identification of Chemical Dependency in a Family   156
    Questions for Family Assessment of Chemical Dependency   156
    Treatment of Chemical Dependency   157
    Recovery   158
    Stages of Recovery   159
    Recovery Plan   160
    Families in Early Recovery   161
    Relapse   162
    Common Patterns in Chemically Dependent Families   163
    Two Parent—CD Parent   164
    Two-Parent—CD Adolescent   165
    ''Good'' Kid/''Bad'' Kid   166
    CD Single Parent   167
    Single-Parent—CD Adolescent   168
    The Golden Years Trap   169
    Adolescent Substance Abuse   171
    Adolescent Substance Use Checklist.   172
    Co-Dependency.   173
    Couples Work for Chemical Dependency   174
    Working With Chemical Dependency in Families: 21 Guidelines   176
    Family Counseling for Chemical Dependency: Summary   178

APPENDIX A: RESEARCH REFERENCES   179
APPENDIX B: PROBLEMS AND PAGE NUMBERS   182
GLOSSARY FOR FAMILY COUNSELING   183
RECOMMENDED READINGS   185
ABOUT THE AUTHOR   187
INDEX   189

PREFACE

This book is about applied family therapy. It is long on how-tos and short on theory and comes from my 30-plus years' experience as a practitioner and trainer in family therapy. I have field-tested virtually all the ideas and techniques in the book—many of which are original—and they rest on a systems-based foundation created by the Structural/Strategic schools of family therapy. All the ideas and techniques flow from the same theoretical foundation—a brief, systems-oriented, goal-directed, problem-solving approach to family counseling. I like this model because of its emphasis on results (rather than exploration) and practice (rather than theory) and because it has a time-proven track record in diverse settings with different problems and family types.

My intention is that both students and practicing therapists will find the book useful. Students should find a refreshing dose of practical knowledge in these pages to go with their voluminous dose of theory in their studies. Practicing therapists will find a wide assortment of interventions, ideas, procedures, and techniques to supplement their practice, something new to try when they are stalled in their therapeutic movement with a particular case. I have taught the contents of this book to many helping professionals in social work, mental health, substance abuse, education, child welfare, intensive in-home services, psychology, psychiatry, the ministry, hospitals, and private practice.

My suggestions to the reader for using the book, which grew from a series of handouts for my training workshops, are to browse through the book, reading here and there to get a feel for what it contains. Then use the contents as a guide for selecting topics that have relevance to the family work you are doing now or plan to do.

Brief and useful are the two criteria I used to include material in this book. Most of the content arose from experience in face-to-face encounters with families, so the book does not follow a neat beginning-middle-end format. In practice, experience and learning are not so easily organized in a linear fashion, nor are they readily categorized; they follow a more random path and have a variety of sources—family sessions, tapes of family sessions, discussions with colleagues, reading, workshop presentations (mine and others), and writing. Whatever their source, our experiences and learning must always, in my opinion, be grounded in actual encounters in the therapy room with families. It is only here that we can discover the value of what we know, or think we know.

The book is divided into six chapters:

Chapter 1—Foundation Ideas—discusses an assortment of useful ideas, procedures, and tips for any professional who does family work in any setting.

Chapter 2—Special Situations—addresses a variety of more specific conditions encountered by most counselors who work with families.

Chapter 3—Counselor Ideas—is an exploration in raising our awareness of ourselves as professionals and how the "use of self" is a critical—and easily overlooked—factor in therapeutic outcomes.

Chapter 4—Techniques—details some of the "tools of the trade," including several old standbys that have been in use by family counselors for years. The major portion of this section consists of techniques that I created to manage particular problems that kept coming up in my family cases. (Note: Techniques are in **_boldfaced italic_** in the text of the book. If you want to read about the technique, please look it up in the index.)

Chapter 5—Multiple Family Groups—is an introduction to a powerful group format of several families together who, with a therapist facilitator, learn from and support each other in the uphill climb toward family change. This group format, which is often referred to simply as MFG, includes the identified patients with their families.

Chapter 6—Working With Chemical Dependency in Families—provides foundation knowledge for the single most frequently encountered dysfunction in a general caseload of families. Substance abuse is often a ''hidden'' problem in distressed families and may not be part of the presenting problems. All family workers need to be alert for, and familiar with, this all-too-common disorder and its devastating impact on family life.

Appendix A is for the research-minded student or professional; it provides a current and comprehensive list of references for the research on marital and family therapy in the text. Appendix B matches presenting family problems with ideas and techniques presented in the book. This section should help to narrow your search for something useful for particular cases. The glossary defines some of the terms used in systems-based family therapy. (Incidentally, the terms ''family therapy,'' ''family counseling,'' and ''family work'' are used interchangeably throughout the text.)

And finally, the index is more helpful than the table of contents in terms of finding a specific topic or technique if you know the name of the item you're looking for.

Some families are difficult to help. Even relatively well-functioning families lie in wait for anyone who sails in, flying the banners of change. I hope you will use this book to search for a specific technique to try with a particular family or to browse for general ideas to supplement your own approach to family work. Whatever your purpose, I wish you and the families you serve a productive and enriching voyage.

About the Second Edition

The original edition of this book was self-published from 1993 to 2010. About every three years during that period, I added new material from my experiences teaching and conducting family therapy. In this second edition, I have written an introduction to each chapter, added new material, removed dated or otherwise not useful topics, added a comprehensive and current research section, and made editorial changes throughout.

My active training practice in family therapy constantly teaches me that busy counselors value brief and useful chunks of field-tested ideas and interventions rather than long narratives on particular topics. They want a manual of practical ideas and techniques, something they can apply immediately to their caseloads or to a particular family. Hopefully, this second edition satisfies that need.

ACKNOWLEDGMENTS

As in most enterprises, a completed project is a team effort. I am grateful to the hundreds of colleague trainees who over the years discovered with me how to approach the case in front of us and whose perceptions and insights always improved my own. A very partial list in this category would include Bev Kovach, Katherine Townsend, Larry Sharpe, Michael Budlong, Rob Young, Richard Martin, Michael McGuire, and Susan Mattox. I also want to acknowledge the invaluable guidance of Marquita Flemming, my Wiley editor, and Sherry Cormier, my developmental editor, who patiently guided me in the tedious process of making a book out of diverse ideas and experiences.

A special thanks also goes to Daphne S. Cain, PhD, LCSW, Chairperson, Department of Social Work, Louisiana State University, for her thorough work in assembling the latest research in family therapy. To Paul Nagy, Clinical Associate, Duke University Department of Psychiatry, a talented trainer and networker, I owe a debt of gratitude for putting the Wiley editors and myself in touch. And finally, my thanks go to my dear friend Mattie M. Decker, EdD, of Morehead State University, Morehead, Kentucky, who had the enthusiasm and patience to review parts of the manuscript and take the trouble to gently nudge me to consider certain ideas in another way.

It was never difficult to find someone who knew as much or more than I did about working with families. To the many unnamed sources in books, articles, workshop presentations, video sessions with families, and conversations about the topic, I offer my appreciation.

CHAPTER 1
FOUNDATION IDEAS

Introduction

This chapter presents some of the foundation ideas upon which the systems approach rests. It is divided into two parts: Part 1 is **Concepts** and Part 2 is **Procedures and Processes.** It is a potpourri of theory and guidelines, with a heavy sprinkling of practical tips and suggestions.

I like to think that theory develops as much from the feet up as it does from the head down. Theory and practice is a two-way exchange: theory provides a framework for thinking, a direction to go and what to look for, while face-to-face experience with families builds up our own personal knowledge about what works and what doesn't. Theoretical constructs are the most helpful in the early stages of learning family work, a period when we need guidance. Over time, however, our practice experience becomes primary and is likely to guide our actions more than textbook theory.

I've always believed that it is the application of our ideas that determines our effectiveness in helping families through their difficult periods. What we know—our body of knowledge, theoretical and otherwise—does not help families. The most knowledgeable person on the methods and theory of all the schools of family therapy will not necessarily be an effective family therapist. How the knowledge is *applied* in face-to-face interactions with families is the critical test.

The content described in this section gives us a place to start—how to convene a family for counseling and have an organized first session, the systems orientation, the assumptions and rationales behind the systems approach, various uses of family work, and a few guiding suggestions and tips about how to apply these ideas in interactions with families. Other ideas and issues in this section are included because they need a prominent place in our thinking about family counseling. Included in this category are ethics and cultural sensitivity, both of which can be overlooked in the myriad details of managing a particular case. Recent research on family therapy is presented for students and professionals who want to dig deeper into the empirical and evidenced-based underpinnings of the family approach to helping.

My suggestion to the reader is to peruse these foundation ideas to see which of them might appeal to you. Then read these topics more thoroughly. The next step is to try them out in family sessions. Some ideas may be selected and become part of your ongoing work while others will simply fade out. Applying them in your practice makes this selection possible.

Part 1: Concepts
Learning Family Counseling

In my training and supervision with colleagues, the most frequent question I am asked is, "What do I do with *this* family?" It's a good and important question, and I try to give my best suggestions. It conceals, however, an even more important question: "How do I acquire the knowledge and skills to do counseling with *any* family? I wish my colleagues would ask this second question more often.

1. Why should I learn to do counseling with families?

    Because significant human relationships are a central part of most people's problems. Our longing for love, our hopes, frustrations, sense of security, fears, and happiness are closely linked to our relationships with our families and significant others.

2. What should I do to learn family counseling?

    Get supervision from a colleague who is more experienced in family work, use video- or audiotaped sessions of yourself, watch other counselors do it, go to workshops, get lots of experience working with families, and find a colleague with whom you can process your sessions. At appropriate times, share with your colleagues what you are learning.

Source: *DeskGallery Mega-Bundle*, Copyright 1995 by Dover Publications, Inc. Used with permission.

3. How long does it take to learn?

    The learning never stops. To start, you need a setting in which you can acquire experience. You can expect one to two years of practice before you begin to feel competent doing this type of counseling. As a foundation, you need 50–100 hours of supervised experience with families, 20–30 hours of watching a more experienced counselor do his or her thing with families, and 4–6 days of workshop training. Read at least three books on the subject.

4. What do I read?

    That depends on what model of family counseling you want to learn. I started with the Structural-Strategic model, which gave me the foundation concepts and skills to learn on my own. I read *Family Therapy Techniques* by Minuchin and Fishman and *Foundations of Family Therapy* by Lynn Hoffman and studied *Problem Solving Therapy* and *Leaving Home* by Jay Haley (see Recommended Readings at the end of this book) plus many articles and handouts.

5. What is some basic information I need to know before starting?

    How to view a family as a system, how to get the family members to come for a meeting, how to conduct a first interview with them, and how to initiate family change while resolving the presenting problem. You can get the foundation knowledge from this book.

6. Should I choose parts from various approaches and put them together?

    Trying to integrate different approaches too early in your learning can create confusion and result in mishmash, scattered therapy. It's like a mechanic taking parts from different automobile models and putting them together to make one car. The thing will run poorly, if at all. Each model has components designed to function together. If you become eclectic too early, taking a little from each "school" of family therapy, you will not learn one model well enough to understand it. Stick with one model until you know how its rationale, procedures, and techniques form a unified whole, until you learn its integrity. Then you can select pieces from other approaches and make informed decisions about how they fit into the one you have learned. With experience, you can determine an approach that works well for you. Develop your own model.

Why Family Work?

I suspect that most professionals who work conjointly with families have their list of reasons for choosing this therapeutic mode. Here is my list.

1. With a symptomatic member (the "identified patient"), everyone in the family is affected. All must accommodate to the problem of one member, whether that member is a child or adult. If the problem is long-standing, the members can develop habitual and unhealthy ways of responding to the problem, causing the problem to intensify, leading to more family dysfunction.*

2. By the time a family reaches the treatment stage, the whole family has been emotionally damaged by the ordeal. All members need support, validation, and a new look at the problem on a family level.

3. How the family members react to the symptomatic member can determine whether the symptoms get worse, stay the same, or get better. In one sense, the family is part of the treatment team for the identified patient.

4. The family's reaction to the problem could be helping to maintain it. This phenomenon, known as "enabling," is the family's unwitting protection of a member from the consequences of his or her behavior. It was brought into focus and named by counselors working with chemically dependent families, but it also happens with problems other than substance abuse. A teenager's irresponsible behavior at home and at school, for example, can be enabled by parents who react to it ineffectively.

5. Family work helps the family view the problem in a different way. The all-important mind-set toward the symptomatic member, or toward the nature of the problem, can be altered with exploration and understanding. A different mind-set, in itself, can lead to family change.

6. Family counseling can have prevention benefits. If current problems are managed more effectively, it can prevent other problems from cropping up in the future. Or if they do appear, the family in counseling has learned better coping strategies to deal with them.

7. Paradoxically, when symptoms subside, the family needs to learn how to live without the problems. Removal of the problems may leave a void to be filled since the symptoms could be serving an important function in the family.

8. Having the family meet together around a problem can be a new and unbalancing experience in itself. Counseling provides a structure for the family to sit down and focus, something they are not always able to do at home. Once they cross the threshold into "treatment," family members cannot deal with their problem in quite the same way. Examples: the "family secret" is out; shame and guilt may diminish; new understanding points to new behaviors.

---

* **dysfunctional:** This is an often-misused word as it applies to families. It doesn't mean "not functional"; it means impaired, incomplete, or painful functioning, but functioning nonetheless. The confusion lies in the prefix "dys-," meaning "bad, ill, or difficult," which sounds identical to "dis-," meaning "not."

Assumptions of a Family Systems Model

The systemic approaches to family counseling in this book rest on these assumptions.

1. Individual problems express themselves in the person's family and social relationships, which, in turn, make the individual's problems better or worse. Most problems are the individual's attempt to adapt to his or her social world and are expressed in relationships with other people.

2. A family is an interacting system.
   a. Family members are *inter*dependent in their behavior. What one member does depends on what others do. Members react as much as they act.
   b. Cause and effect are circular: person A acts; person B responds, which affects A's next move and B's next response, etc. More than two people can be involved in repetitive patterns.
   c. To some degree, what happens within an individual or in part of a family affects the whole family.
   d. A family household is part of a larger system: extended family, friends, work, school, church, neighborhood, community, culture.

3. A well-functioning family has a structure in place, a hierarchy. The parenting adults have more power, influence, and responsibility than the children; older children have more influence than younger children. Different degrees of closeness and conflict exist between different members.

4. The *family* is the unit of change: family relationships, patterns, and structure are the primary focus. The feelings and behavior of each individual are important to the degree they affect family functioning. Family functioning, in turn, affects the way individuals feel and behave.

5. Brief interventions (5–10 contacts) are enough to begin a positive change process. Additional sessions may occur weeks or months later if the need arises.

The Systems Orientation in Theory

Source: *DeskGallery Mega-Bundle,* Copyright 1995 by Dover Publications, Inc. Used with permission.

Families are complex, and to work with them requires an organizing orientation. The systems orientation is the most universally accepted framework.

A system is a group of elements that interact to form a unified whole. Examples of systems include a tree, an automobile, a nation, a family. In each of these systems, the parts interact in ways that maintain an integrity and balance. The actions of one part affect the actions of the other parts, which, in turn, may change the first part; the components of a system are *inter*dependent. In families, you can see members reacting to each other in this circular, interdependent fashion, as in the following:

1. The more a parent questions the teenager about his whereabouts and activities, the briefer and less informative the teenager becomes, which prompts more questions, etc.

2. To the degree the father is strict with the daughter, the mother protects her.

3. To the extent the grandmother spoils the grandchildren, the mother becomes more accommodating with them in order to win back their affections. The father reacts with more authority toward the children, displacing onto them his anger at the permissiveness of his wife and mother-in-law.

Families have the characteristics of social systems, including

*   **a structure and hierarchy.** Different roles are defined for different members, and power is not distributed evenly.

*   **powerful rules of conduct,** many of which are unspoken and unacknowledged.

*   **a set of politics.** Particular members are closer to some members than to others; two members will support each other against a third; one member may temporarily defer to another out of self-interest. The politics may change, depending on the situation.

*   **habitual patterns.** The content of the interaction between members changes, but *how* they deal with the content tends to be repetitive.

*   **a history.** Anyone who becomes involved in a family steps into its history.

*   **influences from the outside**—from the extended family, from the neighborhood, from the work and school community, from the environment.

*   **a tendency to resist change.** A family, like an individual, has a sense of self and will resist a challenge to its self-definition.

The systems-oriented counselor will

1. Treat the *family*, rather than individuals, as the primary unit of change. Individual change is assumed to be created within relationships in the family. ***Mapping*** is a technique that brings family relationships into focus.

2. Use a broad definition of ''family'' to include anyone who may be enabling the problem to continue or who may be a resource for solving it.

3. Be aware that change in one relationship may produce change in another. When the parents begin to work more effectively together, the siblings may get along better.

4. Take a wide-angled view of the physical and social context of the problem—the home, extended family, neighborhood, community, and culture. A systems orientation urges the practitioner toward a broad network focus.

The Systems Orientation in Practice

The counselor works more with the reciprocal relationships between the family members than with the individual dynamics of each member. Even while talking to individual members, the systems counselor is exploring family patterns and repetitive sequences of actions and reactions between members. The family functioning is the target for change.

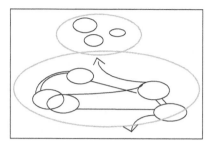

The following examples—which contrast the individual and systems orientations—assume a teenage son is the identified patient; his mother calls for an appointment. Also in the home are father and sister.

Individual Orientation	Systems Orientation
The Counselor:	The Counselor:
Invites the son and mother in for counseling.	Invites everyone living in the home.
Stays central—the "switchboard" for communication in the room.	Is sometimes central but also encourages members to talk to each other.
(To mother): "How do you feel when your son does that?"	"How do you and your husband react together when your son does that?"
Elicits feelings from a member while the family listens.	Does this but also gently directs the talking member to "tell him/her how you feel."
Focuses on individual members, one at a time.	Comments on relationships between members.
Attends only to the person speaking.	Notices all members when one is speaking.
Sees a talkative, dominant wife and a silent husband.	Sees a couple who has co-created a pattern where she talks and acts more than he does.
Assumes that the four people present are the only players in the drama.	Inquires about others who may play a role in maintaining (and solving) the problem.

The systems-oriented counselor is the manager and director of the session—sometimes focusing on individuals, sometimes spotlighting the interaction between two or more members, sometimes stepping back to see the family as a whole. To understand the family dance, the counselor is working with sets of relationships, not individuals acting independently.

Other examples of systemic questions and comments by the counselor:

- To father, while mother and son are talking: "Where are you in this conversation?"
- (To son): "I notice that when you are silent, you may be sending a message to your parents. Could you find out what message they are getting?"
- (To daughter): "How does your mother react when your father and brother have a disagreement?"
- (To mother and father): "Each time the two of you disagree, your daughter interrupts your conversation. Could you find out from her what that's about?"
- "Who outside the home is concerned about the problem?"

Learning to work interactionally and systemically takes some adjustment, since most counselor education and training in graduate school is individually oriented.

The Systems Orientation in Concepts

The person who said, "There's nothing so practical as a good theory" must have been thinking about systems theory. This orientation to family work certainly has practical benefits.

An **Organizing Concept**—Any system, social or biological, consists of various elements and the way they function together. The four characteristics of a system are

1. **Organization:** Elements have specified functions to serve the whole.
2. **Interaction:** The elements act on each other, reciprocally.
3. **Interdependence:** Each element changes, and is changed by, the other elements.
4. **Stability:** A system adjusts to maintain itself over time.

Understanding—Systems thinking aids our understanding of why people act the way they do; it's a good explanatory model. Example: Taken out of the family context, a young person's self-defeating behaviors or low self-esteem make no sense, but they might make sense when seen in the family environment.

Resistance—Systems thinking helps us understand resistance and denial and therefore tolerate them better. Resistance and denial is a system's normal, natural tendency toward stability and survival. Like any other system, a family resists change, even positive change.

Blame—Thinking systemically erases the notion of blame (at least intellectually). Example: Mother is too strict with the child because the father is too lenient, but father is too lenient because mother is too strict. Who is to blame? (There are, however, individual strengths and weaknesses in parenting.)

Interdependence—Thinking systemically reminds us that change in one part of the system affects other parts. Example: When the conflict between father and his daughter eases, the relationship between the mother and son improves.

Complementarity—Systems work teaches the counselor to think in self-perpetuating and overlapping circles. Complementarity is expressed by ''to the degree'' statements. Examples: To the degree he pursues, she distances; to the degree the son is aggressive, the parents retreat; to the degree that mother and son are close, father and son are distant.

Context—Systems thinking reminds us to place problem behavior in a broader context (family, extended family, friends, neighborhood, culture, other professionals). An individual and a family are only subsets of a larger context.

Note: Be patient with yourself. Systems thinking is awkward at first. In our American culture, the perspective on human behavior is individually oriented. We understand human activity more in terms of what's inside the individual person—self-determination, free will, personal responsibility, accountability, etc.—rather than in terms of the interaction with the social and physical environment.

Levels of Systems Interventions

Here is a way to conceptualize systems interventions. Levels 1–5 define the scope of our interventions in a client's "people world." Level 1 is the most restricted intervention, and Level 5 is the broadest. Each level incorporates the levels below it: If we are working on Level 3, we're also working on Levels 1 and 2.

Explanation

Most clients (child or adult) have connections to significant others who influence, and are influenced by, the client (Figure 1.1). These could be mother of the client, father, grandparents, siblings, spouse, children, friends, aunts, uncles, teachers, co-workers, dating relationships, etc. The systems orientation urges us to consider these people in our view of the client's world, even though all of them will seldom be involved in counseling sessions together.

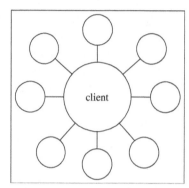

Figure 1.1   Significant Others

The significant others surrounding the client have relationships with *each other* (Figure 1.2), which can also influence and be influenced by their relationship with the client. The mother-father relationship, for example, influences how the child client is parented. For an adult client, conflict between his or her spouse and family of origin can affect the client's marriage.

If we are working exclusively with the individual client, we are working on Level 1. If we are working with the client plus his or her relationships with one or more significant others, we are on Level 2. If we are working with the client, his or her primary relationships, plus the relationships *between* the primary relationships (mother/father relationship with a child, for example), we are on Level 3.

The "people world" of the client doesn't stop there, however. The intimate social group is embedded in a larger system—neighborhood, school, church, community, courts, agencies, etc.—and is being affected by these outsiders (Figure 1.3). If we are working with the influences these outsiders have with the intimate social group, we are working on Level 4; and, as before, if we are considering the relationship *between* the outside people or agencies, we are on Level 5.

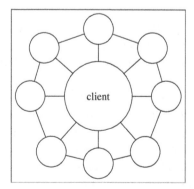

Figure 1.2   Relationships Between Significant Others

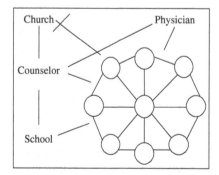

Figure 1.3   Outside Influences

Tanya's Case

Tanya, a 22-year-old single female, presents with depression. She dropped out of college in another state and is now living with her mother, grandmother, and a teenage brother and sister while attending the local community college. She has a steady boyfriend (grandmother doesn't approve of him, but mother does), and they have talked about marriage. She also has a close girlfriend, attends church with her family, and has been strongly influenced by one of her teachers at the community college, who is urging her toward a career in practical nursing. This client is conflicted about her decisions on marriage, her career, and living at home (a busy, argumentative place at times).

How can we characterize this young woman's depression? Is it mostly a reaction to the circumstances in her life, or does it have an organic basis? In this case, it seems reasonable to rule out the organicity (no prior history, no family history). To help her, we need to consider her current life circumstances as the major contributors to her depression: her living arrangements, career decisions, marriage decisions, and how her relationships with others affect and are affected by these decisions.

Some of the work with this client could be individual counseling, offering her a private, impartial sounding board for the changes she needs to make. But at some point, I would want the other people in her life to be a part of the work, since they affect her decisions and are affected by them. Certainly the family who lives in her home and the relationships they have with each other are affected by her depression and are also affected by whether or not she marries and leaves home. I would want to have these people in at least one session to build my own picture of Tanya's family relationships. I could also talk with Tanya about inviting her boyfriend to a session in order to explore that relationship. Her best friend, who is probably her close confidante, may be included in a session or invited just with Tanya. I would also arrange an appointment with a physician to talk about the temporary use of antidepressants. Tanya would be seeing both myself and the physician, requiring us to coordinate and communicate.

In Tanya's case, I have incorporated all five systems levels:

Level 1:   Individual counseling with Tanya.

Level 2:   Tanya's relationships with several other people in her life, especially her mother, boyfriend, and best friend.

Level 3:   The relationships *between* some of these people in her life (mother and grandmother, mother and boyfriend, for example).

Level 4:   I've considered the influences coming from outside the intimate group (teacher at school, church, counselor, physician).

Level 5:   I've considered the relationships *between* the professional "outsiders" (me and the physician, for example).

Most agency professionals are content to stay on Level 1 for adults and Levels 1 and 2 for children. Aligning closely with the medical model, these counselors prefer to focus on the individual patient. This can provide relief, support during crises, new insights for the client, and even new behaviors. For the most part, individual counseling is good.

In many cases, especially with children, I wonder if it's good enough. The best we can do one-on-one for a symptomatic child is to provide nurturance and guidance and sometimes therapeutic drugs. But if the child goes back to a home filled with anxiety, violence, insecurity, and inadequate parental supervision, his or her symptoms will persist and frequently get worse with age. These all-important home conditions are under the control of the adults and parents, not the child client.

To understand a case (adult or child identified patient), I rarely drop below Level 3.

Cause and Effect in Systems

Causation is a tricky subject, even in the physical sciences, where conditions can be carefully measured and controlled. In the social sciences, with minimal control and precision, causation is so complex that sorting out precise cause and effect can turn into theoretical, almost metaphysical, mumbo jumbo. I just try to remember three points.

Point 1. Counselors are not held to the scientific standards distinguishing correlation from causation.

I have a working definition of causality: If A, then B; if not A, then not B; therefore A is the cause of B. I know—this is correlation, not causation. But they often look the same. The substance abuse of a single mother, for example, may not *cause* the abuse and neglect of her children. Rather, the mother's absence; inadequate food, clothing, and shelter; money and legal problems; inconsistency; domestic violence, etc., are the direct causes of the abuse and neglect. If the substance use was removed, however, these problems could be much less serious and may not lead to harm to the children. From my practical, unscientific viewpoint, the substance addiction is a cause of the abuse and neglect.

Point 2. An outcome usually has multiple causes, acting together or in sequence. As counselors, we don't have to help our clients change all the causes for the problem to change or disappear.

To illustrate this at workshops, I hold a pencil over a chair and let it go. The pencil drops to the chair seat. I ask, ''What caused the pencil to hit the chair?'' ''Gravity'' is the usual first response from the audience, but then two more causes pop up: ''Because you let it go'' and ''Because you were holding it over the chair.'' I agree with their answers and make the point that it took *all three* causes to produce the result. If any one of the causes was eliminated, that specific outcome would not have occurred.

Point 3. In human interaction, cause and effect are circular, not linear.

Systems thinking assumes that the cause-effect cycle is circular: He does something, she yells at him, he then becomes quiet, she feels guilty, he acts hurt, she apologizes, he accepts her apology, she feels better, and he feels better—so much better that he might try the ''something'' again later, and the cycle repeats. In this sequence, an action caused a reaction, which changed the next action, causing another reaction, and so on, in a circular fashion. The acts in the chain are dynamically linked and interdependent; each is a cause *and* a result. A similar thing happens within an individual: Does the person's emotional state (depression, anxiety, etc.) cause the drug abuse, or does the drug abuse cause the emotional state? It's best to assume it's both.

The Thing in the Bushes

We see the bushes rustling but can't get a clear picture of what's causing the stir. The amorphous creature stays just beyond our clear view, and even when it's finally spotted, different viewers describe it differently, depending on their perspective. I usually handle the thing in the bushes by avoiding the word ''cause'' altogether and by asking, ''What is happening in this family that results in this problem?'' *Something* is feeding the problem. What we're liable to spot in those rustling bushes is not one entity but a gaggle of the fluffy little things.

Source: *DeskGallery Mega-Bundle*, Copyright 1995 by Dover Publications, Inc. Used with permission.

The Systems-Oriented Program Assessment

The systems orientation can be integrated into any program that offers human services. Here are a few of the characteristics of the ideal systems-oriented helping agency (the "Program"). If you want a rough gauge of the degree of systems orientation of your agency, circle a number for each statement and put a total score at the bottom. (In my opinion, a score above 20 indicates a systems-oriented program.)

	Rarely	Some	Often
1. The Program knows that real progress for their clients occurs in the client's social community, work, school, and home life, not in an agency. The Program's role is to help the client function better within the real-life context of his or her problems.	1	2	3
2. The Program has flexible hours for the staff and stays open in the evenings at least twice a week to accommodate working people and families.	1	2	3
3. Where appropriate, the client's family and significant others are invited with the client to the intake interview, or at least to the second session. Families are not just an afterthought, brought in later to give information about the individual client.	1	2	3
4. The Program has working connections with other helping agencies, groups, and activities in the community and refers clients to them when appropriate. The Program sees itself as part of a larger helping network.	1	2	3
5. The clinical staff members of the Program do more together than just discuss clients at case conferences. They also occasionally sit in on each other's sessions for a second opinion, video- and audiotape sessions for use at staff conferences and training, and occasionally observe each other from behind a one-way mirror. They work as a team.	1	2	3
6. The Program learns how to get around the individualistic, medical model to how sessions are counted for insurance, payment, and data purposes.	1	2	3
7. The Program is not afraid to call a meeting of everyone involved—family, extended family, and relevant staff from its own and other agencies—to identify and solve problems preventing real progress in the case (see **Brief Network Intervention**). The Program knows that helping systems can be just as stuck as client systems.	1	2	3
8. The Program opens its doors to other professionals and offers training in the specifics of Program design, systems-based clinical skills, and innovative management ideas.	1	2	3
9. The Program contributes to community awareness and education in its area of expertise through presentations and workshops.	1	2	3

Code of Ethics

The American Association for Marriage and Family Therapy (aamft.org) sets the ethical standards for family professionals. The current Code of Ethics (July 2001) is published by AAMFT, 112 South Alfred St., Alexandria, VA 22314. The code contains 67 statements of ethical conduct, listed under 8 principles. Only the principles are listed here, but the entire code should be reviewed annually by professionals and their supervisors who work with couples and families.

I. Responsibility to Clients

Marriage and family therapists advance the welfare of families and individuals. They respect the rights of those persons seeking their assistance and make reasonable efforts to ensure that their services are used appropriately.

II. Confidentiality

Marriage and family therapists have unique confidentiality concerns because the client in a therapeutic relationship may be more than one person. Therapists respect and guard the confidences of each individual client.

III. Professional Competence and Integrity

Marriage and family therapists maintain high standards of professional competence and integrity.

IV. Responsibility to Students and Supervisees

Marriage and family therapists do not exploit the trust and dependency of students and supervisees.

V. Responsibility to Research Participants

Investigators respect the dignity and protect the welfare of research participants and are aware of applicable laws and regulations and professional standards governing the conduct of research.

VI. Responsibility to the Profession

Marriage and family therapists respect the rights and responsibilities of professional colleagues and participate in activities that advance the goals of the profession.

VII. Financial Arrangements

Marriage and family therapists make financial arrangements with client, third-party payors, and supervisees that are reasonably understandable and conform to accepted professional practices.

VIII. Advertising

Marriage and family therapists engage in appropriate informational activities, including those that enable the public, referral sources, or others to choose professional services on an informed basis.

Cultural Sensitivity

In one sense, every family is a different culture, with its own worldview, values, rituals, organization, and ways of conducting its business. With every family, counselors are like anthropologists, sitting in the midst of a new culture to learn what it is like.

Culture includes so many characteristics that classifying families by cultural variables is a form of broad stereotyping and should be accompanied by all the caution this implies. In this respect, *all* family counseling is multicultural—every family has identification with some aspects of culture.

Hays (2001) has suggested the acronym ADDRESSING to remind us of the many variables that compose cultural diversity:

Source: *DeskGallery Image Catalog*,
Copyright 1994 by Dover Publications,
Inc. Used with permission.

Age and generational influences
Developmental and acquired
Disabilities
Religious and spiritual orientation
Ethnicity
Socioeconomic status
Sexual orientation
Indigenous heritage
National origin
Gender

Some of these cultural characteristics may present challenges for counselors. The following discussion suggests ways to manage cultural diversity issues in counseling.

Approaching Cultural Diversity

1. When the counselor is culturally or ethnically different from the family, in most cases, an acknowledgment by the counselor of this difference conveys cultural sensitivity and is appropriate in the first or second session. For example, when I, a white person, work with a non-white family, at some point early on I will say something like, "I notice that we represent different ethnic backgrounds. I'm wondering if there is anything you want to tell me that would help me understand your family better."

2. If appropriate, we can make our cultural assumptions explicit and check them out. For example, with a Latino family, I might say, "I am told that in many families from your ethnic origin, the father has the last word. Does it work that way in your family, or does it work some other way." This fairly provocative question is one that not only reveals information about the family but also conveys the counselor's sensitivity to important cultural details.

3. We need to keep in mind the important differences between families with the same or similar cultural influences. For example, it is easy (but incorrect) to assume that working with all Vietnamese families will be the same. While I may see two Vietnamese families in the same day who live in the same geographic region, there are likely to be some important differences between the two families simply because of varying acculturation levels and the unique personalities of the family members. Moreover, it can be stereotypical and misleading to assume that what I know about Asian-American families automatically applies. Not all Vietnamese families are alike, and a cultural description of "Asian families" may or may not apply to the family in front of me.

4. As stereotypes go, this one holds up well concerning role differences of parents in families of any ethnic origin: Fathers have a ''special authority'' with the children, and mothers have a ''special knowledge.'' This stereotype is so universal and generally acceptable, I can even use the phrases with parents at appropriate times. If, for example, I want to include the father more in conversations in the session, I could say to him, ''You have a special authority with your children. What do you think about this?'' Or to the mother, ''With your special knowledge of your child, what do you see?''

5. If English is not the first language of the parents, and the counselor does not speak their native language, I favor using a translator. This is preferable to putting the children in the ''translator'' role, thereby reversing the hierarchy and possibly demeaning the parents in front of their children.

~~~~

At times, dimensions of cultural diversity may challenge counselors' worldviews and values. For example, some counselors may feel uncomfortable working with a family of a different race, ethnic background, or socioeconomic level. Other counselors may feel uneasy with families who have very different religious beliefs from them or who are much younger or older in age. Still other counselors may be challenged in working with families with two lesbian or two gay parents. Some of this discomfort may be from lack of experience, some from differences in deep-seated beliefs and attitudes. None of us will see clients exactly like ourselves. When we commit to being counselors, we also commit to working with clients who represent many different groups, lifestyles, and values. We also commit to being respectful of diversity and of being as nonjudgmental and accepting of clients as possible, regardless of our own backgrounds. Fortunately, in most instances, our training enables us to be accepting of individual differences.

Occasionally, however, counselors find themselves at continuing odds with the worldviews and lifestyles of a particular family. Often, clients are able to sense this judgment from the counselor; family members could feel more marginalized than they did prior to entering the counseling relationship. When this happens, we are presented with a dilemma: refusing to work with a family because of cultural differences can be harmful to the family, yet to continue to see a family in an atmosphere that lacks acceptance can also be harmful.

In these instances, we turn initially to our supervisors and colleagues, seeking consultation surrounding the obstacles in our path so that more damage to the family does not result. To complicate matters, however, our personal blind spots in the area of cultural diversity may prevent us from being aware of our prejudice or bias. This requires that supervisors be vigilant to the warning signs of cultural friction: the counselor's uncharacteristic low interest in the case, humorous references to the clients' behavior and cultural values, body language (especially facial) when talking about the case, and more than usual frustration with the client or family's unwillingness to change. In many cases, consultation and supervision will increase our self-awareness and enable us to work more effectively with the family. If we continue to have differences with a family such that rapport and joining are impeded, referral to another counselor or bringing in one's supervisor or colleague for one or more sessions is appropriate.

In all such cases, the counselor has an opportunity for growth and new learning and may emerge from the episode with increased self-awareness and a little more wisdom.

Uses of Family Counseling

Family counseling is well suited to the trend toward time-limited, more effective therapies. It is suitable for a wide variety of family, couples, and individual problems. This model is a brief, goal-directed, problem-solving approach with a systems orientation.

- **Brief:** This model is designed to accomplish worthwhile goals in 5–10 one-hour sessions with the family. More sessions may add effectiveness to the treatment.
- **Goal-Directed:** The counselor and family set goals together, usually arising from the presenting problems.
- **Problem-Solving:** This approach helps family members solve their current problems and gives them tools for continued improvement, especially with communication, closeness-distance, and parental management of the family. It is not an in-depth, insight-oriented model.
- **Systems Orientation:** Each of us has an intimate social group that affects, and is affected by, our behavior and mental health. The family-as-system assumes that family members affect each other interdependently, in a circular, repetitive pattern, sometimes leading to symptoms for one or more members. The systems approach also casts a broad net, looking at how the family interacts with its social, cultural, and physical surroundings.

Family counseling can be used

1. As the main therapy. Everyone living in the home, including the identified patient, is seen every session. Generally, family counseling requires fewer sessions than individual therapy.
2. As a supplement to individual therapy, to gain information about the client's family situation and symptoms.
3. During a client crisis or relapse. As treatment becomes more short term, families take on more responsibility for crisis management and caretaking.
4. During a *family* crisis that affects a client's progress.
5. To prevent a client crisis. This is accomplished through the ***Brief Network Intervention*** technique, which convenes the family members and others in a client's life (including professionals) to prevent a particular crisis from developing.
6. To avoid or shorten inpatient treatment or to help the family manage during and after hospitalization.

Treatment recommendations

1. If the client is a child or adolescent, family work is the treatment of choice.
2. If the client is an adult with marital or partner issues, most sessions should be with the couple together.
3. If the individual client is an adult who has relationship problems with parents, other family members, a friend, or a lover, at least one or two sessions should include these people. Relationships are easier to understand when they are observed firsthand by the counselor.

Forms of Family Work

Family work can be used in a variety of forms. The guidelines and techniques in this book will be helpful regardless of the setting or the type of family work you practice.

Couples and Family Therapy

Family therapy consists of face-to-face meetings with families, or portions of families, for the purpose of resolving problems brought to the therapist. It can take different forms, depending on the practice setting in which it is done and the theoretical orientation of the practitioner. The six major schools of family therapy currently practiced are Behavioral, Structural, Strategic, Communications, Psychoanalytic, and Experiential. Therapy meetings usually last about an hour, occur weekly, and span from a few sessions to several months or longer. In some theoretical schools, the systems orientation is used; in others, it is not.

Family Counseling

Counseling is distinguished from therapy by the length of time and depth of treatment. Counseling is briefer and is usually (but not always) applied to less serious and long-standing family problems. Most family counselors subscribe to one of the previously mentioned six theoretical schools. The approach in this book has a combination of the Structural and Strategic schools as a foundation. Family counseling (including marriage and couples work) can be practiced in most settings in which individual and group therapy are conducted. The terms ''counseling'' and ''therapy'' are used interchangeably in this book.

Family Interviewing/Clarifying

Interviewing and clarifying usually take place during one or two sessions with a family in order to gather information or explore family issues. Collateral information about the primary client is needed mostly in schools, hospitals, inpatient or outpatient treatment centers, and hospices. Family interviewing and clarifying by themselves are not intended to resolve family problems.

Informal Contact

Informal contact is any social contact with a family for the purpose of involving them in the agency's activities or to keep them involved with the client or student. It is used in such places as schools, hospitals, churches, residential child care, and inpatient centers. The primary purpose is to obtain information and to build rapport and trust between the agency and the family members.

Family Work in Different Settings

For each setting, I've listed how family work is used, along with a few of the obstacles to its use—some procedural, some attitudinal—that I have observed.

Mental Health Agencies

Uses of family work
1. For treatment of a variety of children and adult presenting problems.
2. To better understand the family and social situation of the individual client.
3. To manage a family crisis or family dynamics affecting the individual client.

Obstacles to overcome
1. The medical model (one-on-one treatment) is deeply embedded, beginning with the charting and billing procedures and extending into the clinical methods.
2. Accordingly, paperwork and reporting procedures discourage family work.
3. Most of the staff's training and education have been in individual and group counseling; few are trained to work with the family as the unit of treatment.

Department of Social Services (DSS)

Uses of family work
1. For Child Protective Services investigations.
2. To work through family problems to keep the family together.
3. To prepare a child and family for the child's return home from out-of-home placement.

Obstacles to overcome
1. Child protection is the primary goal, which often leads to excluding the child's family.
2. Many workers are reluctant to convene the family or network during in-home visits, preferring to see whoever is present during the visit.
3. DSS is overwhelmed with so many cases that its criteria for child abuse and neglect are extreme.
4. The chemical dependency of parents is too often seen as a collateral rather than a causative factor in child abuse and neglect.

Residential Child Care

Uses of family work
1. To keep the family engaged as a resource for the child.
2. To work with family problems that resulted in the child's placement.
3. To prepare the family for the child's return home.

Obstacles to overcome
1. Historically, residential facilities grew out of the concept of removing the child from the family and offering alternative ''parenting.''
2. Most group homes and residential campuses are child-centered, preferring to protect the child rather than engage his or her significant family. This is slowly changing to a more child-in-family approach.
3. Agency policies work against engaging the family, with little or no informal family involvement in the cottage life or campus activities.

Schools

Uses of family work
1. Parent conferences, to solicit parents' help for a student's school problems.
2. Family interviews, when a more in-depth look or a referral is needed.
3. Social work assistance to the student and family.
4. Brief family counseling for family disruptions and crises.

Obstacles to overcome
1. Some parents are difficult to get to conferences.
2. Parents often see the school, not themselves, as responsible for their child's behavior.
3. Schools are reluctant to become involved in family affairs.
4. Schools are not staffed to do family counseling.

Hospitals

Uses of family work
1. To help the family understand and manage the patient's illness.
2. To help correct family habits that may contribute to the illness.
3. To prepare the family for the patient's return home.

Obstacles to overcome
1. The medical model is narrowly focused on the patient's body parts.
2. Family relationships are often seen as complicating the medical treatment.
3. Hospitals are not trained or staffed to handle the psychosocial and emotional factors in the patient's healing.

In-Home Services

Uses of family work
1. To prevent expensive out-of-home child placement.
2. To help change family patterns that threaten to dismember the family.
3. To work on problems that contribute to family abuse, neglect, and violence.

Obstacles to overcome
1. In-home services have become too brief, except for family stabilization.
2. Workers usually lack a holistic, systemic view of the family.
3. Workers are reluctant to structure the interviews (who attends, etc.) in the family's home.

Private Practice

Uses of family work
1. To assist individuals who present with family or interpersonal problems.
2. To bolster the individual's social network by including others in the sessions.
3. For briefer resolution of individual problems.

Obstacles to overcome
1. Therapists are quick to accept the paying client's preferences about how the work should proceed; excluding significant others may be the client's, not the therapist's, preference.
2. The practitioner may become inducted (sucked in) by the client's negative view of his or her family.
3. Managed care is cutting into the profitability of private practice.
4. Many insurance companies do not reimburse for family counseling.

Suggestions for Family Work in Different Settings

Public Social Workers (DSS, In-Home Services, etc.)

The multi-problem families in these settings have environmental and economic pressures that put stress on family relationships. Another characteristic is that family roles may be defined loosely—for example, a cousin may be treated like a sibling. Family bonds can be strong.

1. To define the relevant family system, cast a broad net. Work with the family living in the home, plus (where appropriate) extended family, neighbors, friends, and the social network.

2. Support the parent(s) or adults in the home acting as parents. If the parental stress is lessened, the relief will flow down to the children. Find adult support for the single parent.

3. Stay problem-centered. For many of these families, the primary concerns are being safe, surviving, and easing a hard life, not enriching family relationships.

4. Chemical dependency is rampant and is often a direct (not collateral) cause for abuse, neglect, and parental incompetence (see chapter 6).

5. Home visits are essential, and the safety of the worker must always be considered. Once rapport and trust with the family are established, begin to put the adults in charge of the home, with your coaching and support.

6. Don't do for them what they can do for themselves. Helping too much is seductive, since they need so much.

7. Find close colleagues and supervisory support. Working with these families can be stressful; the helper needs the relief of talking to colleagues about his or her cases.

Residential Child Care Professionals

Where possible, a functional family is the best permanency plan for most children in placement. After a round of ''group home drift,'' most children return home anyway.

1. Because you develop close ties with the child in placement, you have a natural and normal bias. This can lead to taking too much responsibility for parenting the child, overprotection of the child, and overidentifying with the child's anger at the family.

2. If DSS has custody of the child, it has the ultimate authority. Work with the agency closely and carefully.

3. Family reunification should be ruled out before any other placement is considered. Parents are often ambivalent about parenting their child. They don't set out to harm their children, but they're not sure they want the responsibility of parenting. I believe that, except in the worst cases, the residential facility should address and resolve the parental ambivalence in 90 days or less and determine whether reunification with the family is an option. (If it is an option, it will often, of course, take more than 90 days to return the child home.)

4. Treat the parents as the experts on their children. To the degree you overfunction by taking the expert role and the responsibility for ''fixing'' the child, the parents underfunction.

5. Watch the six-month time frame: After the child has been about six months out of home, you sometimes have to ''sell'' the child back to the family.

6. Because of physical and emotional danger to the child, some children cannot be returned home to their families. If the child's family is not available, find ways to help the child deal

with his or her feelings about family relationships. You can take the child out of the family, but you can't take the family out of the child.

7. Start with family sessions early in the child's placement. When the family is engaged at the outset and made a full partner in the care of the child, family reunification is more possible.

Public Mental Health Staff

1. Most mental health centers were created around the individual, medical model of treatment. The charting, billing, and record-keeping functions encourage individual, not family, treatment. Separate, individual treatment of a child is helpful, but whether it is helpful enough is another question. Returning an improved child to an unimproved family holds little promise.

2. Family counseling often consists of the problem person and one other family member: for example, the identified patient child and the most available parent, without the other parent (if applicable), siblings, others living in the home, or influential extended family members. The identified patient could be a depressed adult in an unhappy marriage or partnership, without the partner being included. Returning an improved partner to an unimproved partnership also holds little promise.

3. Most of the mental health staff members have the experience and ability, but not the confidence, to do marital and family counseling. The lack of confidence comes from inadequate supervision in family work, insufficient training, and lack of encouragement and support by management.

4. Effective family work requires a slight shift in working hours. Centers should provide evening hours 2–3 days per week.

Private Practitioners

There is a built-in ethical problem in private practice: The clinician may believe that couples and/or family therapy is the preferred mode of treatment in a given case but fail to insist on it because the paying client is resistant to the idea.

1. Even though private practice contains some of the most talented and experienced professionals in the helping field, many have had no formal training in systems therapy and fail to use this model when indicated.

2. Many private practitioners work alone, even though they are in a practice with other professionals. Everyone's time is valuable, so they don't take adequate time to talk to each other about their cases. As a result, private practitioners often drive home after work talking to themselves.

3. When couples therapy is used, children are frequently omitted from all sessions. This can make the couples work less effective for several reasons:
   a. The conflicts are often the result of the couple's parenting functions.
   b. Children in the home are affected by, and affect, the parents' relationship problems.
   c. Children are often valuable assets in couples therapy because the parents (and therapist) need to hear the children's side of the story.
   d. The presence of children in one or more of the sessions is a reminder to the couple to do the hard work of change for the sake of their children.

Rationales for This Approach

Rationales are reasons for what we do with families. Like hypotheses, they may be wrong in a given case, but we need them anyway. Sometimes our rationales are based on our theoretical orientation, sometimes on our experiences, sometimes both. Here are some of the rationales for my approaches.

1. **Seeing the whole family together (at least everyone living together).**

   You can't understand the nature of a family by talking to one or two of its members. In a family, realities are based on individual truths, and each member will have a slightly (or radically) different one. To be valuable to families, counselors need their own "truth," which can only be developed by seeing the family function together.

   Assuming a four-person household (two parents, two children), too often "family" counseling consists of seeing the mother and the problem child. This is not *family* counseling and is as confusing as watching a play with half the characters missing. The mother-child subset of the family provides more questions than answers and keeps the counselor at least four steps away from understanding what's happening in the family:

   1. What's the father's role with the child?
   2. What's going on between the parents?
   3. How do they parent the non-problem children?
   4. How does the family function together as a unit?

2. **Keeping parents in charge of their children.**

   I do this more than most family counselors. My reasons:

   1. Parents care about their children and want the best for them.
   2. The parents must cooperate with plans for their child if the plans are to work.
   3. Parents know their children and their family situation better than we do.
   4. If the professional takes the one-up, knowledgeable, expert role regarding what is best for the child, the counselor will also be handed the responsibility for "fixing" the child.
   5. Children want their parents to succeed as parents.
   6. This approach confirms and supports the parents, which is good for children to see.
   7. The counselor's relationship with the child and family is brief. The parents' relationship with the child is for a lifetime.

3. **Paying special attention to the adult relationships in the family, especially the primary parents.**

   The parent-parent relationship is, in my opinion, the most important relationship in the family. If this bond is solid and supportive, the children get consistent messages from both parents, the children cannot "split" and manipulate the parents, and they learn what a loving, cooperative relationship is all about. This assumes, of course, that the parents have decent parenting skills and are making decisions in the best interest of the children.

4. **Attending to all children in the home, regardless of who the identified patient is.**

   The welfare of their children motivates most parents, and strong motivation is needed for the changes the adults have to make. Having all children in the home at most sessions reminds parents (and counselor) that the children are being affected, directly or indirectly, by everything the parents do or don't do. Also, *all* children in the home need to be looked at, not just the identified patient child. In a troubled family, the "good" child is also suffering.

Bedrock Beliefs About Families

I have several bedrock beliefs about families. They grew from my experiences, both professional and personal, and so far they have not let me down.

Parents care about the welfare of their children.

No matter how angry, withdrawn, or abusive the parents are, they will choose what they believe is good as opposed to what they believe is bad for their child. Their intentions are usually honorable. The problem, of course, comes when the parents behave inadequately as parents, coming mostly, I suspect, from the poor parenting they received in their families of origin. Also, most parents have been dealt a difficult hand since they have had no real preparation or education to take on one of the most difficult things human beings do. I have much admiration for parents who manage to do it well.

Children want their parents to succeed as parents.

No matter how angry and resentful the children are at their parents, and despite runaways, severe conflicts, and emotional cutoffs, children want the security of nurturing, limit-setting parents. The problem, of course, comes when the children engage in a struggle for their freedom (starting at about age two) and later when they try to differentiate from their parents and become their own person. This adolescent struggle is often a conflict-ridden time and can last from months to a lifetime.

Family members want the same things: security, love, to get along.

No matter how much conflict exists over how these needs should be met. In the family journey, members are different travelers, seeing the landscape from different windows, all trying to get to the same place. Their common emotion—longing to belong—is usually just below the surface and can often be reached in family sessions.

Children are a major reason why families exist.

In the family "body," if parents are the brains and muscles, children are the heartbeat; they keep it alive with new blood. If children are in the family picture, I use the parent-child bond to motivate parents, and I have found no stronger motivation for family change than the love (and guilt) of parents toward their children.

The family is always partially right.

No matter how poorly the family is functioning, any outsider looking in is viewing only a snapshot in the dynamic history that led to the current situation. Given the set of conditions family members are working with—their circumstances and backgrounds—many of us would act in similar ways. They're doing the best they can.

Families have much strength and resilience.

They have survived a long time without us. The family bonds are sturdy and can endure much testing and crises. In most families, it takes a shakeup or crisis to bring about change, a natural process in all systems.

A Theory of Change

Source: *DeskGallery Mega-Bundle*, Copyright 1995 by Dover Publications, Inc. Used with permission.

A theory of change is useful for family work. It guides our actions and gives meaning to our experiences with families.

I believe we all have a personal theory of sorts, a set of beliefs and assumptions about families and what helps them change. Whatever our theory, we should be congruent—our *beliefs* about change and our *actions* to promote change should match. Here is my own theory about what conditions help families change.

1. **Discomfort**

Without some level of discomfort, people have no reason to do things differently. Feelings such as anger and fear are disturbing, and they energize us to take action.

If I believe this, I should not ignore, minimize, or try to take away the family discomfort. Since counselors would rather help people get rid of their pain; it's easy to allow the family members to avoid what hurts. To help people stop running, turn around, and face the thing they're running from is not easy and requires all the courage and patience we can muster.

2. **New Experiences**

Experiences are anything we perceive through our senses, plus our emotions and thoughts. Experiences are primary; they are the raw material for change.

If I believe this, I should create opportunities for new experiences during sessions. One way is to set up conversations between members that they don't usually have or help them have the same conversations in new ways or not have a conversation at all, as with the techniques of *Sculpting* or *Drawings.* To do this, members need prompting, encouragement, support, feedback, and sometimes here-and-now coaching.

3. **New Understandings**

New understandings (insights) can come before behavior change, but just as often they happen after. They are promoted by honesty between the members, by new expressions of feelings, by new information, and by observations from the counselor.

If I believe this, I should take full advantage of my position outside the family and offer my (relatively) objective feedback at the appropriate time, without attempting to interpret, label, or change. Sometimes, just getting a firm grip on the obvious and holding a mirror up to the family is valuable:

1. ''The two of you seem to have differences on how to approach the problem.''

2. To wife: ''Your husband has been silent on that topic.''

3. ''In the past few minutes everyone has been talking at once. Is this the way it is at home?''

4. **Hope**

People need to believe there's a way out of the problem, that it's possible for them to overcome their difficulty. Hope gives energy.

If I believe this, I should stay in touch with my own hope that families can change, and I should use this energy to generate hope in the session—by finding the family strengths, showing realistic optimism, normalizing members' behavior and feelings, and using appropriate humor. If I don't have hope that the family can change, can I expect them to?

Children Raise Adults

I've never known exactly what the phrase from Wordsworth's poem—"The child is father of the Man''—means, but it sounds important. Of several possible interpretations, I choose this one: Children raise adults. This is not as crazy as it sounds, especially if you consider the strong maturing influence children have on parents. I've seen children get parents to be more responsible, move out of a dangerous neighborhood, quit smoking, change their exercise and diet habits, have a better relationship with their parents, and recover from drinking and drugs. Children, especially young ones, are little change agents, and their power is in opposite proportion to their size.

We all know that children are important in families, but how do we make this idea work in family sessions? One way is to mention every child in the home every session, whether or not the children are present. This keeps the family unit as the level of focus, since everything that happens between the parents will sooner or later affect their children. In couples therapy, for example, Jennifer, age 6, and Brian, age 8, may not be brought to the sessions by the couple, but their absence doesn't make them irrelevant. Ask questions like, "Where were Jennifer and Brian when that happened? How much do they know about what is going on? How much do you want them to know? Do you think the problems you are having affect them?"

Source: *DeskGallery Mega-Bundle*, Copyright 1995 by Dover Publications, Inc. Used with permission.

If young children are in the family session, another way to make them important is to let them contribute through techniques such as ***Drawings***, ***Sculpting,*** or other movement and games rather than just through verbal expression. The main language of children is metaphor and play. If children do the ***Circle Method,*** for example, show the drawing to the parents: "What do you suppose Brian meant by putting his dad partly outside the circle?"

Everyone who is partnered and has children wears two hats: partner/spouse and parent. When dealing with spouse issues, it is sometimes easier to find agreements and successes of the couple in the parent arena, since regardless of their differences and conflicts, the welfare of the children provides a strong common concern. Get the couple (where appropriate) to put on their parent hats: "How have you worked out the disciplining of your children?"

During a session, give parents a chance to be parents. Instead of you correcting their child, comment on what you see, and let the parents correct the child's behavior. If Jennifer, for example, is in the corner writing on your office wall, make a profound comment to the parents: "Jennifer appears to be writing on the wall." If Brian keeps interrupting one or both parents while you are talking to them, say, "Brian is interrupting as we talk." Let the parents decide what to do, and watch them be parents. If parental support and coaching are required, provide them.

If you are unclear whether the children should be hearing a particular topic of conversation between you and the parents, ask the parents for guidance: "Are you okay with Jennifer and Brian hearing this?" If you are uneasy about the children hearing a conversation (argument, etc.), say to the parents, "I would prefer that we discuss this without the children. Can I take them over there and give them some drawings (toys, etc.) to keep them occupied?"

I have much respect for the integrity of the parent-child bond, and I rarely do anything with children in a family session without going through their parents, either by encouraging the parents to attend to the child's behavior or by getting their permission before I do something. Keep parents in charge of their children.

Neglected Relationships in Family Counseling

If a child is the identified patient, we usually focus mostly on the parent-child relationship in family work. This is important, but other relationships are also important as a resource for helping the family.

Parent-Parent

In two-parent households, this is perhaps the most important relationship in the family:

1. It influences virtually all significant parenting decisions.
2. When parents are divided on one or more parenting issues, their children are likely to "split" them, that is, take advantage of their disagreements for the child's own purposes, or even play one parent against the other.
3. If parents are having relationship problems, they may detour their conflict through one or more children by fighting about the child rather than dealing directly with their issues with each other.
4. When parents are divided, the children may get conflicting messages ("I don't care what your father said, I want you to do it this way!"). If one parent says "yes" and the other says "no," either way the child moves will disappoint one parent. It's a lose-lose proposition for children, and it makes them anxious.

I always work with the parent-parent relationship, urging the parents to speak with one voice and to present a consistent, team-like message to their children. When parents act together, it increases the parental leadership tremendously. And when they don't, problems are likely to arise.

Grandparent-Grandchild

Today, many households with children are being held together by grandparents, especially single-parent households. Whether grandparents and grandchildren live together or not, however, the bond between them is special. For grandparents, it's a chance to enjoy their grandchildren without having daily responsibility for them, and for grandchildren, it's a chance to experience the grandparents' love and "spoiling." This relationship also adds depth to the child's three-generation family experience and sense of belonging.

I have a bias—I believe that children should have a relationship with their grandparents, even if one or both parents are in conflict with the grandparents. This adult conflict may have a deep history, but it can rob a child and punish a grandparent. If the parent has legal custody, however, he or she must be kept in the controlling role around grandparent-grandchild contact. I let my bias be known, when appropriate, and offer to help with the adult conflicts to avoid penalizing the child.

Sibling-Sibling

Siblings are a child's first peers. Sometimes a sibling will be more influential on a child than the parents are, especially if the siblings are teenagers. An older sibling is a role model; a younger sibling is someone for the older one to protect and teach. Also, during their lifetime, children will know their siblings longer than they will know their parents. The *Sibling Talk* technique is one way to put a light on this special relationship.

Getting a Grip on the Obvious

1. Family members *feel* their family but they can't *see* their family. Client families are often blind to their own structure, patterns, and repetitive interactions, which result in symptoms for one or more members. They don't see their interdependent behavior.

2. Except to give us factual information, family members are not talking to us, even though they appear to be. They are using us to talk to each other.

3. You can't help children by trying to take their parents' place. Keep the parents in the parental role in a family session (unless you plan to go home with the family and do it for them).

4. Regardless of how parents act, they care about what happens to their children.

5. Regardless of how angry or disruptive children act, they care about their parents. They also want them to succeed as parents.

6. Parents and children are not peers. During parent-child dialogues and negotiations, give the parents more authority (and responsibility).

7. You can't solve all the problems in the family. In fact, *you* can't solve any of them.

8. It's better to ask one question at a time, keep it brief, and not answer it for them.

9. Don't always talk directly to the person(s) who you want to receive the message. If you say it to someone else, the target person listens better.

10. Rule of 20/20: If you lean forward in your chair by 20 degrees or more for a total of 20 minutes or more in a one-hour session, you're probably inducted (sucked in, too close).

11. When you can't think of what to do in a specific moment, just make an observation, without interpreting (''I notice that when you two [parents] disagree, your son interrupts a lot''). Sometimes, just hold a mirror up to the family.

12. Observations and impressions that we keep to ourselves are of no use to the family. Be careful about when and how you say something, but don't be too secretive.

13. Some of our uneasiness in family sessions comes from a belief that we aren't supposed to meddle in another family's business. We aren't sure we have permission to be there. Work with respect and sensitivity, and you will have all the permission you need.

Experience Is Primary

We learn to do things through our experiences, and everything else—reading, discussions, watching others do it, workshops, etc.—is just preparation for learning, not the learning itself. We benefit from these inputs, but we learn primarily from our own experiences, not someone else's. Before trying family work, if you read all the family therapy books, listened to all the audiotapes, watched all the videos of master therapists, and studied all the various and conflicting theories, you would emerge a little smarter, but no wiser, and too confused to stir a muscle. Learning a complex skill requires personal trial and error.

I should have known. My dad used to say, "I don't care how many times you're told something, you have to experience it for yourself." My family trainer was fond of repeating, "You've got to put in your hours" (in the therapy room with families). Another saying goes, "The map is not the territory," meaning, I suppose, the talk is not the walk, the theory is not the practice. All this advice was warning me that experience is primary, and that you learn through doing, bit by bit, over considerable time. No one becomes Virginia Satir overnight, not even Virginia Satir.

The American Association for Marriage and Family Therapy (AAMFT) recognizes the importance of putting in your hours and requires 1,500 hours of face-to-face experience in some form of family work (plus 200 hours of training) before the organization will certify a family therapist. Fifteen-hundred hours is an hour every workday for over *six years*.

Our experiences gradually change us. Here is my opinion about the stages counselors go through in learning family work through their supervised experiences:

1. **Wide-Eyed Wonder:** "I'm open to anything."
2. **Experimentation:** "This is harder than it looks."
3. **Familiarity:** "I've seen this before."
4. **Confidence Building:** "I think this might work."
5. **Adolescence:** "Don't tell me; I've got it."
6. **Journeyman:** "I'm sometimes inept, and that's OK."
7. **Maturity:** "I've learned a lot, and have a lot to learn."
8. **Wide-Eyed Wonder:** "I'm open to anything."

As T. S. Eliot said, "[t]he end of all our exploring [w]ill be to arrive where we started. And know the place for the first time."

Traditional education seems to favor a certain sequence—theory first, then experience. We studied butterflies in the classroom and then went outdoors to see butterflies. We study counseling theories in graduate school to prepare for doing counseling when we get to the real world; students are lucky to get any supervised experience at all. In contrast, my trainer had me in the room with a family within three hours of our "education" about family work, and every time she arrived for training, we had an observed family session. I, of course, had no idea what to do, but after those first sessions, I was all ears. Aside from motivating us, our experiences gave us good reality testing for the ideas we were hearing in our education.

Of course, in actual practice, learning goes back and forth between the preparation and the actual learning—between learning *about* it and *doing* it. Education and experience inform each other in a constant interplay. In the skills arena, experience without supervision and education is an inefficient way to learn, and education without experience is nearly useless.

Too Many Variables

A variable, in scientific jargon, is any condition that can vary.

Recently, I sat with a father, stepmother, and their 15-year-old daughter, who was classified as mentally retarded and who had recently been harming herself and threatening others. The parents were seeking help for her at a mental health center. Of the dozens of conditions that can vary from one family to the next in a case like this, I chose to focus on

1. The people who live in the girl's home (father, stepmother, two younger siblings)
2. How long the problem has existed
3. The parents' clues about when her behavior is deteriorating
4. The parents' agreements/disagreements on how to manage the child
5. The action plan by the parents if the daughter threatens self or others
6. The way the parents talk to the child, and who initiates the conversation
7. The strength of the conflict between stepmother and patient
8. The agreements (often unspoken) between the parents regarding who takes the parenting lead with the daughter
9. How the two younger siblings in the home react to the daughter
10. The influence of the biological mother
11. And so on

Considering the above variables, notice

1. They are too numerous to list completely.
2. The family has more control over the variables than the treatment provider does.
3. The information we collect will largely depend on what variables we explore. I chose to focus mostly on the relationship variables in the case and how the relationships affected the way the family handled the girl's problems.

Also note that most of my exploration of the variables is hypothesis testing. I'm exploring certain areas and ignoring others because I have an opinion or bias to check out. I wanted to know, as I do in every blended family, if the biological parent or the stepparent took the lead in parenting the identified patient. In my experience, if the biological parent withdraws and turns over the primary parenting to the stepparent, the child often acts out his or her anger.

I am fond of saying that every intervention in a family is an experiment. We try a particular input to see how it affects the variables. But unlike a scientific experiment, we have limited power to manipulate and control the variables, and we therefore have minimal control of the outcome. The input side, where we do have some control, is our main responsibility.

And that is responsibility enough. We have been given a difficult job—changing human behavior—and few of us will do it as quickly or as well as we're expected to by the lay public, the law, and the insurance companies. We are responsible for caring about what we do and doing the best we know how; for consulting with supervisors and colleagues; for keeping up our skills and knowledge base; for maintaining professional ethics, standards, certifications, and licensures; for sometimes working with clients we don't especially like; for doing stacks of paperwork; for being held accountable to our clients, supervisors, and administrators; and for working with impossible cases. We have our own set of variables to look after.

Too-Brief Family Counseling

This is an efficient, one-session model that should appeal to busy counselors. Use any two of the tenets of this model, and your goal of one interview will probably be achieved. Use all 12, and your goal is assured. (If your intention is to have more than one session, this approach is not recommended.)

1. Encourage everyone to express all their feelings about each other. Quickly get everything out in the open, no holds barred.

2. Do not tolerate boring stories, details, anecdotes, and crises situations you have heard many times before from other families.

3. Dispel their superficial views about what's wrong in the family. Explain the underlying dynamics of the problem.

4. Find out who's right, and help them defend their position against the others.

5. Ignore their strengths and successes. The family is here because of their weaknesses and failures.

6. Disregard the power structure in the family. It's probably not working anyway.

7. Aggressively defend a scapegoated family member.

8. Go directly to the underlying parental conflict that is feeding the family problem.

9. Explain to them the systemic underpinnings of their behavior: their circular causality, negative feedback loops, and cybernetic epistemology.

10. Be an expert, full of ready answers. Also be an expert on *their* family.

11. Assign a homework task that they have been unable to do in the past. If the presenting problem is communication, for example, say, ''During the coming week, I want you to spend one hour a day together examining your areas of mutual conflict.''

12. After the interview, follow them out of the counseling room, into the halls, and out to the parking lot. Use this extra time to explain how you have helped them in spite of themselves. As they drive off, wave a final good-bye.

Traveling Pairs of Concepts

Some pairs of ideas about parenting sit side by side and travel well together; others don't belong on the same train.

Control/Nurturance

These two travel well together. Parents need to establish control before they can nurture. This is obvious to anyone who has tried to nurture a young child who is having a tantrum, but it also applies to out-of-control teenagers who do whatever they want without regard for others or themselves. Unless parents establish some limits and control the teenager's behavior, giving the child what he or she needs—love, attention, guidance, consistency, protection, limits—is difficult at best. Establish control and limits (hopefully in a loving way), then nurture.

Source: *DeskGallery Mega-Bundle*, Copyright 1995 by Dover Publications, Inc. Used with permission.

Love/Objectivity

These two don't go together. Love, by its nature, is subjective. Objectivity, by its nature, is dispassionate, rational, detached. Love explains why parents can't stand aside and see what is happening with their child or distort the truth or enmesh their child and smother their autonomy. "Parental objectivity" is an oxymoron. As counselors, we need to allow parents the normality of being irrational about their children.

Parent/Friend

These two don't go together. I hear parents—often single parents—proudly say that they're their child's best friend. With good intentions, these parents try to mesh these incompatible roles. Friends don't tell you to clean your room or fuss at you for a bad report card or provide food, clothing, and shelter. Trying to be both parent and friend is confusing to children and weakens the parent's authority. If a single parent is the child's best friend, the child has lost both parents.

Responsibility/Authority

These two go together. It's frustrating, even crazy-making, to have the responsibility for doing a job but not the authority to do it. Many parents of problem children are in this dilemma. They have the responsibility to raise their children, but their authority has been eroded by trying to be their child's friend, by guilt, by inconsistent or mixed messages, or by another adult who has a strong influence on the child, among others.

Parenting/Guilt

These seem to go together. A warning should be placed on the child's birth certificate: "The parents of this child will feel intermittently guilty during the child's lifetime." Parental guilt is so common that I consider it normal and easy to understand. The world's most difficult job is too difficult to be done without mistakes, and sometimes the child will pay for these parenting mistakes. Managing guilt is part of the parents' job description, and if it isn't managed, it can control the parents, making them too lenient, too inconsistent, too accommodating, too apologetic, or too something.

Research on Marital and Family Therapy*

Does family counseling work? This question is too general to answer—it depends. For what specific problems? With what populations? Using what methods? Conducted how and by whom? With what outcome criteria, measured by what means? When it comes to research, the details are critical. Fortunately, we have decades of research studies (along with their details) to guide our practice.

The next few pages contain a summary of the empirical evidence on family-based interventions with a number of common clinical and medical conditions. (References are found in the Research References at the end of the book.) Overall, research suggests that utilizing family-based treatments, especially with children, enhances or extends positive outcomes (Dowell & Ogles, 2010). Moreover, including family-based interventions does not drastically increase the costs of services (Crane, 2008).

Two valuable sources used extensively for this research summary are Alan Carr's reviews of the effectiveness of family therapy and systemic interventions, including family therapy in conjunction with other family-based approaches (e.g., parent education/training), for both child and adult problems (Carr, 2009). Carr utilized meta-analyses, systematic literature reviews, and controlled research trials in his reviews of the literature. With child problems, he found evidence that supports the effectiveness of systemic interventions, either alone or as part of multimodal programs, for childhood sleep disturbances, feeding and attachment problems in infancy, child abuse and neglect, conduct problems, emotional problems, eating disorders, and somatic problems. For adults, he found that couples and family therapy are effective "either alone or as part of multimodal programs" for relationship distress, psychosexual problems, domestic violence, anxiety disorders, mood disorders, alcohol and drug abuse, schizophrenia, and adjustment to chronic physical illness (Carr, 2009, p. 46). Carr's findings, along with other research, are summarized in the following pages.

Research Findings on Specific Disorders

1. Problems of Infancy and Early Childhood
   a. Attachment Problems
      Brief (15 sessions or fewer over 3–4 months), highly focused, family-based interventions (that involve fathers and mothers) specifically aimed at enhancing maternal sensitivity to infants' cues are "effective in improving maternal sensitivity and reducing infant attachment insecurity" (Carr, 2009, p. 6).
   b. Feeding Problems
      Family-based behavioral modification programs are effective in ameliorating severe feeding problems and in improving weight gain in infants and children, including children with developmental disabilities (Carr, 2009).
   c. Sleep Problems
      Family-based behavioral modification programs and pharmacological interventions are effective in the treatment of children's sleep problems; however, only systemic interventions (that include family therapy, parent training, and/or multisystemic therapy that engages extended family or wider family networks in efforts to ameliorate familial problems) have long-term positive effects on children's sleep problems (Carr, 2009).

---

* Credit goes to Daphne Cain, PhD, LCSW, Chair, Department of Social Work, Louisiana State University, for this section on research and for the Research References at the end of the book.

2. Childhood Disorders
   a. Attention Deficit Hyperactivity Disorder (ADHD)

A multimodal approach that consists of family, school, and psychopharmacological interventions is the most effective (Abikoff et al., 2004; Carr, 2009; Hinshaw, Klein, & Abikoff, 2007; Jensen et al., 2007).

   b. Conduct Problems

Behavioral parent training is effective at ameliorating childhood behavior problems and can be maintained for over one year with periodic follow-up sessions (Carr, 2009). Teaching parents cognitive behavioral techniques to increase children's prosocial behaviors (attending and positive reinforcement) while also reducing antisocial behaviors (ignoring, time-out, and contingency contracts) is critical to this process (Carr, 2009, citing Patterson, 1976). Moreover, behavioral parent training may be enhanced by including child-focused therapy to improve child self-regulation, problem solving, and emotional coping (Carr, 2009). Behavioral parent training is less effective with parents coping with mental health problems, for parents who have limited social supports, and among parents with high levels of poverty-related stress (Carr, 2009, citing Reyno & McGrath, 2006). When such factors are present, concurrent parent-focused interventions aimed at ameliorating the effects of these factors should be considered (Carr, 2009).

   c. Delinquency

Functional Family Therapy (Alexander, Sexton, & Robbins, 2000) in combination with prenatal care, home visitation, bullying prevention, drug and alcohol prevention, mentoring, life skills training, and reward systems for graduation and work are effective at ameliorating the risks for delinquency (Zagar, Busch, & Hughes, 2009).

   d. Separation Anxiety Disorder (SAD) and School Refusal

Structural Family Therapy is effective in the treatment of SAD (Mousavi, Moradi, & Mahdavi, 2008). Moreover, school refusal, which is frequently due to SAD, can be effectively treated with behavioral family therapy (Carr, 2009; Heyne & King, 2004).

   e. Obsessive Compulsive Disorder (OCD)

Family-based exposure/response cognitive behavioral strategies are effective in the treatment of OCD among young people (Barrett, Farrell, Dadds, & Boutler, 2005; Carr, 2009; Storch et al., 2007).

   f. Adolescent Anorexia Nervosa

There is "growing evidence that family-based treatment models are indicated for recent onset child and adolescent anorexia nervosa and that specific forms of family therapy are more effective and user-friendly with certain types of patients and families. Family therapy models that are initially symptom-focused and resource-oriented bring about more positive results than deficit-based models that do not consider the individual symptom" (Cook-Darzens, Doyen, & Mouren, 2008, p. 168). For a review of the research on family interventions with adolescents with anorexia nervosa, see Le Grange and Eisler (2008).

   g. Adolescent Bulimia Nervosa

Family therapy is as effective as cognitive behavioral therapy and is more effective than supportive therapy for adolescents with bulimia nervosa (Carr, 2009; Le Grange, Crosby, Rathouz, & Leventhal, 2007; Schmidt et al., 2007).

   h. Juvenile Obesity

Family-based behavioral intervention is more effective than dietary educational programs in promoting weight reduction among obese juveniles (Carr, 2009; Jelalian & Saelens, 1999).

i. Juvenile Sexual Offenders

Community-based multisystemic therapy (MST) adapted for juvenile sexual offenders evidenced significant reductions in sexual behavior problems, delinquency, substance use, externalizing symptoms, and the need for out-of-home placement (Letourneau et al., 2009).

j. Depression

The combination of family therapy with group-based parent and child psychoeducational sessions is effective in the treatment of major depression among children (Diamond, Reis, Diamond, Siqueland, & Isaacs, 2002; Carr, 2009; Lewinsohn, Clarke, Hops, & Andrews, 1990; Sanford et al., 2006; Trowell et al., 2007; Weersing & Brent, 2003).

k. Grief and Bereavement

A combination of family and individual treatment is effective in the treatment of grief/bereavement reactions, including grief reactions associated with parental loss (Carr, 2009; Cohen, Mannarino, & Deblinger, 2006; Kissane & Bloch, 2002).

l. Bipolar Disorder in Adolescents/Early Adulthood

While psychopharmacological treatment is the primary treatment for bipolar disorder, conjoint psychoeducational family therapy is an effective intervention to prevent relapse (Carr, 2009; Fristad, Goldberg-Arnold, & Gavazzi, 2002).

m. Alcoholism and Other Drug Addiction in Adolescents/Early Adulthood

Deas and Clark (2009) conducted an analysis of published research (from 1990 to 2005) on the current state of treatment interventions for alcohol and other drug (AOD) use among adolescents. Overall, they found that the majority of current treatment options utilize "family-based interventions and multisystemic therapy, motivational enhancement therapy, behavioral therapy, and cognitive-behavioral therapy" (Deas & Clark, 2009, p. 76). Moreover, these interventions have evidence to suggest effectiveness. Additionally, Multidimensional Family Therapy (MDFT) (Liddle, 2002) in combination with a peer group intervention with young teens demonstrate effectiveness in reducing substance use, substance use problems, delinquency, and internalized distress (Liddle, Rowe, Dakof, & Henderson, 2009).

3. Child Abuse and Neglect

a. Physical Abuse and Neglect

Effective treatments to reduce the risk of physical abuse and neglect of children include therapy that is "family-based, structured, extends over periods of at least six months, and addresses specific problems in relevant subsystems and includes children's post-traumatic adjustment problems, parenting skills deficits, and the overall supportiveness of the family and social network" (Carr, 2009, p. 7). Specific manualized approaches that demonstrate effectiveness in reducing the risk of subsequent physical child abuse include cognitive behavioral family therapy, multisystemic therapy, and parent-child interaction therapy (Carr, 2009).

b. Sexual Abuse

"Trauma-focused cognitive behavior therapy for both abused young people and their non-abusing parents has been shown to reduce symptoms of post-traumatic stress disorder and improve overall adjustment" (Carr, 2009, p. 8, citing Deblinger & Heflinger, 1996). It is recommended that therapists working with sexual abuse survivors carry small case loads (fewer than 10), that services be provided to families for at least 6 months, and that along with regular family therapy sessions, the non-offending parent receive parent-focused intervention along with child-focused interventions (Carr, 2009). Furthermore, a thorough assessment of the child's environmental needs is recommended, and a separate living environment for the offending party is necessary, at least until he or she has completed treatment and is deemed to be at low risk to re-offend (Carr, 2009).

4. Mood Disorders in Adults
   a. Depression
      Evidence on the efficacy of couples therapy as a treatment for depression is inconclusive (Barbato & D'Avanzo, 2008). Barbato and D'Avanzo conducted a meta-analysis using 8 controlled trials (567 subjects) on the efficacy of couples therapy as a treatment for depression. There were no statistically significant differences found between couples therapy and individual psychotherapy on depressive symptom levels. However, results reveal that "relationship distress was significantly reduced in the couple therapy group" (Barbato & D'Avanzo, 2008, p. 121).
   b. Bipolar Disorder
      The primary treatment for bipolar disorder is pharmacological (Carr, 2009); however, concurrent family therapy is effective in reducing relapse (Carr, 2009).

5. Anxiety Disorders in Adults
   a. Panic Disorder
      Partner-assisted, cognitive behavioral exposure therapy is as effective as individual cognitive behavioral treatment for panic disorder with agoraphobia (Byrne, Carr, & Clarke, 2004; Carr, 2009).
   b. Obsessive Compulsive Disorder (OCD)
      Systemic couples or family-based approaches are at least as effective as individual cognitive behavioral therapy (Carr, 2009; Renshaw, Steketee, & Chambless, 2005).

6. Marital Problems
   a. Marital Dissatisfaction and Conflict
      Wood, Crane, Schaalje, and Law (2005) conducted a meta-analysis of 23 studies on marital and couples therapy and determined that both behavioral and emotionally focused couples therapy are effective but that emotionally focused couples therapy is more effective with more highly distressed couples (Carr, 2009). Moreover, Snyder, Wills, and Grady-Fletcher (1991) found insight-oriented marital therapy to be more effective over the long term (4 years post-treatment) at preventing divorce than behavioral marital therapy (Carr, 2009).
   b. Spouse Abuse
      Based on a small body of empirical evidence (6 experimental studies), it appears that "carefully conceptualized and delivered couples treatment appears to be at least as effective as traditional treatment for domestic violence, and preliminary data suggests that it does not place women at greater risk for injury" (Stith, Rosen, & McCollum, 2003, p. 407).

7. Sexual Disorders
   Sensate focus exercises (Masters & Johnson, 1970) in combination with directed masturbation are effective treatment in most cases of female orgasmic disorder (Carr, 2009; Meston, 2006). The combined use of medications (such as Viagra) and cognitive behavioral sex therapy is more effective than the use of medications alone for cases of male erectile disorder (Banner & Anderson, 2007; Carr, 2009).

8. Alcohol Abuse in Adults
   Community Reinforcement and Family Training (Smith & Meyers, 2004) and behavioral couples therapy (O'Farrell & Fals-Stewart, 2003) are among the most effective treatment approaches for alcohol abuse (Carr, 2009; Miller, Wilbourne, & Hettema, 2003).

9. Physical Illness
    a. Juvenile Asthma
        Psychoeducational family-based interventions are more effective than individual therapy in treating poorly controlled asthma in children (Brinkley, Cullen, & Carr, 2002; Carr, 2009).
    b. Type 1 Juvenile Diabetes
        Family-based interventions that are appropriate for age and life cycle stage are effective at helping juveniles control their diabetes (Carr, 2009; Farrell, Cullen, & Carr, 2002).
    c. Chronic Illness
        Systemic interventions for people with chronic illnesses such as dementia, heart disease, cancer, chronic pain, stroke, arthritis, and traumatic brain injury are more effective than standard care (Carr, 2009; Martire, Lustig, Schultz, Miller, & Helgeson, 2004). Systemic interventions may include family therapy and psychoeducational groups for caregivers. Additionally, it appears that couples therapy is particularly effective at alleviating depression among chronically ill patients (Carr, 2009).

10. Schizophrenic Disorders
    a. Systemic Family Therapy (SFT) appears to be effective in the treatment of schizophrenia. Patients treated with the Milan School model of SFT had an improved clinical course and better medication compliance at the end of treatment (12 months) than patients treated with routine psychiatric treatment (Bressi, Manenti, Frongia, Porcellana, & Invernizzi, 2008).
    b. A meta-analytic study of 25 interventions revealed that psychoeducational family interventions are effective at reducing patient relapse as measured by rehospitalization or a significant worsening of patient symptoms (Pitschel-Walz, Leucht, Bauml, Kissling, & Engel, 2001). Best outcomes were found with longer-term family interventions (longer than 3 months).
    c. In a large study combining four meta-analyses, Pfammatter, Junghan, & Brenner (2006) found that ''compared with medication alone, multi-modal programs which included psychoeducational family therapy and anti-psychotic medication led to lower relapse and rehospitalization rates, and improved medication adherence'' (Carr, 2009, p. 62).

Part 2: Procedures and Processes
Recruiting Families for Counseling

Who decides who attends the first session? If the family (or one member) decides, the counselor may be playing into some of the splits, conflicts, and coalitions that are part of the problem. Family counseling goes better when the counselor decides who needs to be present (initially, everyone in the home). The following are several working guidelines that will improve the chances of getting families in.

Make Recruitment an Agency-Wide Issue

Recruiting families for counseling is not a contest between the counselor and one or more family members, although at times it seems that way. Getting families in also involves the agency management, the receptionist staff, and the record-keeping procedures.

Agency management controls the important resources: space, time, policies, and money. A different space may be needed because many counselors' offices are not large enough for a family; the working hours may need to include more evening appointments; the treatment policies determine the amount of firmness counselors can use in recruiting families; when required, time and money are needed for training.

The receptionist staff who receive phone calls for referrals are a vital—and frequently overlooked—component in a treatment system. If they do not understand the rationale for working with family units, they are not likely to convince a client to bring everyone in the home for the first interview. These initial contact people should be included in at least some family case conferences, clinical meetings, and training workshops.

In public mental health organizations, record keeping is individually oriented and may require opening a new chart on each person who attends family sessions. This extra paperwork discourages counselors from recruiting families. Someday, the *family*, not the individuals, will be allowed as a treatment unit. In the meantime, an expedient answer to this problem is to keep an individual chart for the identified patient and to include the family members as collateral contacts.

Get Administrative Support

Marriage and family therapy (MFT) is an important supplement to a clinical program. Here are some ideas to use when talking to your administrators about increasing the use of MFT in your program:
1. MFT is evidenced based and well researched for a wide variety of problems. For a recent research survey, see pages 32–36.
2. The average time spent with clients can be calculated for each counselor or agency. I suspect that MFT is 25–40% briefer than individual counseling. This faster turnover means more clients served per year but not more clients on the rolls at any given time.
3. Shorter treatment and higher client turnover result in lower cost per client served.
4. More people receive treatment at the same expenditure of staff time. A session with a family of four takes about the same time as a session with an individual.
5. MFT has prevention benefits. If a family with a problem adolescent, for example, can make progress in counseling, the likelihood that problems will develop later in younger siblings or in other members can be decreased.
6. Since MFT is more of a team effort than individual therapy, it produces positive change in how the staff members work together.

Recruit Missing Members

A family will often present itself for counseling in fragments: an individual with marital or partnership problems, a mother with an acting-out teenager, a young adult who lives with his or her parents. The counselor may want to involve the missing members if the work is to be effective.

Source: *DeskGallery Mega-Bundle*, Copyright 1995 by Dover Publications, Inc. Used with permission.

1. During the initial phone call, ask the caller for the names and ages (of children) of everyone living in the home. Say to the caller, ''The way we work (or ''Our policy . . .'') is to see everyone living in the home at least once to get a clearer picture of your situation.'' Ask the caller to invite the other members to the first interview.

2. If the above effort to recruit everyone living in the home fails, agree to see whomever the caller wants to bring. Example: A mother who wants to bring only her problem son; also in the home is the mother's spouse/partner and daughter.

   a. At the first session, put empty chairs in the circle to represent the missing spouse and daughter.

   b. During the interview, join with the persons present and in need. But also talk about the missing members: ''What does spouse and daughter think the problem is? What would (your spouse) say about that? How does the situation affect your daughter?''

   c. Ask, ''Who can get your spouse and daughter to come to the next session?''

   d. The father's attendance at family counseling is sometimes a problem, perhaps due to his work schedule or because he disagrees with the mother's approach to the problem. Since you want to promote parental teamwork in reaction to the problem child, his presence is important.

   e. If other attempts fail to include the father, write down some questions for father (''What is your major concern in the family?'' ''How do you see your son's problem?'' etc.). Give them to the mother to take to the father and have her bring his answers to the next session.

3. If you get the family's permission to phone the missing member directly, include some of these ideas and statements:

   a. Hear their story and viewpoint.

   b. Emphasize the importance of that member to the family and to the problem solution.

   c. ''I am trying to be impartial, which is difficult when I have only one side of the story.''

   d. ''All I know about you is what I hear from your _____ (wife, son, etc.).''

   e. If he refuses to attend with his family, ask to see him for an individual session ''to get his view of the situation.'' During the individual interview, emphasize his importance in helping his son by attending family sessions.

   f. If he still refuses, ask his opinion about what should be talked about in the sessions and about his views of the problem and the solution.

4. Other recruitment suggestions:

   a. In the first session with a partial or a complete family, join well. Support their strengths and successes without minimizing the problem. Go with the problem they bring you, even though you believe it's a surface issue. The overriding goal of the first session is to have a second session.

   b. Don't be afraid to gently use leverage (DSS, legal, etc.) when necessary and available.

   c. If the identified patient is a child or young person living at home, it is especially important to get both parents, if available, to come to counseling. You can get their written permission to work with their child, including an agreement by the parents to participate in the treatment when requested.

d. If other methods fail to engage the missing member(s), place a tape recorder in the empty chair and make a recording of the session (with the adult family member's permission). At the end of the session, give the tape to the client to take to the missing member(s). ("They will cooperate better if they know what's going on.").

e. If the family members don't return after the first interview, call them. If they reveal that something you did (or didn't do) decreased their motivation for counseling, apologize, if appropriate, and ask to be given a chance to correct your misunderstanding at another session.

Conducting the Initial Family Interview
The ReSPECT Sequence

ReSPECT is an acronym that helps us remember the sequence in the initial interview:

Re: Recruitment
S: Social
P: Problem
E: Exploration
C: Closing
T: Talk to colleagues

1. **Recruitment**—Recruitment is included in the sequence of steps in the first interview because without effective recruitment, there won't be a first interview, at least not with the right family members. During the first contact (usually by phone), collect certain information (the presenting problem, who lives in the home) and set the appointment for the first session.

2. **Social**—When the family members arrive, greet them and ask them to be seated in a prearranged circle of chairs. Ask each member about themselves in a polite, "small-talk" fashion, gathering information about school, work, hobbies, etc.

   a. Begin with one of the parents. If both parents are present, begin with the one who did not make the initial call; this balances the information sharing and draws in the (presumably) less involved parent/spouse. Proceed from parents to oldest child to youngest child. This sequence of addressing members of the family supports the natural hierarchy of the family unit.

   b. Discourage discussion about the presenting problem until a social response is obtained from each member.

   c. Find out about the extended family (grandparents, aunts/uncles, etc.). Depending on the amount of contact with the family and their availability, these members may be asked to attend one or more future sessions.

   d. Usually, about 3–5 minutes is enough time to complete the social stage. The purposes of this stage are to

      1. Begin the counseling in a friendly, non-threatening way.
      2. Give the family a chance to adjust to space, place, and person.
      3. Show that everyone in the family will be considered important and attended to by the counselor.
      4. Collect information about each family member and about others who may be involved with the immediate family.

3. **Problem**—After the social exchange between you and family members, ask each member how he or she sees the problem.

   a. The sequence is the same as that in the social stage: begin with the parents and proceed from oldest to youngest child.

   b. Ways to ask about the problem:

      "What is your major concern in your family right now?"

      "How can I be of help to you?"

      "How do you see the family situation now?"

   c. Hear each person's view of the problem. If you like, summarize to the speaker your understanding of what he or she said. Make no attempt at this point to help the speaker see the problem differently or to offer solutions.

   d. Ask questions of a person to clarify an unclear statement of the problem; however, don't urge the person to reveal information or feelings that he or she may not want to disclose this early.

   e. Gentle control of the session is important; do not allow extensive discussion between the members until everyone has been given a chance to express the presenting problem.

   f. The Problem stage clarifies the family's motivation for counseling, establishes the therapeutic contract, and gives permission to explore certain areas of the family's functioning.

4. **Exploration**—This is the stage to explore the presenting problem in more detail (who, what, where, when) and to observe how the family functions. The Exploration stage is the main part of the first interview, taking most of the time.

   a. Ask any question that will clarify the family situation for you. It's best, however, to avoid certain topics or questions if the members have too much difficulty with them. Save such topics for later, when you have developed more of a relationship with the family.

   b. At some point in this stage, you want a shift from the members *describing* the problem (in Stage 3) to *interacting* with each other around the problem. This usually occurs spontaneously, since they often have different, and often conflicting, ideas about the problem. If the interaction between the members doesn't occur spontaneously, encourage two or more members to talk together concerning some aspect of the problem.

Source: *DeskGallery Mega-Bundle*, Copyright 1995 by Dover Publications, Inc. Used with permission.

   c. If appropriate, ask non-participating members to join the conversation between two other members ("Where are you in this conversation?"). This will reveal everyone's involvement in the topic and give information about each person's relationship to the others (who sides with whom, who is most active and inactive, who has the apparent power, etc.).

   d. The Exploration stage gives valuable information about family patterns. It also prepares the family members for future sessions when you will sometimes become less active to allow them, with your support, to do their work directly with each other.

5. **Closing**—The counselor wraps up the session.

   a. Create motivation for the family members to return, pointing out their strengths and their current efforts to improve the family. Present the hope that in these meetings, they will find relief from their problem.

   b. Set the appointment for the next interview.

6. **Talk with colleagues**—As written elsewhere in this book, I believe it's important to discuss our cases with colleagues and supervisors (see Colleague Consultation in Chapter 2). Simply telling another person about your session or your case will often trigger an idea about a direction to go with the family. It's not necessary to discuss every session with colleagues to get this benefit.

Initial Interview Summary

Date: _____

Counselor: _____

Living in the Home: (names and relationships; ages of children)

Follow this sequence (ReSPECT):

1. **Recruitment:** Ask for everyone living in the home to attend the first session.
2. **Social:** Gather social information from each person (work, school, hobbies, etc.). Also, get information about the broader family system and who else might be involved. (Family Data below).
3. **Problem:** Ask each person to define the problem the way he or she sees it.
4. **Exploration:** Learn more about the problem, and allow family members to talk to each other on a relevant topic. Listen and observe all members, and support their efforts.
5. **Closing:**
   a. Support strengths and positives in the family; give them hope.
   b. If appropriate, explain your treatment program and policies.
   c. Set an appointment for the next session.
6. **Talk to colleagues:** Discuss your case with a supervisor and/or colleague.

Family Data: List others with whom the family has contact, including parents, grandparents, in-laws, aunts, uncles, friends of the family, and other helping professionals.

Tips for the First Family Interview

The first interview with a family is usually not the most interesting session, but it's one of the most important. For one thing, it can determine if there will be a second session. It also sets the stage for later interviews by showing the family what to expect and what is expected.

First Session

1. The purpose of the first session is to understand, not change, the family.
2. Avoid getting wrapped up in paper.
3. Have a plan or sequence of steps to ensure that everything gets covered. The **ReSPECT** sequence (previous page) does that.
4. Be a good listener. Just ask questions and ''soak in'' what they tell you without challenging their perceptions or trying to change their minds.
5. Check out everyone's viewpoints, and don't let the talkative member take all the time. All members need to feel their input is valued.
6. However, give more attention to the parent(s). They are the architects of the family.
7. If a non-parent member (child, adult child, or grandparent, for example) is obviously influential and has the ability to bring the family back, you must join carefully with him or her.
8. Notice who is apparently aligned with whom around the problem situation. Against whom?
9. Ask, ''Who else knows about the problem?'' This gives information about who is involved.
10. Gently maintain control of the session so you can gather your information while letting the family members feel a guiding hand.

Bodyspeak

As counselors, we know that the client's body language and meta-communication (*how* something is said) is as important, if not more so, than what they say. Usually, I find it's best to just take this in as information. If we point out a client's body language immediately, it can make him or her uneasy and suspicious. Besides, sometimes a twitch is just a twitch.

Here are a few nonverbal communications to look for in the first, and later, sessions:

1. Who is missing?
2. In a two-parent household, do the parents look at each other when one is talking? If they don't, it may (or may not) mean parental splits and conflicts.
3. Communication is often expressed by our bodies before the words are shaped by our mouths. If someone moves noticeably, they often want to speak.
4. Who shifts in their chair? Around what topics?
5. Who moves their chair slightly and in what direction?
6. Facial expressions are telling: smiles, frowns, confused looks, grimaces, squints. A subtle eye roll by the wife while the husband is talking could speak volumes.
7. Do the children look scared and speak only when spoken to? If so, it could mean unhealthy secrecy in the family.

Four Basic Tools for Family Counseling

1. **Enactment:** An in-the-room transaction between two or more family members around one of their real-life issues. The counselor sets up the conversation (or allows it to happen).

   Purposes and examples:

   a. To establish parental authority and parenting teamwork. <u>Example:</u> "To be clear with your son, decide together now what the two of you will do if he comes home late again. I will listen while you talk together."

   b. To help the child negotiate with parents. <u>Example:</u> "Find out from your parents what it will take for them to get off your back."

   c. To include a silent, detached member. <u>Example:</u> "Your husband hasn't expressed an opinion about that. Would you find out from him what he thinks?"

   During enactments, several things are happening simultaneously:

   a. The counselor, as observer, is receiving information about relationships, communication styles, strengths, weaknesses, and problem-solving ability.

   b. Family members are practicing more direct communication with each other and learning firsthand about how each other thinks and feels.

   c. The counselor, from a non-central position, is communicating to the family members that they must work together to change their relationships. The counselor cannot do it for them.

   Comments:

   a. Be directive in creating enactments. Tell them (politely) what you want them to do.

   b. Keep enactments relevant (a topic they consider important).

   c. If necessary, physically shift yourself in the room to keep the participants from talking directly to you.

   d. During enactments, monitor the interaction, support, clarify, challenge, and help them stay on the topic.

2. **Segmenting:** Working with a portion of the family at a time.

   Purposes and examples:

   a. To draw boundaries around subsystems. <u>Example:</u> Get the parents' permission for the children to leave the room while the parents work out agreements together about the children's activities or so the parents can discuss spouse issues.

   b. To remove distractions. <u>Example:</u> Young children may be placed in the care of a colleague and removed from the room (with parents' permission) if they are distracting the parents from important issues.

   c. To discover a "family secret" or pattern of communication that is blocking progress. <u>Examples:</u> Spouses may speak more freely when seen individually; children interviewed without parents may give information they would not reveal in front of parents.

   Comments:

   a. Get both parents' permission before doing anything with their children.

   b. Give a reason for the segmenting. To parents: "I would like to talk with you about how you make decisions together about your children. Can your children wait for us in the waiting room?"

3. **Task:** Between-session homework for the family.

   Purposes and examples:

   a. To start a new process between members. <u>Example:</u> Father and daughter plan to do something together without mother (go to a movie, etc.).

    b. To clarify boundaries around subsystems. <u>Example</u>: Mother and father ''have a date,'' leaving the children at home.

    c. To reestablish role modeling of parents. <u>Example</u>: Father teaches the son about cooking by fixing a meal with him for the family.

    Comments:

    a. Tailor the task to each family: members' activity preferences, their schedules, etc.

    b. Keep it simple and easy, to encourage a success.

    c. Make a specific plan with the family for the task (who, what, where, when).

    d. Assign everyone a role in the task, to make it a family commitment.

    e. Inquire about the task at the beginning of the next session. If the task wasn't completed (or only partially), discuss it thoroughly. This lets family members know that the tasks are important. Talking about an uncompleted task also gives information about how the family functions.

4. **Unbalancing:** Interrupting habitual interactions in a family by creating alternative interactions in the room.

    Purposes and examples:

    a. To test the flexibility of the family. <u>Example</u>: Encourage the parent who talks least about the children to talk more about them.

    b. To interrupt enmeshment. <u>Example</u>: Ask a father who is overinvolved with his son to sit aside (with the counselor) and listen to his wife and son discuss a particular topic.

    c. To interrupt a severe power imbalance. <u>Example</u>: The husband is overtalkative and domineering, the wife is silent and submissive. The counselor gently and temporarily sides with the silent wife. Alternatively, the counselor can join with the husband, gently pushing him to change his wife's behavior by changing the way he acts toward her.

    Comments:

    a. When making an unbalancing move, be sure to note everybody's reaction, not just the members who are directly involved.

    b. If it is too difficult for the family, back off. Two tries are enough, unless you have a strategic reason to continue.

General Guidelines

The physical setting for counseling is important.

a.   The way family members arrange themselves in the room will influence their interaction together. (It's difficult to get a detached father or sullen teenager to be involved in the session if he or she is hiding in an overstuffed chair in the corner.)

b.   If possible, the chairs should be of the same height, moveable, and placed in a circle.

c.   The room should be large enough to allow the counselor to get up and move around, or to get out of family members' way when they are productively engaged with each other.

d.   If your office is not suitable, find another space for family work: the group room, conference room, reception area after hours, etc.

Work with the relevant family system.

a.   Everyone in the home should attend the first session: "*The way we work is to meet with everyone in the home to get a clear idea of how we can help.*"

b.   During the first interview, inquire about extended family (siblings, grandparents, aunts, uncles, etc.) and significant others (friends, professionals, etc.). A good question for this is, "Who else knows about the problem?" Obtain enough family information to allow you to view the family's problem in a larger social context. You may also want to include some of these people in a later interview.

Include the family as early as possible.

a.   If the problem is initially presented for individual counseling and you believe that family or marital treatment is more appropriate, no more than 2–3 individual sessions should be held before getting the family/spouse in. If you have a long-standing counseling relationship with the individual member, the family may resist attending because they assume that you are biased toward the individual member's viewpoint. They could be right.

b.   If you have more than three sessions with the individual member, refer the family—including the identified patient—to a colleague for conjoint family counseling. You may or may not choose to continue the individual sessions with the identified patient.

Get the family in.

a.   It's best to start counseling with the family rather than with an individual. If the identified patient comes alone, get his or her permission (release form) for you to contact family members by phone to invite them to the second session.

b.   During the initial phone contact, try to avoid letting the caller determine who comes to the first session. You want to see everyone living in the home. Exception: If the presenting problem is in the spouse relationship and the parents insist on leaving the children out, comply with their wishes. However, the children should be present in a later interview to give a broader view of the relationship patterns in the family.

c.   During or immediately after a crisis is the best time to get family members into treatment. They are the most receptive for help at this time and the most susceptible to change.

Recruit missing members.

a.   Always discuss a member's absence at the beginning of the interview (empty chair in circle): "I thought Janet was coming today. What happened?"

b. You may want to try to let the family get the missing member in (''Who can get Janet to join us?''). If this doesn't work, get permission for you to contact the missing member by phone to invite him or her to the next session.

c. When phoning the missing member, emphasize the importance of that person to the counseling (''Your family needs your help.''). Also, let them know that you are striving to be impartial, which is made very difficult when you have only one side of the story (''All I know about you is what I hear from your wife, husband, children, etc.'').

d. It may be necessary to offer the missing member an individual interview to get his or her private opinions of the situation. One or two of these interviews may be required to get the resistant member to the family sessions.

Keep the presenting problem in focus.

a. Stay with the problem presented for treatment. Switching problems (for example, from a child's school problem to parental conflict) can quickly lead to confusion, denial, anger, and leaving counseling. You can usually find a way to work with the relationships in the family by staying with the problem presented for treatment.

b. Later, when the presenting problem improves, you can ask about focusing on a different problem.

Join with the family.

a. *Joining* is the activity of making a connection between the counselor and family members; establishing rapport and trust; seeing their reality, individually and collectively. It is the same counselor-client process that must occur in any form of counseling. However, its importance in family work is even greater because of the need to gain everyone's cooperation in spite of multiple and often conflicting viewpoints within the family.

b. Joining includes
    • listening well
    • pointing out positives
    • matching their mood (at least initially)
    • using their words and metaphors
    • accommodating (in a variety of ways)
    • communicating understanding
    • expressing genuine concern
    • gently challenging
    • giving hope

c. The most hostile or uncooperative member must be joined with carefully, especially if that member is one who has the power to stop the family counseling.

Get the family members to talk to each other.

a. Families tend to talk directly to you rather than to each other, keeping you in the center of conversations. This centrality of the counselor is appropriate most of the time, but there also needs to be some interaction *between* members around their important issues. It may take some kind of directive and physical shift by the counselor for this to happen: ''Decide together now about _____. I'll get out of your way while you talk.''

b. While they are talking to each other, you can—from a more detached position—monitor the interaction and
    • observe relationship patterns, strengths, flexibility, etc.
    • help them stay on the subject

- support their efforts
- clarify
- question and challenge
- bring others into the conversation (if appropriate)
- protect the conversation from intrusion by others (if appropriate)
- move toward problem solving and resolution

c. Don't answer a question that could or should be answered by someone else in the session (Member to counselor: ''Why do you think he does that?'' Counselor: ''That's a good question. Ask him.'').

d. Be cautious about encouraging ''emotionally divorced'' parents to talk to each other about sensitive issues. This may be difficult for them at first, and pushing for it too early could create resistance to the counseling.

Search for strengths.

a. All families who come for counseling have strengths and positive attributes—they do many things right. Families without competence would not have survived as a family unit and certainly would not have enough cohesion to be in counseling together.

b. To focus entirely on problems and weaknesses in a family is a therapeutic error. Families are likely to change, not because they believe something they are doing is wrong, but because they feel supported in their efforts to change.

c. Set up *Enactments* between members, then find and report out positives and strengths in their interaction (''You have differences on that issue, but it's obvious you have the ability to stay with something important even when it's uncomfortable.'').

d. Use *Positive Reframing.* This is a technique based on the assumption that for every negative behavior, thought, or statement, there is a positive intention or characteristic of the person being expressed. For example, an argument could be reframed as strong desire to communicate with each other. An angry ''He's never at home!'' could be reframed by the counselor as, ''I can see that having more time with him is important to you.''

e. It's better not to be long-winded with positive reframing and praise. Be brief and sincere.

If the Presenting Problem Is a Child or Young Person

General Approach

a. In a two-parent family, some behavior problems in young people are the family's way of denying or diffusing conflict between two other members, often the parents. The guiding direction for you is to push, with benevolent and patient skill, to get the parents to *work together* to take charge of the young person's problem behavior. In this way, you are working on the parents' relationship while focusing on the problem of the young person. If this focus is maintained, it will often bring the parental conflicts and disagreements to the surface so they can be resolved. If the parenting relationship improves, the child may be free to give up his or her symptoms. (The variations on this approach for single-parent, blended, and separated/divorced families are discussed under **"Therapeutic Themes by Family Type"** on p. 60.

Source: *DeskGallery Mega-Bundle*, Copyright 1995 by Dover Publications, Inc. Used with permission.

b. When the parenting adults begin to work together to set limits on the young person, expect the child to temporarily get worse ("testing the limits"). *Be sure to warn the parents that this will happen.* Explain that this is normal; their child's behavior will become worse before it gets better: "This is your child's way of testing you to see if you are serious about the change."

Join thoroughly with the parents.

a. In this approach, it is essential that the parents feel supported by the counselor in their struggle to change the problem behavior of their son or daughter. The counselor must join well with the parents; if their cooperation is lost, helping the family or the child becomes unlikely.

b. Do not join the young person against the parents, even if you believe the child is right. The question is not who is "right" but what helps.

If the identified patient is a teenager:

a. Keep the parents in a responsible parenting role with their adolescent. They, not the counselor, are the experts on their teenager. If you accept the responsibility for changing the adolescent, parents tend to remove themselves and turn over the treatment to professionals ("fix my kid"). Reframe the problem behavior of the child in a way that enlists the parents' involvement (*Strategic Child Assessment; Problem Reframing*).

b. Repetitiously support the teenager as becoming an adult who is learning, with the parent's help, to be more self-directing and responsible.

   • If the identified patient is an adolescent substance abuser with a driver's license, ask, "Do you allow your son/daughter to drive an automobile?" If the answer is yes, discuss it at some length. This is the number one cause of death among teenagers; do not let the parents dismiss it as an unimportant detail.

   • The parents must stop the driving until everyone, including the counselor, is sure that the young person is not driving while impaired.

Do not allow a child or adolescent to be openly disrespectful to parents during a session.

a. Give your support to the parents to get them to stop tolerating the child's disrespectful behavior (open defiance, name-calling).

b.   If that doesn't work, announce to the parents the rule that ''During family sessions, I do not allow young people to do that. What you do in your own home is your business, but here that kind of behavior is not acceptable.''

c.   If that doesn't work, ask the parents to have the young person leave the room and wait in the reception area. Whenever a young person is asked to leave the room, especially if he or she is agitated or upset, an available colleague should check on the young person or, better, invite him or her to talk with the colleague in private (to get his or her side of the story, find out what happens at home, etc.).

d.   Notice that in the above interventions, the counselor always goes through the parents to deal with the young person's behavior. This is consistent with the direction of keeping the parents in charge of their children.

Source: *DeskGallery Mega-Bundle*, Copyright 1995 by Dover Publications, Inc. Used with permission.

Parents are not to blame.

a.   Parenting is an impossibly difficult job, and for parents to entirely escape feelings of guilt is rare.

b.   I assume that parents feel some guilt, whether they admit it or not. Guilt is often the driving emotion behind the behavior of many parents.

c.   Address the parental guilt by statements such as

•   ''You are not responsible *for* your son's behavior, but you are responsible *to* your son.''

•   ''You're not the problem, but hopefully you will be part of the solution.''

•   ''We want to help you use a different way to help your son.''

If the Presenting Problem Is a Marital or Couples Issue

Define the problem.

a. In defining the problem, allow each person to be somewhat general in the beginning, to protect them from having to reveal information or feelings they are not ready to talk about. The problem should, however, be specific enough to allow the counseling to proceed. For example, ''We have problems communicating'' is too general. Counselor: ''How will you know when you are communicating well together?''

b. Encourage the couple to stay on current issues rather than have extended and detailed arguments about past events.

Keep the broader system in mind.

a. In a couples conflict, there are sometimes others (in-laws, extended family, friends, etc.) who are, in some way, playing a part in the struggle. Find out who else is involved. If appropriate, and with the couple's permission, you may want to include one or more of the others in a later session.

b. Examples of questions:

   1. ''Who else knows about this problem?''

   2. ''When you want to talk to someone besides each other about this, who do you go to?''

   3. ''Do you believe this problem has an effect on anyone else? If so, who?''

Meet their children.

a. If the couple has children, get the parents' permission to include them in at least one session. Make it clear that you will respect the parents' wishes for the children not to be included in certain conversations; the parents will control what their children hear.

b. Including the children in one or more sessions has advantages. It allows the counselor to

   1. Reveal the effects of the problem on the children

   2. Motivate the couple to solve their relationship problems for the benefit of the children

   3. Get the children's input and opinions

   4. Show the children that the family's problems are being worked on

"Take sides" carefully.

a. You need to strive for a position of impartial involvement with the couple.

b. If you take sides with one, have a therapeutic purpose for doing so, and make the temporary coalition explicit: ''On that point I will have to agree with your _____ (wife, husband, partner, etc.).''

c. If you temporarily take sides, find something in the opposing viewpoint to join with, if not immediately, then later in the same session.

Ask about sex.

a. The couple's sexual relationship should be discussed, even if they have not included it in the presenting problem. It's best to wait until some rapport and trust have been established (3+ sessions) before introducing the topic.

Source: *DeskGallery Mega-Bundle*, Copyright 1995 by Dover Publications, Inc. Used with permission.

b. Suggested opening: ''One important part of an adult relationship is how you function together sexually. Even though you did not present this as a problem, it is too important not to mention. How is your sex life together? Do either of you have any concerns you want to talk about?''

c. If one or both partners admit to a sexual dissatisfaction, determine if the problem can be resolved within the context of the couples counseling or if specific sex therapy is needed. Examples of questions:

    1. ''Has the problem you brought to counseling affected your sex life?''

    2. ''Have either of you noticed any change in your desire to have sex together?''

    3. ''Do you talk together about your sexual relationship?''

    4. ''How often do you have sexual relations? Is this frequency satisfactory to you both?''

    5. ''Who usually initiates sexual activity?''

d. If either partner shows reluctance to continue on this topic, suggest separate interviews to obtain more information. This would be accomplished with the help of an opposite-sex colleague: A male counselor interviews the man, a female interviews the woman. Assure the couple that nothing will be revealed to the other partner without explicit permission.

e. During the separate interviews, determine if referral to a qualified sex therapist is needed and desired. If the couple is referred, you may want to continue the couples counseling concurrent with the sex therapy or resume couples counseling after the sex therapy is completed.

General Clinical Suggestions

Use repetition.

a. Important therapeutic messages need to be repeated. Repetition of a therapeutic theme (for example, overinvolvement of one or both parents with their children) is necessary when they are too caught up in a process to see what's happening.

b. Repetition can be done with different words and in different contexts. It can become the "melody" of a song that is recognizable even though played with different keys, instruments, and arrangements.

c. <u>Example</u>: Parent-child interactions in the sessions can occur in ways that discourage the child's autonomous behavior, like when a parent speaks for a silent child, when a child always seems to get his or her way with the parents, when a parent consistently sits closer to a child than to his or her spouse, or when parents repeatedly and ineffectively lecture their child during the session. All these transactions may indicate some form of parent-child overinvolvement. The counselor can intervene in each of these seemingly different incidents and still be addressing only one theme: parent-child enmeshment. Usually, it is not necessary to make this theme explicit ("You're overinvolved with your children."). Your repetitive process with the family speaks the message.

Good questions to ask:

a. "What have you tried to solve the problem? How did that work?"

b. "What is likely to happen if the problem isn't solved?"

c. "What makes the problem work?"

d. "What will you do the next time he/she does that?"

e. Instead of the question, "How do you *feel* about ... ?" try "What do you *do* when ... ?" This maintains an action focus and gives information about how the members react to each other—the actual behaviors that maintain the problems.

Segmenting the family: Working with a portion at a time.

a. Segmenting helps to draw boundaries around subsystems in a family (parental, spouse, or sibling subsystems). Examples:

  1. Asking the parents' permission to have the children leave the room while the parents work on appropriate rules for the children to follow. After decisions are made, the children return to the room and the parents (together) inform them of their decisions.

  2. Asking only the parents to attend a particular session, leaving the children out.

  3. Arranging individual interviews with conflicted spouses. This may enhance the joining process and reveal important information.

b. If you are taken aside by one member before or after a session or are called on the phone between sessions, keep the conversation brief and

  1. Encourage the member to deal with his or her concerns during the next family session or

  2. Get the member's permission for you to bring up his or her concerns during the next session: "Is there anything you told me today that you do not want discussed with your family the next time we meet?"

Don't try to "win" an argument you can afford to lose.

a. Avoid having an argument with a member unless there is a strategic purpose for doing it. Your strong disagreements show the family member(s) that either you do not understand their situation or you are a stubborn person, or both.

b. If you believe it is necessary to express an opposing belief, gently do so, but later find something to join with the member(s) about. This protects the counseling from a ''I'm right, you're wrong'' power struggle.

c. Join more thoroughly with the most resistant member, especially if that person is a parent or spouse who has been pressured into coming for counseling.

If the counseling gets stuck:

a. Redefine the problem. If the counseling has no definite direction, it could be because everyone has forgotten where it's supposed to be going.

b. If two or more members reach a block in their communication, become more central yourself, drawing the attention to you and away from each other.

c. Get up and move around or leave the room for 3–4 minutes. Sometimes a fresh perspective helps.

d. An effective way to change interactions between people is to add or subtract. For the next session, you can add family members (or relevant others) or can reduce the number attending. A different mixture of people will usually change what happens in the session.

Use the team approach.

a. Even though I believe that co-therapy (two counselors in the room in each family session) is usually unnecessary, it is important for counselors to work together. I do not recommend doing family counseling without colleague support.

b. Ideally, this is accomplished by a colleague(s) observing the session through a one-way mirror and processing with the counselor afterwards.

c. If observation of live interviews is not possible, try ***Colleague Teamwork***:

    1. Video- or audiotape the sessions (with the family's permission) for later review by the counselor, colleagues, or supervisor.

    2. Invite a colleague to sit in for one session. The reason for this, of course, would be explained to the family (''We frequently work as a team in improving our help to families.''). This would be necessary only when the counselor wants a second opinion.

Source: *DeskGallery Mega-Bundle*, Copyright 1995 by Dover Publications, Inc. Used with permission.

Discuss mistakes.

a. Our therapeutic mistakes can be viewed as the family's way of teaching us something about them.

b. While working with something as complex as a family, counselors will usually make mistakes. The real mistake, however, is not that a mistake is made but that nothing is learned from it.

c. The vast majority of therapeutic errors are correctable. The one that may not be correctable is when the family leaves treatment prematurely. In all such cases, ask yourself, ''Could I have done something to prevent that?'' A discussion with colleagues can facilitate this learning.

d. Frequently, therapeutic mistakes are not recognized as such by the counselor. What he or she did made perfectly good sense to that person. This is where our colleagues can help, when we are willing to listen.

Termination

a. In many cases, it is appropriate to terminate the counseling by lengthening the interval between sessions: ''Together you are doing some nice work on this problem. I don't believe it's necessary to meet next week, so let's make our next appointment two (three) weeks from now.''

b. When family members return in two or three weeks, and if they're still doing well, give them your phone number at the end of the session and ask them to call if they need to return.

c. If the family members decide to terminate and you believe it's too early, try to keep them in counseling. If they are reluctant, it's best to point out the positive changes they have made and let them go. Reason: If you make it reasonably easy for them to leave, they are more likely to return if necessary.

d. After successful (or unsuccessful) termination, the family will usually appreciate the counselor calling after 3–4 weeks to see how things are going. This also gives you information and feedback and accelerates your learning.

Session-by-Session Guidelines

The First Interview

1. Understanding the family, not changing it, is the purpose. Having a *second* interview is the goal.

2. Follow the **ReSPECT** sequence or some other guide to an orderly first session.

3. Define the family system. Who else may be part of the problem (or solution)?

4. Ask about missing members (who live in the home but are not present). What do they think?

5. Keep parents or caretakers in the central role by getting their permission before doing or saying anything significant with their child or children.

6. Report out strengths and successes as a family. If children act well, compliment the parents.

7. Be ready to stop a line of questioning or a topic if it's a struggle for them. Accommodation to their moods, views, attitudes, and behaviors is greatest in the first session.

8. Contract for 3 sessions (2 more). ''At that time, we will decide about continuing.''

9. Build a bridge to the next session: ''Next time, I want to find out more about . . . ''

The Second Interview

1. Make a brief social contact with each person before starting.

2. If they don't start, you can begin with an open-ended question. Examples: ''What's important to you today? How did it go last week? Who wants to start today?''

3. If a member who was not at the first session attends, do a brief social talk with that member (asking about job, school, etc.) and find out his or her view of the problem.

4. Milder basic tools and techniques are appropriate in this session: ***Enactments, Segmenting, Sculpting, New Talk, Circular Questions,*** and others. (After this second session, all techniques in this book are appropriate.)

5. During this session, begin pursuing a direction based on your understanding of the family structure and functioning. Is one parent closer and more protective with the teenager than the other parent? Does this cause conflict between the parents? If you suspect a particular family pattern, check it out without trying to change it. But be ready to let go if your inquiries are too difficult for them.

6. In general, give parents (or other adults) more talking time than children, even if the parents are not talkative and the children are. Parents need to have more authority and responsibility than their children.

7. Allow family members to talk to each other. If necessary, use ***Enactments.***

The Third Interview and Beyond

1. Often, the third session is different: A small crisis has happened, members show more emotion, a quiet member gets more expressive, a hidden conflict pops to the surface, or some other shift occurs. Family sessions are more familiar, the members feel safer, and they let their guard down.

2. The process from the third session and beyond is circular: Learn about the family; develop hunches about what part of the family functioning may be contributing to the presenting problem; check out your hunches with exploration and techniques; gradually focus more and more on the hunches that are confirmed; develop new hunches, etc. While doing all this, never stray too far from the family's expressed concerns (the presenting problems). Most families come to counseling to solve a problem, not for random exploration or to achieve self-actualization as a family.

Session Checklist for Family Counseling

Source: *DeskGallery Mega-Bundle*, Copyright 1995 by Dover Publications, Inc. Used with permission.

After a session, you can use this checklist to monitor yourself. You can also use it while observing a colleague's session (live or videotaped) and refer to it in your post-interview discussions together. If you use this form for several interviews, you will have a good idea of your strengths and the areas you need to work on.

- ☐ Made a brief introductory statement about the purpose of the interview (first session).
- ☐ Helped the family members define their needs and concerns.
- ☐ Defined the relevant family system.
- ☐ Collected detailed information about the nature and history of the identified problem.
- ☐ Interrupted chaotic interchanges.
- ☐ Shifted approach when one way of gathering information was not working.
- ☐ Used short, clear communications.
- ☐ Stayed relevant to their concerns.
- ☐ Structured or directed interaction between family members.
- ☐ Engendered hope.
- ☐ Used appropriate self-disclosure.
- ☐ Demonstrated warmth and empathy.
- ☐ Conveyed sensitivity to their feelings.
- ☐ Spoke at a comfortable pace.
- ☐ Concentrated more on the interaction of the family than on individual dynamics.
- ☐ Used *Positive Reframing,* and reported out strengths.
- ☐ Rearranged (when appropriate) the physical seating of family members.
- ☐ Helped the family establish appropriate boundaries.
- ☐ Encouraged the family to find its own solutions.
- ☐ Explored current feelings and reactions to each other in the room.
- ☐ Focused more on process (how) than content (what).
- ☐ Used own affect to elicit affect in family members.

CHAPTER 2
SPECIAL SITUATIONS

Introduction

Every family is a special situation. After responding for a while to these unique groups—these little subcultures—you notice that some situations and circumstances occur repeatedly across different families, with different problems, in different settings. These diverse experiences allow us to generate some principles to guide us when the situations occur.

Everyone who works with families must address some common issues: family resistance and denial, enmeshment, powerless parents, and ''hidden'' parental conflict. We also need to respect the differences between a single-parent family, a two-parent family and a blended family. Their structure and circumstances are not the same, and we learn to apply slightly different approaches to each of them.

In this chapter, special attention is paid to working with adolescents in family sessions. Teenagers can be challenging—raising teenagers has been compared to being nibbled to death by ducks—and many families have trouble with the ambivalence, mood swings, and experimentation of these young people. It can be an agitated time for a family and can spawn problems that go beyond the parent-teenager relationship—problems between the parents, for example, or between the grandparents and parents, or even between the siblings.

We will not successfully negotiate these special situations and dynamics every time, but common sense tells us that some things work better than others and that being a successful helper does not depend on being successful every time. Nothing we have will work for everybody, but everything we have will work for somebody. Our task is to acquire an assortment of ideas and skills and to match them to the special situation in front of us.

My suggestions to the reader are to find the topics that are familiar to you, which you have seen in your practice with families. Then take from those pieces what you can use to add to your own style and approach, perhaps making your interventions more on target.

At a crafts fair I attended years ago, I watched a craftsman fashion sturdy, simple furniture from wood using only a hatchet and a shaving knife. As he chopped away at a table leg, I asked him how he did it. He replied, ''It's simple. You just hit right where you're aiming, and the more you practice the luckier you get.''

Therapeutic Themes by Family Type (Child Identified Patient)

Biological Two-Parent

Theme Work on the parental relationship while keeping the child's behavior as the central issue. The goal is parental agreement, teamwork, "speaking with one voice," and consistency with the child.

Rationale Some child problems are the result of parents who are in conflict about how to parent their child or children. One parent, for example, is lenient to balance the strictness of the other; the other is strict to balance the lenient one. This gives the child two conflicting messages about their behavior, plus it puts the child squarely in the middle of the parents' disagreements (triangulation). It also keeps the parents tense and angry with each other, which can have serious consequences for the family functioning and the emotional climate in the home.

Blended Family

Theme Same as the biological two-parent family *except* keep the biological parent in the more central, responsible role concerning the child.

Rationale In most blended families, it is natural for the biological parent to be more emotionally close and protective of the children than the stepparent.

If the parents haven't negotiated the stepparent's role with the children, the stepparent may be doing things with the child that the biological parent doesn't agree with, which sets up conflict between the parents. The stepparent, at least in the early part of the remarriage, should be working with "borrowed authority" with the children (borrowed from the biological parent). All stepparenting should be with the biological parent's agreement and approval.

Single Parent

Theme Help the parent find adult support (family, friends, dating partners, adult groups, church).

Rationale Many single parents have a tough job, trying to make a living and be both parents to their children. This places much stress on the parent, often making him or her exhausted and irritable. The parent needs to look after his or her own adult needs, have friends, and have some clean fun. If this doesn't happen, the parent may pass on his or her fatigue and irritability to the children.

Also, many children of single parents are accustomed to having more responsibility and freedom. One or more may even become their parent's "friend," emotional confidant, peer, partner, almost spouse substitute. When the parent allows the child to become a peer or friend, it is difficult to maintain one's authority as parent—being both a friend and a parent is a dual and conflicting role. If a single parent is their child's best friend, parental authority is compromised.

If the parent receives adult support, he or she is more likely to act like an adult and take charge of the children. In addition, the parent is also more likely to get interpersonal needs met in more appropriate ways.

Separated/Divorced

(This assumes the identified patient child is spending time in the homes of both parents.)

Theme Be careful whom you invite to the sessions.

Rationale Ex-partners meeting together with current partners can produce a tense meeting. The adult history and ''politics'' are so thick that parents may be unable to cooperate in setting consistent rules for the child in both households. In the initial session, if you are not sure about the adult relationships in the family, invite only the family members in the home of the parent who is seeking services. In this meeting, you can find out about the adult relationships and decide who should be present for later sessions.

Same-Sex Parents

Theme Work on the parental relationship while keeping the child's behavior as the central issue, as in the biological two-parent family. Encourage parental agreement, teamwork, and consistency with the child. Recognize that not all same-sex parent families will look the same. There may be one biological parent with an adoptive parent partner, a biological parent with a partner who has not adopted the children, or a guardian instead of a biological parent.

Rationale Regardless of the particular constellation of the same-sex family, keeping the focus on issues of the child identified patient is still important. Some of the child problems may result because the parental team is in conflict about how to parent the child, in effect ''splitting'' the parental team. It may also be useful for the child to discuss openly in the session any feelings he or she may have about having to moms or two dads. This is done, of course, without overemphasizing this alternative family structure.

Blended and Single-Parent Families

Here are a few of the dynamics that lie hidden in many blended and single-parent families. Because the issues are often outside awareness or are unacknowledged, they can generate a variety of problems.

Blended Family

Central Issue The emotional bond between the biological parent and children can be much stronger than between the stepparent and children. The older the children were at the time of the remarriage, the more this is true. This can lead to numerous problems, including the stepparent feeling left out and unaccepted by the children, the overprotection of the children by the biological parent, and disagreements between the spouses on how the children should be parented.

Clinical Suggestion While allowing the biological parent to remain in the more central, decision-making role with the children, help the parents find a way to include more of the stepparent's influence in parenting. This can be done by the stepparent exercising influence through the biological parent or the biological parent allowing more direct interaction between the stepparent and the children. There is little use in encouraging a totally equal parenting partnership, as you might do in a family with two biological parents.

Central Issue The biological parent hasn't given full permission for the stepparent to parent the children. As a result, the stepparent either withdraws from parenting responsibilities—leaving the biological parent without help—or becomes overactive with the children, ineffectively trying to correct the ''mistakes'' of the biological parent. Either way, the stepparent is angry at having no real authority.

Clinical Suggestion During a session, get the biological parent to tell the stepparent under what conditions he or she will accept the stepparent's help in parenting the children. The stepparent can accept or reject the terms, but the issue needs to be out in the open so their expectations can be examined.

Central Issue One parent becomes a ''friend'' to the children while the other does the disciplining and limit setting.

Clinical Suggestion Discuss how friendship and parenting are not alike in several important ways: friends don't enforce house rules or administer discipline; friends don't break up arguments between siblings; friends don't provide food, clothing, shelter, and transportation. Get the ''disciplining'' parent to acknowledge to the spouse his or her resentment at being kept in the role of bad guy. Patiently coach the parents into discovering better ways to stand together and support each other. The goal is a united front by the parents.

Central Issue The children can put great stress on a new partnership and purposely make it difficult. It is normal for them to test the parents' resolve to make the new relationship succeed.

Clinical Suggestion The primary bond for the blended family is the parents' relationship. Get the parents to explore ways to convince the kids that the parents will stand together and provide a secure and loving home for the family.

Single-Parent Family

(Note: To simplify the language, I will assume the single parent is a mother. If the single parent is a father, the principles also apply.)

Central Issue The mother becomes overly close to one or more of her children, sometimes seeking emotional support from them. At other times, she reverts to the authoritative parental figure. These inconsistent and conflicting roles of peer/friend on the one hand and disciplining parent on the other can make children anxious, insecure, and resistant to the parent's authority.

Clinical Suggestion Help the parent find *adult* support (extended family, friends, adult groups, etc.). This begins with the mother's adult-adult relationship with the counselor. Encourage the parent to allow the children to improve and expand their peer relationships (so they won't be so dependent on mother).

Central Issue The mother is overwhelmed with parenting and ineffective at disciplining and setting appropriate limits with her children.

Clinical Suggestion Join in a clear alliance with the parent, offering faith in her abilities to parent and giving her strong support in taking charge of the children. To balance somewhat, act as negotiator between parent and children to help the children get their mother to meet their appropriate needs. But keep the mother in the decision-making role and clearly in charge.

Central Issue If the mother has a steady partner, the children often act toward the couple with jealousy, anger, and resentment. The kids can make it difficult for the couple to have a relationship.

Clinical Suggestion Work with the mother/partner relationship (without the children present). Encourage the couple to talk to each other about her expectations of the partner's role with the children, to discuss their future together (and whether or not marriage may be an option), to explore how their interaction affects the children, and to decide how to manage their sexual relationship. Explain to the couple that this clarification will reduce the confusion, anxiety, and hostility of the children. When they reach some agreements and clarification, bring the children in and ask the mother to explain the agreements to them.

Central Issue The single parent takes care of the children but doesn't take care of him- or herself. Single parents sometimes neglect their own needs, not realizing that the children are receiving parenting from a stressed-out, tired parent. If the parent is not getting his or her needs met, the children are not receiving the best the parent can give.

Clinical Suggestion Say to the parent, "When you travel by plane with a child and the cabin suddenly loses pressure, what do they say you should do with the oxygen mask when it pops down from the overhead?" (Put yours on before assisting the child.) Emphasize the importance of self-care—adequate rest, alone time, social time, etc.

Blended Families: Tips for Two Common Scenarios

I have admiration for blended families who successfully manage their complex set of loyalties and relationships. But sometimes things go wrong. Out of a number of potential problems, here are two common scenarios and some general tips.

Scenario #1 With a biological mother and stepfather, she naturally has a stronger emotional connection with the children than he does. She wants him to be a father to her children, but she may not like the way he parents them. And when conflict and tension bubble up between the stepfather and children, she is caught in the middle. Trying to manage this go-between role, she may give her husband mixed messages, assuring him that he has authority with her children but also at times undermining his authority by secretly siding with the children. This causes trouble every time.

In a private session with the parents, address the mother's dilemma and her stressful position in the family ("Ever feel like you're caught in the middle?"). During the session, create an enactment between the parents by saying to her, "Tell your husband under what conditions you will allow him to help you parent your children." This issue has never been fully worked through, and it takes some negotiation, since he doesn't have to agree to all her conditions.

Scenario #2 With a biological father and stepmother, this problem happens often: the father has given the primary parenting of the children to the stepmother. The father's detachment confuses and angers the children, which they take out on their stepmother, causing much conflict. This fray has a secondary gain for the children—it keeps the dad involved—but the greater the conflict, the more the dad detaches, leaving her even more alone with the children. In this situation, stepmothers get frustrated and angry at both the children and the husband.

The goal here is to work with the parents to bring the biological father back in as the primary decision-making, disciplining parent. At a minimum, he needs to let the children know, by his *actions*, that he firmly stands behind whatever parenting decisions his wife makes.

General Tips

1. Some remarried couples try to put the stepparent in an active parenting role too quickly. A newly blended family (less than 2 years) is still struggling with their roles and relationships; they haven't blended yet. In these cases, refer to the stepparent as the "polite stranger" regarding his or her parental role. Using these phrases cautions the couple to go slow in creating an active parenting role for the stepparent.

2. Find out how the children refer to their stepparent (mom, dad, Franco, Lilly, etc.), and use their terms. If you refer to the stepparent as the child's "mom" or "dad," the child will often correct you in a flash ("He's not my dad!"), creating an unnecessary side trip.

3. If the children were teenagers or older at the time of the remarriage, they may never fully accept the stepparent in a direct, active parenting role. If appropriate, educate the parents that this happens frequently and is quite normal.

4. For a family problem with an out-of-control teenager who is in conflict (sometimes physically) with the stepfather, in a private conversation with the parents, get them to consider a "cooling-down" period: Both parents agree that the stepfather does not discipline, or even actively parent, the teenager for a specified time (maybe 2–3 weeks). Instead, he goes to the mother when he wants action taken with the child. This agreement puts the crisis on hold, provides relief for everyone, and reduces the dangerous interactions between the stepfather and teenager until the family can be helped to manage better.

The Powerless Parent

Description

A powerless parent is usually a single parent who seems to be unable to control her* child. The child responds only momentarily, if at all, to the parent's corrective efforts. The child is oppositional and unruly, home life is chaotic, and the parent is exhausted. The child is in charge. The powerless parent syndrome seems to have one or more of the following origins:

1. The parent apparently believes that she has no right (or responsibility) to set appropriate limits on the child. Or, the parent tries to make friends of her child. Her philosophy appears to be, "The more I let him do what he wants, the more he will like me."

2. The parent feels guilty toward her child; the guilt comes from not being a perfect parent, from separating from the child's father, from raising a child with a disability, or from another source.

3. Another influential adult, who is lenient and protective toward the child, is co-parenting. This other adult could be the divorced other parent, a grandparent, or someone else. The single parent attempts to maintain discipline but is undermined by the lenient co-parent. The child knows this. A saying in family work goes, "If a child is taller than a parent, they're standing on someone's shoulders."

Suggestions

The counselor needs to give an extra dose of support, consistency, and gentle firmness to the powerless parent. While doing this, it is important to keep the processes parallel—your behavior toward the parent is what you are modeling for her about how to act toward her child. If you are encouraging her to be gently firm and consistent with her child, you must be gently firm and consistent with her. The medium is the message.

1. *Believe* the parent can be in charge. You need a genuine faith in her ability to regain control for the child's good, the family's good, and for her own good.

2. Start with successes. What does this parent do well ("How did you get him to go to bed last night?")? Keep searching until you find examples of successful control.

3. During the sessions when the child misbehaves, look at the parent, not the child. This will put pressure on the parent. She will be a bit miffed at you, so be prepared to do relationship repair when needed.

4. Keep the parent in the central, decision-making role. Do nothing with the child without going through the parent. Child (to counselor): "Can I play with the toys?" Counselor: "Ask your mom."

5. Find out about the parent's adult support network. For the parent to stand firm with the child, she may need the support and advice from other adults (friends, siblings, her parents, etc.).

6. Explore the parent's background. You will often find some influence, crisis, or trauma that has shaped the parent's behavior toward her child. Maybe insight will help.

---

* For purposes of my example, I have assumed a single mother with one undisciplined child. If the single parent is a father, the principles are the same. It is also important that medical conditions for the child's behavior have either been ruled out or are under treatment.

The Parental Mind-Set

Source: *DeskGallery Image Catalog*, Copyright 1994 by Dover Publications, Inc. Used with permission.

Parents often arrive at the counselor's office with a young child in tow who "doesn't act right." They may describe the child as "bad," "aggressive," "mean," "irresponsible," "lazy," or other such term. The parents label the child and take themselves out of the interactional equation. In the parents' minds, the child acts that way on their own, no matter what the parents do.

The Professional's Mind-Set

First, let's acknowledge that not all problem behavior of children is psychosocial in origin. Some reasons for the child's behavior might be organic or medical. The counselor must rule these out by asking about medical conditions—physical checkups, pediatrician visits, hospitalizations, and medications. Also, some causes might be genetic in origin. Children are born with different temperaments, different activity levels, different reactivity, different predispositions. Of course, even when the problem behavior is medically or genetically based, the parents' *reaction* to the child can make all the difference in whether the problems get worse, stay the same, or get better.

If you rule out medical conditions, the most common underlying emotional states of problem children, in my experience, are a mixture of fear, anger, confusion, and sometimes depression. The fear is closely tied to insecurity; they don't feel a foundation of safety, and they are scared that they or someone else in the family will be hurt. The anger and confusion result from the child being kept off balance by the parents' inconsistency or by the secrecy and deception in the family. Depression in children will usually manifest as sadness and withdrawal but is often punctuated with angry acting out. And sometimes, children just act out the tension, anxiety, and conflicts in the family.

What to Do

If the parents view the child as chronically "bad," they are usually angry at him or her—not just irritated when their disruptive behaviors occur but more continuously angry, like they might be toward an adult. Their anger leads to more mindless, and usually inconsistent, punishment for the bad behavior and much yelling or lecturing, all of which does little to change the child's behavior except in the wrong direction.

The counselor's challenge is to gently shift the angry parents' mind-set from "bad" child to "upset" child. This is an important shift, since parents will usually soften their reaction to their child if their mind-set is that he or she is "upset." In this reframing of the problem, we help the parents look at the *underlying emotions* driving the behavior. This needs to be done with minimal challenging of the parents' perceptions, especially at the beginning, and sufficient care that the parents don't feel blamed. Initially, this is accomplished by matching the parents' way of seeing the problem: "I see what you mean; she is very challenging."

To accomplish the reframing of the child's behavior from "bad" to "upset," several techniques in this book are especially appropriate: **Strategic Child Assessment** and **Child Diagnosis** are individual assessments of the child, the results of which are explained to the parents in a way that gets the parents' cooperation in solving the problem. This can be combined with **Draw-a-Dream,** a drawing made by the child that looks at his or her underlying fears. **Worried Child,** a technique to help the child express his or her emotions to the parents, may also help.

Parent-Child Enmeshment

Enmeshment is when two or more family members are too close—they seem to be inside each other's heads and hearts. (In its extreme form, I call it "enmushment.") Enmeshment between parent and child is perhaps the most common form in families.

What's Wrong With Parent-Child Enmeshment?

For one thing, the child doesn't mature normally. Since he or she spends so much time in the adult's world, a child enmeshed with an adult may appear to be more mature than he or she actually is. But the child has missed some of the peer relationships, childhood play, and misadventures that are part of growing up. Enmeshment also tends to produce "entitled" children, whose spoiled behavior may cause trouble with peers and friends. On the parent side, normal development is also inhibited, since the parent gets too many interpersonal needs met though the child, which blocks other growth-promoting ties with family members and friends. In an enmeshed relationship, neither member has room to grow. On the family level, enmeshment can generate conflicts, especially if one parenting adult is enmeshed with one or more children and other parenting adults are not.

How to Spot Enmeshment

No single behavior will establish enmeshment, but any of these items point in that direction.
1. A parent consistently answers questions or "elaborates" when you're talking to the child.
2. Parent(s) are overly attentive toward the child in the session, frequently touching the child and noticing his or her every move.
3. The parent encourages a child, too old to be "lappable," to sit in his or her lap.
4. The parent speaks to the child in a younger (or older) way than is appropriate for the child's age.
5. You find out that the child sleeps with the parent(s).

What to Do

1. Beginning in the second or third session, gently raise awareness of the parent-child over-involvement by first establishing conversational boundaries.
    *   Invite the enmeshed parent to listen to you talk with the child. It will be hard for the parent to stay silent, giving you a chance to comment, "Letting your child speak without your help seems to be difficult for you."
    *   Create an **Enactment** between the child and the less-enmeshed parent while defining the enmeshed parent as "a listener." When the enmeshed parent interrupts, gently remind him or her to "Let them work this out."
    *   If the children are about age 10 or older, try **Sibling Talk,** where you help the parents stay out of a conversation between two of their children ("While we listen, tell your brother how you worry about him sometimes."). Gently block interruptions by either parent.
2. Once the parental awareness of conversational boundaries is increased, start conversations with the parent(s) about other relationships.
    *   In a two-parent family, encourage more parental togetherness ("When is the last time the two of you had a 'date' without the children?").
    *   Encourage the parent(s) to allow their child to develop age-appropriate friends.
    *   Encourage an enmeshed single parent to have friends and time away from children.
3. Have a private conversation with the single parent, finding out about his or her best friend, social activities, dating interests, and how the parent enjoys him- or herself without the children.
4. Since adult support for the single parent is a major theme in these families, get the parent's agreement to bring an adult family member or friend to the next session.

"Split" Parenting

Sometimes, symptomatic children are produced when both parents or parent figures are not together in the way they parent the child. One can be strict, sometimes to balance out the other lenient parent (who is also balancing the strict one). This gives the child conflicting messages and produces tension and arguments in the home, which children often act out in their behavior (the symptoms). The child's problematic behavior feeds the parental split, resulting in more bad behavior, and round and round it goes. If this occurs in a family with a child identified patient, regardless of age, here are some guidelines:

1. Find out the details of the child's problem behavior (when, where, how, even why). If appropriate, use the **Strategic Child Assessment** technique.

2. Sort out how the parents usually react to the child's problems. What action have they taken to solve the problem? During this discussion, notice the *differences* in how each parent views the behavior and how each reacts to it: "You seem to have different ways of loving your child."

3. As the sessions progress, gently push for parental unity—the parents coming together to agree on appropriate consequences for the child's problem behavior ("speaking with one voice").

4. If deep-seated parental differences exist, they will usually be revealed when you encourage parental unity. If these differences surface in the counseling sessions, get the parents' permission for the child to leave the room while "the two of you develop a plan you want to follow." When a plan is decided, ask the child to return to the room and have the parents explain it to the child.

5. When parents begin to present consistent, unified, limit-setting messages, the child will usually get worse: "This is your child's way of testing to see if you are serious." The child is losing power, and it is normal for him or her to temporarily resist. Explain this to the parents.

6. During the period of counseling, crises and setbacks will usually occur as a natural part of the family's life. While helping the parents through these, gently work on the theme of parental unity.

Comments

1. Explore, and attend to, the behavior of all the children in the home, not just the identified patient. If the other children are doing well, use this to reinforce parental competence.

2. Don't focus entirely on the parents providing *negative* consequences to the child's bad behavior (To parents: "You have been clear with your son about what you will do if he continues to get into trouble in school. But what will you do if he *improves* his school behavior?"). Keep the parents in charge of consequences, but help them give incentives for good behavior.

3. Discourage open disagreements and arguments between the parents at home in front of the child: "If your son sees this, he may get worse." Encourage them to save disagreements for times when the child is not present or simply go to a location—out of earshot of the child—to work out their disagreements.

4. When parents decide on limit-setting instructions to the child (as in item 4 in the preceding list), ask the "lenient" parent to take the lead and do most of the talking to the child. This difference lets the child know that change is in the air.

5. For dangerous behavior (teenage substance abuse or aggressiveness, for example), both parents must be on board with limit-setting consequences. If a limit is enforced by one parent and the teenager's rebellion causes harm to someone, you don't want the other parent saying, "I told you so." If this happens, the blame, anger, and guilt can damage the family.

Parental Denial

Parental denial of their child's problems is understandable. It brings up disturbing feelings of guilt and responsibility for parents to believe that their child is emotionally or behaviorally disturbed, is in trouble with drugs or alcohol, is oppositional at school, is engaging in dangerous behavior outside the home, or whatever form the problem behavior takes.

However, if parents refuse to acknowledge and act on the high-risk behaviors of their children, no intervention will be made, no serious parental limits will be set and maintained, and the child will continue the antisocial or self-destructive behavior until someone gets hurt. I have seen parental denial of their teenager's problems so strong—in the face of obvious signs—that the child was allowed to run with dangerous friends, be promiscuous, break the law, and fail in school. Some children end up incarcerated or hospitalized before the parents admit to a problem.

There is another form of parental denial that is even more common. Some parents are quick to discount the impact of family problems on their child. Many parents will sincerely deny that their relationship difficulties, arguments, tension between adults in or out of the home, even spouse abuse has had an effect on their children.

I don't believe it. Children are extremely sensitive to emotions in the home, overt or "hidden." The child may not be able to put the issues into words or may not understand the cause of the disruptions, but it's best to assume that they *feel* everything that goes on. These feelings (anxiety, anger, depression) frequently result in behavioral and emotional problems for the child and family.

If parents are denying the dangerous or unhealthy activities of their child:

a. Be calm, be patient, be persistent, and use facts (suggest drug testing, for example).

b. Don't be afraid to "tell on" the child to the parents if you find out that the child is doing dangerous things. Explain to the child that confidentiality does not extend to harm to self or others. Of course, give the child a chance to tell the parents first in your presence during a session. (Under informed consent, you would have notified both child and guardian or parent of this in the initial session.)

c. One way to do this is to get the parents to ask the child about the dangerous behavior in question while you listen. This conversation is worthwhile for its information value to the parent, even though the child may not be totally honest.

If parents are denying the impact of a parental or family problem on the children:

a. Show benevolent skepticism. Gently get the parents to explain how arguments between them do not reach the ears of their child, how the child does not know that two or more people in the home are not getting along, or that mom or dad aren't doing well.

b. During a session, focus on the child or children to get to their emotions. A private interview with the children (if the parents give permission) may be helpful.

c. For any type of parental denial, some of these techniques are appropriate:

1. *Strategic Child Assessment*
2. *Worried Child*
3. *Strategic Predictions*
4. *Alter Ego*
5. *Drawings*
6. *Sculpting*
7. *Brief Network Intervention*
8. *Expert Colleague*

Difficult Parents

Once we build a relationship with the child in treatment, it is easy, even natural, to become somewhat disappointed at the child's parents. I often hear, ''It's the parents who need counseling; this child is the healthiest one in the family!'' This attitude is easier to adopt if most of what we know about the parents and family comes only from the child.

Most of the children and adolescents we see in counseling are in homes that are heavy on conflict and tension and light on security and stability. But by exploring the histories of many families, I have come to understand that most parents who don't give their child what he or she needs didn't get what they needed as children in their own families of origin. Incompetent parents were usually parented incompetently, so they never learned how to do it well. As helping professionals, this gives us a choice about our attitude: Do we view parents as *perpetrators* of their child's problems or as *victims* of their own inadequate childhood?

Reasons to build a relationship (''joining'') with the parents of a child or teenager in counseling:

1. The first step in helping a child is to put the parents on the ''treatment team.''

2. The best long-range ''therapist'' for a child will always be a competent parent. Our professional relationship with the child is very temporary.

3. If a single parent has legal custody, that parent is usually the child's best hope for a family life.

4. The therapeutic work with the child is easier when a good relationship develops between us and the parents.

5. It's good for children to see us respecting their parents, even though the child may be angry at his or her parents.

6. When trust is developed with the parents, it's much easier for them to accept the help they need to change their parenting behavior or to seek their own counseling.

7. An extra dose of joining is often needed with parents who fear or mistrust you or your agency's motives. Also, if child custody is an issue, our legal system encourages an antagonistic relationship with parents. We need to rebalance by connecting well with them.

How to Join With Difficult Parents

1. Briefly explore the parent's childhood (see the ***Parent's Childhood*** technique). This is good relationship building, plus it may give you compassion.

2. Respect the parent-child bond; it is strong and special. Notice how most children in out-of-home placement want to return home regardless of how they are treated.

3. You can be an ''expert'' on counseling, child development, and child management, but always keep the parents as the experts on their own children.

4. Keep the parents in charge of their children when they are together in a meeting or session with you. Until legal custody is removed, the parents have the responsibility for their children, including the children's behavior in your office.

5. Take every opportunity to acknowledge the parents' appropriate authority with their children. Responsibility and authority go together.

Child Diagnosis in Plain English

Definition

Through child assessment and discussion with parents, the counselor frames the child's problems in everyday language in a way that puts the problem behavior in a *relationship* context between the parent and child.

Purpose

This intervention is more appropriate for young children and pre-adolescents and is especially useful when the parent(s) ascribe all the problems to the child and none to the way they parent their child; the parent takes him- or herself out of the equation. This intervention attempts to put the parents back in the equation, urging them to change their child by changing the way they respond to the child's problems.

Background

If organic/medical causes are ruled out, I have found that the following five emotions/behaviors of children accompany most behavior problems. They can occur separately or in combination:

1. Fear—A basic feeling of insecurity about being cared for. The child doesn't feel safe. Behavior problems are basically acting out this anxiety.

2. Anger—Frustration with the parents' behavior or at others in the family. The parents respond to the child's anger with more anger, setting up a vicious circle—the child's and parents' anger feed each other.

3. Confusion—Parents are inconsistent in setting limits and supervising the child's behavior. The child is kept off balance and randomly tests the parents' resolve.

4. Manipulation—The child has learned how to manage the parents. For example, the child learns that if he or she complains enough or has a tantrum, the parent will get tired and give in; or the child thinks, "I don't have to mind Daddy because Mom will take my side."

5. Modeling—The child is imitating the moods, behavior, and attitudes of the parent(s) or other family member(s).

Procedure

1. Do a problem assessment with the parent(s). Find out from the parents or parent figures about the child behaviors they are concerned about. A problem assessment includes:

    a. What are the specifics of the problem behaviors?

    b. How long ago did the problems start?

    c. When do the problems occur/not occur?

    d. What is the parent's "theory" about the causes of the problem behavior?

    e. Does anyone else in the family have a "theory" about the causes?

2. Assess the child alone. After talking with the parent(s), ask permission to talk to the child alone to "determine the causes for the disruptive behavior." When assessing the child, explore his or her feelings and thoughts about what is happening in the home plus anything else the child will tell you.

3. Diagnose. Return to the parents with the assessment information and a "diagnosis." This is a critical piece in this procedure and may take some discussion (without the child). In a two-parent home, be sure both parents are present.

Examples

Here are some brief examples of "diagnosis" statements and suggestions to parents for each of the emotions/behaviors of the child described earlier. The parents' skepticism and resistance to these ideas and suggestions may lessen with time; if necessary, let them think about it between sessions. In a two-parent household, the parents need to help each other with the following action steps:

1. **Fear** "My assessment of Jimmy revealed that he is deeply afraid of something, even though we know he has no reason to be. His deep fear is keeping him stirred up inside and makes him desperate and unpredictable. Let's talk about how you can help Jimmy feel safe."

2. **Anger** "As we know, Jimmy is sometimes aggressive and defiant toward you and his siblings. After getting to know him, I found that he has a lot of anger and frustration, and it's making him act poorly. Because anger has to go somewhere, it comes out in his behavior. For the next two weeks, each time he gets angry or aggressive, can you talk to him *calmly* to discover where this anger is coming from? This will take patience on your part, but it may reveal something important."

3. **Confusion** "In my assessment of Jimmy, I discovered that he is testing you to see if you are serious. Sometimes he thinks you are serious when you correct or supervise him, and at other times he thinks you're not serious. For the next week, can you show him you are serious *every* time?"

4. **Manipulation** "My talks with Jimmy revealed that he will take advantage of some situations to get what he wants. He has learned that he can outlast you—if he has a tantrum long enough and is very persistent, you will get tired and he can have his way. For the next week, can you outlast him and show him you won't give in?"

5. **Modeling** "Because Jimmy looks up to you, he tries to imitate you. When you become understandably frustrated and angry with him, he does the same with you; he believes he's supposed to act that way. For the next two weeks, I want you to teach him a different way to act by being kind and gentle, even when he becomes angry and aggressive. Hopefully, he will begin to imitate this new behavior."

Comment

I haven't seen this intervention produce radical positive change in a child's behavior, although if this occurs, it's certainly a bonus. The real purpose is to help parents become more aware of how their reaction to the child largely determines whether the problems get worse, stay the same, or get better. It broadens the parents' view of the problem, brings them closer to looking at their own behavior toward the child, and puts their child's behavior in context, rather than them believing that the "bad" behavior originates within the skin of the child.

The Three Worlds of the Adolescent

Most adolescents inhabit three interconnected worlds—family, school, and peers. When doing family work with an adolescent identified patient, all three worlds need attention.

Rationale

The adolescent's relationships with his or her parents will usually be conflicted if the child is failing at school. And if the young person drops out of school, it sets him or her on a developmentally abnormal track. Likewise, stable family relationships won't last long if the adolescent is running with peers who are influencing him or her toward rebellious, trouble-making activities. One area of the teen's life affects the others.

Here are some considerations in the three areas of the child's life.

Family

1. Are appropriate parent-child boundaries established (parents are not so emotionally close or so distant that they have lost control of the child)?

2. In households with two parenting adults, are the parents in agreement? Do ''hidden'' conflicts and disagreements between the parents result in different messages to the child about his or her behavior? (The goal is unified parenting.)

3. In stressed families, all children are affected, not just the identified adolescent. Are the other children in the home being considered in the family sessions, even the non-problem, ''good'' children?

School

1. Do parents monitor school attendance and homework? Does the child have a good place to study at home, and are TV watching and other distractions such as computers and cell phones controlled by the parents?

2. Are one or both parents staying informed about the child's school activities by maintaining contact with teachers and counselors?

3. Do the parents sign the student's report card, and, if appropriate, grant or remove privileges based on grades?

Peers

1. Do the parents know their child's best friend? Do they know the friend's parents?

2. Are the parents aware of the general whereabouts and activities of their child?

3. How much control over the child's choice of friends do the parents have? How much do they want (and need)?

4. Have the parents established and maintained appropriate curfews?

Family · School · Peers

Source: *DeskGallery Image Catalog*, Copyright 1994 by Dover Publications, Inc. Used with permission.

Source: *DeskGallery Image Catalog*, Copyright 1994 by Dover Publications, Inc. Used with permission.

Source: *DeskGallery Image Catalog*, Copyright 1994 by Dover Publications, Inc. Used with permission.

Managing Adolescents in Family Sessions

1. Put the parents on the "treatment team."

   This model of family counseling assumes that families run better when the parents, not the children, are in charge. (I've seen many families where a disruptive adolescent is in charge; these families usually don't run well.) As counselors, we join thoroughly with the parents and keep them in the central, responsible, decision-making role; this allows us to enter the family in a way that brings about change.

2. Don't let the adolescent dominate.

   Don't let adolescents dominate the session by their disruptive behavior. If the adolescent starts name-calling or other disrespectful behavior toward the parent(s), take a firm stand: "What you do in your home is your business, but I don't allow that here." If that doesn't work, get permission from the parents for the young person to talk to another counselor outside the session (or just leave the room temporarily): "Mike is trying so hard, he's getting in his own way."

   Even a silent adolescent can dominate a session, drawing everyone's attention to get him or her to speak. If the adolescent is uncommunicative after several tries to include him or her, let go and frame the silence to the adolescent as protection for the family: "I guess you figure if you don't talk, you're protecting the family from an argument. Maybe you'll get something out of listening to me talk with your parents."

3. Acknowledge the adolescent's position.

   Family counseling is hard on an adolescent who is the identified patient. The adolescent often feels ganged up on and unduly blamed for all the family chaos. This child often knows that others in the family are contributing to the family problems; everything is not all their fault. They sometimes rebel at this unfair treatment. The counselor should find opportunities to offer support to the adolescent.

4. Temporarily become the adolescent advocate.

   We need a way to balance somewhat our strong empowering of the parents. One way to do this is to temporarily become the "adolescent advocate" by asking permission of adolescents for you to help them talk to their parents about something they want from the parents. Just ask young people to turn to their parents and ask for something they want—a thing, maybe, or a privilege or some favor. Let the parents respond. If they say "no," say to the adolescent, "Your parents have said no to that. Find out if there are any conditions under which they would say yes." (Parents may say no to extended weekend curfew but may say yes to the request if the child's school grades improve.) This intervention temporarily takes sides with the young person while still keeping the parents in charge. It may take several tries before the parents agree to a request by the child.

5. Gently spread the focus.

   A way to extend the problem beyond the adolescent identified patient is to say to the adolescent's *sibling*, "How is it that you can have a good time and stay out of trouble with your parents, but when your brother tries it, he gets into trouble?" This question acknowledges that the siblings have their fun and that they are imperfect children just like their brother. The counselor needs to patiently bring the family to the realization that what's happening in the family affects all the children, even the quiet, "good" ones.

   If parents appear to be denying that the problem adolescent's behavior is somehow related to anything in the family, you can say, "Mike's behavior may not be a family problem, but it's obviously a problem for the family." This turnaround in terms acknowledges that everyone is involved in some way and that the problem is at a family level, not just a one-person issue.

Couples Work

These are a few tips I try to keep in mind when doing marriage and couples counseling. They are general guidelines and apply to married or unmarried couples, with or without children, heterosexual or gay, living together or apart.

1. Small things matter. Don't sit closer to one member of the couple than the other. Also, if you find yourself aligning more with the disclosures of one, find some way to join the other, if not immediately, at least before the session ends.

   Reason: In couples work, the counselor's impartiality is a crucial and ongoing issue. Two people in conflict are acutely aware of where the third party stands (or sits).

2. In the initial stages, it is appropriate for the counselor to be central in the couple's communication—the counselor is the ''switchboard'' for communication, with most of the talk going through the counselor.

   Reason: The couple is having a hard time communicating effectively and needs the structure of a third party to talk to. Talking directly to the counselor also reduces interruptions by the other partner.

3. Even though you are mostly central in the first couple of sessions, encourage (or simply allow) the partners to talk directly to each other several times.

   Reasons: 1) You need to *see* how they interact, rather than just hear a description of it, and 2) You are preparing them for later in the counseling when you will be more of a coach on the side during their attempts to communicate directly to each other, which they must learn to do. If you don't prepare them for this early, they may have difficulty with direct communication later in the counseling.

4. Try to hold your interpretations and deeper insights until you have joined them in the details of their story.

   Reason: Each member is anxious to justify his or her position to you and the partner. They are not free to hear your insights, interpretations, or what ''they are really struggling about'' until they have done this.

5. The term ''power struggle''—to label their conflict—is usually not helpful.

   Reason: The struggle for power in a relationship is behind the scenes in most conflicts and can even take on a life of its own. It's best not to validate it with a name.

6. It's okay to give directives to guide and coach their communication. Tell them what to do in a given moment: ''That sounds important. Tell ____ (spouse or partner) while I listen.''

   Reason: You are teaching and shaping their communication process while you stay with their content. When done appropriately, couples and families don't mind nudges.

7. Find out who else is affected by their conflict and disagreements. Examples: ''Who else knows what's going on between you?'' ''Who else is affected by your relationship?''

   Reason: When a couple is emotionally focused on each other, they are often unaware of the impact on those around them. These, or similar questions, can heighten the couple's awareness of the social context of their struggle (children, in-laws, friends) and broaden their perspective.

8. Don't be reluctant to use metaphor when appropriate, such as ''Draw your relationship,'' or ''Change the distance between you.'' See ***Sculpting and Movement.***

   Reason: Sometimes it helps to step off the well-traveled highway of words and shift the medium to something more expressive and playful.

9. If you assign a homework task early in the counseling, keep it simple and easy.

    Reason: They need a success together. A homework task that may appear easy to you (''Have a date during the coming week when you don't mention your disagreements'') may be too difficult for them, setting up a failure.

10. A more functional task might be to ask them not to discuss a particular heated and chronic conflict issue until they see you again: ''It may be best to handle that topic in our sessions, at least for now.''

    Reason: If they try to resolve their tough issues between sessions, it can lead to bitter feelings and produce conflict in other areas.

11. Once a counseling relationship has been established (3–4 sessions), if they haven't mentioned their sexual relationship, ask about it.

    Reason: Some couples are reluctant to bring up this topic, but it's too important to ignore.

12. Find areas of agreement and cooperation. Any area—except the ones they're having trouble in—is good: parenting, work, household management, family finances, leisure time activities, social life, and so on.

    Reason: They need to be reminded of the ways they have worked together successfully in managing their lives.

13. If they have children, find out about them (names, ages, personalities, school work, etc.). It's also a good idea to invite their children to a session: ''We've talked about your children. When will I get to meet them?'' Of course, the parents have a right to refuse to bring them. If they do refuse, ask again at a later session.

    Reason: You, and the couple, need to look at how their relationship is affecting their children; you also need to see the couple as parents. You may find successes here.

14. Don't do couples counseling when one member is having an acknowledged affair with another person. The partner must agree to end the affair during the duration of the couples work, or they (and you) are wasting your time.

    Reason: A person having a current affair is only half there: One foot is in the couple's relationship, and the other is out. An affair is not defined by having sex or by seeing the other person. It is defined by *communication*—in person, by phone, letter, Internet, through a third party, or by passenger pigeon. If the spouse and third party are communicating in any way, the affair is continuing.

Couples Counseling: Additional Tips

1. Keep the presenting problems in focus so that the counseling has a destination.

2. Help the partners discover the positive aspects of their relationship; focusing on nothing but problems and weaknesses makes their efforts seem hopeless.

3. Keep them on current issues, not past disappointments, unless the past issues add appropriate emotion to the session.

4. When you are ''caught in the middle,'' move yourself and have them talk to each other.

5. Think of the couples' relationship as being embedded in a larger social network. Who else could be involved—children, parents, in-laws, grandparents, siblings, friends—in a way that helps to maintain the couples' conflict?

Source: *DeskGallery Image Catalog*, Copyright 1994 by Dover Publications, Inc. Used with permission.

6. Point out complementarities (the ''dance''). <u>Example</u>: ''I notice that when you question him about his actions, he becomes more silent, which makes you question more.''

7. Remember, you are part of a triangle. Be careful about balance and impartiality; if it is necessary to side with one on a particular issue, later join with the other on another topic.

8. If you get stuck:

   a. Consider a session of separate interviews to discover the block.

   b. Include a colleague as observer, either in or outside the room (videotape, audiotape, or one-way mirror, all with the client's prior permission).

   c. Enlarge the system: Ask them to bring in their children or their parents (or anyone else who appears to be involved) for you to meet.

   d. Go back to basic communication skills training.

   e. Establish the ''rules of fair fighting.'' Make a list of rules to fit their situation.

9. A case in which couples counseling may not be indicated, depending on the circumstances, is when the couple is not living together and has little contact with each other.

Closed Families

Source: *DeskGallery Image Catalog*, Copyright 1994 by Dover Publications, Inc. Used with permission.

A closed family is one in which the family boundaries are rigid and impermeable. Influence from outsiders is minimal, and family members don't establish important relationships beyond the immediate family. These families are a little scary, since all problems are magnified—anxiety is keener, depression is deeper, child problems are worse, arguments and domestic violence more intense. Because of its self-contained, locked-in nature, a closed family heats up quicker and stays hotter longer. The counselor's job, along with working on the presenting problems, is to open a window, better yet a door, to let a fresh "people breeze" in the home.

In my experience, closed families are mostly two-parent households, with one parent who is rigid and inflexible, ruling the family autocratically. He or she is a dominant presence in the sessions, by being highly verbal and talking for everyone or by maintaining a self-assured silence. This autocratic parent is sensitive to new people and ideas influencing his or her family.

What to do

1. Be careful. Any outsider who enters these families will make the autocratic parent suspicious and vigilant. This member is the family "doorkeeper," and if you don't get past him or her, you don't get in the family.

2. The way into the psychosocial heart of these families is *through*, not around, the powerful autocratic member. He or she must be kept in charge of their family, at least initially. We can't diminish their control by trying to ignore it. In some cases, I have asked the permission of the autocratic parent before even talking to his or her children in the session.

3. Find out about extended family: grandparents, siblings of the parents, cousins, and so on. Also, the **Circle Method** technique may help. The counselor and family need to open and expand their views of the "people world" of the family.

4. If the identified patient is a child, use the **Strategic Child Assessment** technique to frame part of the problem: "After our assessment of your child, we discovered that he/she doesn't have a best friend, which is unusual for a child of his/her age." Even if the identified patients are parents, we can usually gain access to the family through the parents' concerns for their children.

5. Ask the family (with everyone present), "Is anyone in the family afraid of someone getting hurt?" The way family members answer this question is as important as what they say. Either extreme—strong verbal denial or stony silence—is telling. If you get a "yes" answer (of sorts), segment the family by meeting privately with the concerned members for more explanation. After this assessment, if you determine that the safety of one or more family members is in jeopardy, first talk to colleagues about your concerns and possibly get a colleague to sit with you in a session with the family (see **Colleague Teamwork**). Then you can decide together if a report to the Department of Social Services, in compliance with your state's laws, is the appropriate action to take.

Friends as Family

I like this definition of "family": "The we of me." Certainly, friends fall into this category. In addition to the other benefits friends provide, this "family of choice" can also be an outside sounding board for what's happening inside the family. Here are some ideas about how friends can be a resource in family work.

Single Parents

The therapeutic theme for single-parent families is to encourage adult support for the single parent; this support is as likely to come from friends as family. When appropriate, I favor inviting the single parent's "best friend" to a session to create a visible reminder of the importance of the parent having supportive adult relationships. An added bonus is that when a friend is present with the single parent, the parent is less likely to get stuck in a conflicted, peer-like exchange with the child. With the other adult present, the parent becomes more adult, more parental.

If you do get another adult to attend a session with a single parent and his or her children, pay special attention to the adult-adult bond. Find out about them, and emphasize the support they draw from each other. It's good for the children to see their single parent having a close adult relationship.

Friends of Teenagers

The identified patient teenager in a family often feels alone and ganged up on. When everyone sees him or her as the "bad guy" in the family, the teenager often becomes angry and defensive. On some of these occasions, I have managed to get the family's permission to have the teenager's friend at a session, and the friend proved to be the most valuable member in the meeting. Friends will often point out the teenager's self-destructive behavior in a more direct and powerful way than the parents, and, as we all know, a teenager's peers can be more influential than the parents. Whether or not it's productive to have the friend at a session depends on the nature of the friendship and the parents' reaction to the idea of the friend attending, both of which would be determined before the counselor extends the invitation.

A common and vexing problem often pops up when parents become critical of their teenager's friends. Instant conflict usually results, since teenagers will quickly defend their friends. At times like this, I want to gently challenge the parents to get to know their child's friends in a more direct way. One idea is to encourage the parents to invite the friend to their house for a meal or in some way create direct contact between the parents and friend. This suggestion, even though it may not happen, is a much-needed advocacy for the beleaguered teenager.

An Adult Client

Counselors often see an adult client who has no immediate or extended family in the area. Knowing that loneliness and isolation often contribute to their problems, counselors can help the client shore up, or even create, their support group of friends. Try to get one or more friends to attend at least one session with your individual client. The goal is to leave the client with more and better social resources than he or she had when entering counseling.

Friend of the Family

This is a concerned other, a person who is informed about the family situation and who wants to help. In this category can be a long-time friend of the parent(s), a minister, a neighbor involved with the parents and children, or anyone who has a relationship with the whole family, not just one member. The friend's value to the family is the different perspective and greater objectivity he or she brings to the problems at hand, plus the trust he or she has built with all the family members.

Family Resistance

To introduce this stubborn topic, a few *Positive Reframes* may help. Resistance to change is an attempt by an individual or family to

- avoid discomfort, failure, or shame
- maintain stability and familiarity
- keep one's cherished sense of self
- maintain pride, self-esteem, and self-confidence
- be careful, go slow, and avoid impulsive decisions

Resistance to change must be in our genes; it seems to be part of human nature. Even more stubborn than resistance in individuals is family resistance, because it adds an interactional level of complexity, expressed by the maxim, "The whole is greater than the sum of its parts."

After some general comments on the topic, I have listed 10 common problems—with resistance at their core—that are encountered by family counselors, along with suggestions for handling each problem. Most of this topic was adapted from *Mastering Resistance* by Carol Anderson and Susan Stuart (New York: Guilford Press, 1983). I also added some items from my own experience.

Discussion

1. Resistance is defined as all behaviors, feelings, patterns, or styles that operate to prevent change. It may appear to reside in one member or to be distributed throughout the family.
2. It may be open or hidden, conscious or unconscious. Most resistance is probably outside of awareness. What is important in resistance is not the intent of the behavior but the function the behavior serves to prevent change. The silent, passive member may not consciously try to prevent progress but may be expressing anger or hopelessness. The silence, however, may serve to resist change.
3. It is best to view resistance as a product of the interaction of the counselor and family, not as an integral part of the family. Most resistance, however, is not provoked by the counselor but rather is an inevitable part of the interaction between counselor and family.
4. To recognize and manage resistance, the single most important skill to develop is an awareness of patterns and sequences of behavior in the family. Taking a pattern-level view makes dealing with resistance less complex and more manageable than attending to each piece of behavior separately.
5. When chronic resistance is encountered, examine your interaction with the family. Did you miss some important issue, get caught in an alliance with one part of the family, or ask the family to change too much or too fast? We look here first because we have some control over *our* part in their resistance—we can change what we do.

Denial

1. **Slow down.** When denial is obvious, slow down and ask the family to slow down ("Changes shouldn't be made too quickly.").
2. Give the least-denying members plenty of time and support to talk about their viewpoint. Gently and overtly side with the least-denying members to help them be heard by the family. This must be repeated several times.
3. Use techniques such as *Sculpting, Drawings,* or *Alter Ego.*
4. If you must counter denial directly, do so carefully and flexibly. It's usually best not to try to break through denial in one conversation. If the denial is entrenched, let it go and get back to it later. A direct and persistent challenge can make denial stronger.

Chronic Arguing and Bickering

1. **Be direct.** Go to the issue the bickering seems to be hiding. This insight may take the conversation to a new level. If not, little is lost; the family will just continue.

2. **Reframe.** ''Verbal fighting is your way of keeping each other involved.'' ''Loving and fighting are similar because they are both ways to keep the relationship intense.'' ''It's your way of getting some psychological space in the relationship. You need more breathing room.''

3. **Insist on ''I statements.''** This takes constant reminding but can serve to unbalance the family's normal style of communicating.

4. **Establish a rule.** The family can't go to another issue until one is resolved. This gives the counselor permission to interrupt irrelevant bickering (in order to enforce the rule).

The Blame Game

1. **Common sense solutions.** Suggest that blaming won't help. Or use logic: ''What would happen if blame was proven? How would it help? How would it make it OK?''

2. **Redirect the competitive energy.** Pick the most flexible person in the argument (''strongest,'' ''most ready,'' ''most able to change'') and ask that person to be the initiator of change. Explain by saying, ''This may not be fair, but it will work.'' Make specific suggestions as to what the person should do.

Disruptive Children

1. **General.** It is usually best to keep disruptive children in the session (at least for a while) to give the parents an opportunity to deal with them. This provides the counselor and family an opportunity to learn more about how the behavior works in the family. It's also a chance to teach parents new behaviors and to demonstrate that they can be effective with their child.

2. **Get the parents to take charge of their children.** Examples:
   a. ''It's the job of parents to set limits and the job of children to test them.''
   b. To parents: ''I can't concentrate on what you're saying with Manuel being so active. Can you help him settle down?''
   c. To parents: ''Would you let me take your child (or children) to the corner of the room and ask them to do some drawings while we talk?''
   d. Sometimes the child is disruptive to protect the family from talking about difficult issues. Get parents to deal with their child's anxiety by explaining the situation to him or her.
   e. Teach parents behavioral techniques to use at home such as token economies, charts and lists, granting and removing privileges, contracting, time out.
   f. If you want to model how to set limits with the child during the session, get the parents' permission (''Is it OK if I talk with Cassandra about her interruptions?''). Be sure to give control of the child back to the parents before the session ends.

Overtalkative Member

1. **Positively reframe the speaker.** ''You are helpful but are taking too much responsibility. Let me see how the others see the situation'' or (to other members) ''You are making the talker do all the work. Can you help him out?''

2. **Use nonverbal techniques** such as *Sculpting* and *Drawings*. This equalizes participation.

3. **Use key words to interrupt.** When Bob (the talker) mentions another family member, interrupt and bring that member into the conversation (''Is that the way you see it?'').

4. **Explore the issue openly.** ''What would happen if someone interrupted Bob?''

5. Ask Bob to sit next to you and listen while two (or more) other family members talk together. Give them a topic to discuss. If he interrupts, gently remind him to ''let them work it out.''

6. **Get permission.** Interrupt Bob and get his permission for you to talk with another member about the topic being discussed.

Sullen or Hostile Teenager

1. Ask the silent adolescent not to participate.
   a. To teenager: ''You're in no mood to talk now, so maybe you can just listen and get something out of me talking to your parents.'' Be sure to choose a topic with the parents that is important to the teenager (thereby getting the teenager to stay involved).
   b. Label the teenager as not ready to participate, the family as not ready for him or her, or the silence as a positive function in the family, such as protecting the family from arguments.
2. **Set the rules for the conversation.** In the case of verbal abuse and name-calling, set limits early before the situation escalates: ''If we are going to talk about this, I can't allow name-calling.''

Intellectualization

1. **Use an intellectual style,** searching for rational, logical explanations. Find out family members' ''theories'' about what is causing the problems. Label feelings as facts; this gives permission to talk about feelings.
2. **Ask another member to comment on the intellectualization.** ''What do you think about what he's saying?''
3. **Use the *Alter Ego* technique.** Sit behind a family member and talk for him or her. Instructions to the member: ''If I say anything you disagree with, stop me immediately and correct what I said.'' With this technique, the counselor can gently create more emotion in the room.

Scapegoating

1. **General.** Scapegoating is a process in families (or other systems) in which the family blames an individual for the family problems. It serves the function of avoiding other, more difficult or sensitive issues. Do not try to protect the scapegoated member (the identified patient); keep him or her as the presenting problem. Rescuing the member usually doesn't work because both the family and the scapegoat resist. Also, it may be worse for the scapegoat if he or she is protected by the counselor since the family may take it out on that person at home.
2. **Relabel.** Give positive connotation for the scapegoat's behavior. Example: This ''sensitive'' child is acting that way to distract the parents from more painful issues or to protect the family or someone in the family (''incompetent'' youth giving the parents someone to help).

Hopelessness

1. **Hear them out.** Listen to all the past failures, what they have tried or therapies that failed. If they aren't heard through, all reassurances by you will sound false, and they will believe that you do not understand their hopeless situation. Also, this gives information to make the current intervention something different from past attempts.
2. **Become more hopeless than they are.** Admit to defeat. Nothing can be done to change the presenting problems. The counselor apologizes for not being able to help. The family may respond by proving the counselor wrong. (This paradoxical strategy should be used after other things have failed.)

CHAPTER 3
COUNSELOR IDEAS

Introduction

Encouraging self-awareness in clients is at the heart of many models of therapy, regardless of the mode of therapy—individual, group, or family. Throughout the helping process, we want our clients to be open to self-reflection and to practice new ways of thinking and acting. If we are asking our clients to do this, we should be doing it too.

Like our clients, counselors have the tendency to keep trying to make the old way work, and if it doesn't, we can usually find reasons it didn't within the *clients*—"They weren't ready to change." Sometimes this is true, but sometimes it's ourselves we need to look at—our style, manner, beliefs, expectations, sense of timing, and other counselor variables, many of which affect the relationship we have with our clients. And research tells us that these relationship issues are as important to outcome as the particular model of counseling we are practicing.

This section gives us a glimpse at a few of the elements to consider in the development of counselor self-awareness, especially our styles, our use of self, our growth as a counselor. It also addresses some of the more out-of-awareness aspects of the helping relationship such as our underlying fears about family work and that ubiquitous little sinkhole waiting for all helpers—*induction*. Induction is a process whereby our own histories and emotions interfere too much with our objectivity, rendering us, at least in its extreme forms, less valuable and available to our clients. Our impartiality may also be compromised. Unwittingly, we become "stuck" and are not able to move the clients forward, partly because we're in their way. To make matters worse, induction is usually unconscious on our part, and it often takes discussions with a supervisor or colleague to help us see it.

For this section, my suggestion to the reader is to try to find yourself in these pages. Some of the information may apply to you, some of it may not. If you do find yourself in these pages, read the topics and do a little self-reflecting. That's what I did when I wrote, and my self-awareness increased. While not eliminating my blind spots altogether, self-reflection did make them less insidious and controlling. And more importantly, this little sojourn into my professional self made the journey more familiar and less threatening and increased my chances of being open to learning from clients and colleagues.

Fear of Family Work

Why should we fear learning to do family counseling? I'm not sure of all the reasons, but I know that as a trainee, I did fear it, and I know that most of those I teach get nervous being placed in a situation with families where they are being trained. Maybe if we can identify and name the fears, they will be less powerful.

Fear of the Unknown

This fear is built into us and is expected. If a counselor is doing family counseling for the first time and he or she has no anxiety about it, I am curious. Lack of fear of the unknown is not normal.

Fear of Intrusion

Getting into a family's personal affairs is something we have been taught since childhood not to do. Now, here we are sitting right in the middle of the family's business and asking all sorts of personal questions about topics that are difficult for them. We are not entirely sure we have permission to be there.

Fear of Inadequacy

Being observed conducting a family session, via live session or video recording, is intimidating at first. Will the supervisor think I am inadequate? Most therapists are not used to being so exposed and having their work directly observed; we are accustomed to therapy being a more secretive, confidential enterprise. Being in the learner's seat is a vulnerable spot.

Fear of Vulnerability

The avoidance of vulnerability is perhaps our greatest obstacle to learning. Letting in new information can be exhilarating but also threatening—it implies we don't know enough, plus the new information might threaten what we already believe to be true. It seems that the more ''expert'' we become, the less inclined we are to consider new ways of working. Also, during family sessions, we are vulnerable to the family members. Will they do something I can't handle?

Fear of Family Ghosts

We all have family issues. Occasionally, the family's problems trigger our own family stuff. (''The father in this family reminds me of what I don't like about my father.''). When this happens, the counselor's awareness can be greatly sharpened by exploring these feelings with trusted colleagues.

~~~~

From the trainee's viewpoint, all of the previously mentioned fears are real, even visceral, and they are easy to understand. But having been through the training process myself, and having helped a large number of others through it, I have a different perspective. I know the fears of trainees will turn to excitement in a short while and that their vulnerable feelings are largely paper monsters, offering no real threats. But I must be careful to respect their fears until they are replaced with a measure of familiarity, comfort, and even confidence. This happens in stages, of course, but starts within the first few hours of training.

Now we can learn together. As a supervisor, my image soon changes from working with a trainee to working with a colleague. We are both learners on a journey with *this* family; I've never seen one quite like it before.

Inexperienced vs. Experienced Family Counselors

I don't believe that anyone can pre-scribe the exact counselor behaviors that are the best with a given family. However, over the years I have noticed that, with families in general, inexperienced and experienced family counselors do things differently. It seems that experience gradually takes us from the left column to the right column.

Source: *DeskGallery Image Catalog*, Copyright 1994 by Dover Publications, Inc. Used with permission.

Inexperienced	Experienced
1. Lets the caller decide whom to bring for the first family session.	States who should attend the first session (everyone in the home).
2. Tends to see a family as a democracy, with members having an equal vote.	Sees a family as a hierarchy, with adults having more responsibility and power than children.
3. Each session is a new beginning; works mostly with recent issues that upset the family.	Each session is cumulative; works the current issues into broader relationship and structural changes.
4. Talks a lot. Silence is seen as dead time and is often uncomfortable for both family and counselor.	Talks less, to allow the family to come forward. Pauses and silences are seen as vital time needed to absorb, feel, and understand.
5. Is ambitious about the amount of change the counseling can accomplish.	Is satisfied with smaller, clearer, more focused goals.
6. Is polite and non-directive.	Is respectful and more directive.
7. Members' expression of feelings to the counselor is seen as an end in itself.	Expression of feelings is a means to an end and should lead to something new.
8. Individually oriented. Does not usually encourage (or notice) interactions between members.	Sees patterns in the way family members speak and interact together. Notices the reactions of all as one talks.
9. Gently gives honest feedback to family members before laying the groundwork: "The truth will set them free."	Knows that honesty needs a foundation; attends to timing and family readiness: "The truth will set them off."
10. Lets the family switch issues and topics often, going with whatever is hot at the moment.	While accommodating to the family, selects the issues and topics that speak to a broader theme or goal.

A Novice's First Family Interview

I am fortunate to have the videotape of my first family session. It was made over 30 years ago, and one day I became curious enough to play it. I saw myself on tape trying to be calm and confident, which I wasn't, and giving the appearance to the family that I knew what I was doing, which I didn't. Watching my awkwardness was uncomfortable, but I suffered through the whole tape to remind me of where I started. Here is how it went:

"By the way, John," Bev said, "the family comes in at four o'clock." Bev was my family trainer. We hired her to train myself and three other counselors in how to use family counseling in our inpatient substance abuse treatment center in South Carolina.

"What?" I said. "I can't see a family. I don't know how to do family therapy. You've only given us three hours of training, and all we did was talk about models, theory, and stuff like that!"

"I know," she said, "but it's not that difficult. Just put some chairs in a circle and invite them to sit down. Beginning with the parents, ask each person about themselves (*Social* stage), then ask about their main concerns and how they see the problem (*Problem* stage). Sometime during the session, let them talk to each other so we can see the strengths and problem areas in their relationships (*Exploration* stage)."

"Okay, but I thought family counseling is about solving a family problem, in this case the alcohol problems of their son. Won't they expect me to know how to solve the problem?"

"Yes, family counseling is about helping them solve problems, and yes, they will probably expect you to help. But before a family will follow you, you must follow them. In this first session, you need to learn about them, to make an honest effort to understand their special situation, and to gain acceptance by the family."

"You mean I don't have to fix the problem, just find out about them and what they've been through?"

"That's right."

"Well, that doesn't sound too hard."

"It isn't. The hard part may come later when we try to interrupt the enabling, splits, alliances, and other family patterns which could work against their recovery as a family. Your team members and I will watch from behind the one-way mirror and videotape the session. Briefly explain to the family that this setup is how we work. If I want to talk with you during the session, I'll knock on the door and you come out."

"Okay," I said, thinking that skills such as these are best learned in private.

The family—mother (Judy), stepfather (Sam), and 25-year-old son (Jerry)—was expected in five minutes. I set four chairs in a circle and nervously waited. At four o'clock, Judy and Sam walked in—without their son. "Bev didn't prepare me for a missing member," I thought. I invited the couple to sit in the circle and made some nervous small talk while waiting for Jerry. A few long minutes passed before he shuffled in from the inpatient unit ("Sorry, I almost forgot") and sat in a chair across the room from us. I remember thinking insightfully that Jerry doesn't want to have this interview. I summoned him over to the circle, and the session started.

I recalled Bev's instructions for the social stage: "First, ask each person about themselves."

I talked first with Judy, a petite, attractive lady with a gentle disposition. She was unemployed at present; her previous work had been as a receptionist in a doctor's office. "I enjoy meeting people," she said. She and Sam had been married for 13 years, the second marriage for both. I failed to inquire about Jerry's natural father.

I then asked Sam about his work, and he gave me his complete career history, all the way up to his latest job as salesman in a manufacturing plant. I didn't help shorten this lengthy monologue by the questions I asked during the rare pauses. Judy and Jerry politely listened as if that was their fate when Sam talked. I skipped Jerry in this stage of the interview, explaining to the family that I knew about him from my work in his treatment program.

Bev's voice came back to me: "Ask about their main concerns in the family." I started this problem-definition stage with the vague question, "How do you see what's going on in your family?" After some fumbling around, this confusing question was picked up by Sam: "Jerry and I have never been close...." During Sam's detailed description of his relationship with Jerry, Judy added, "But there's always been affection between them."

I then asked Judy the same fuzzy question. She gave me a relevant history of Jerry's drinking problems, his inability to hold a job, and his failures to make it on his own since age 18. He now lived with the parents, in an irresponsible, impulsive way, his life filled with questionable peers and mysterious activities. Both parents knew that Jerry drank a lot and that he would often be unable to stop at appropriate limits, but until the past year, no one had thought of calling this alcoholism. Judy found excuses for his behavior, and Sam would give in to keep the peace with Judy. This went on for several years until the latest crisis, when Jerry was arrested for drunken driving and resisting arrest. At the stepfather's urging, Judy consented to inpatient treatment for Jerry, who complied because it would look good for the judge during his court hearing a month away.

During Judy's recounting of their problem history, I suddenly remembered Bev's instructions to encourage them to talk to each other instead of to me. I also silently questioned, "Why should they talk to each other when they came to *me* for counseling? Besides, if they do, I may lose control of the session." But the pressure of being observed by Bev, my co-workers, and the video camera got to me.

I abruptly stopped Judy in the middle of her informative history and asked her to talk to Jerry instead of to me. This was awkward for Judy—telling her son something he already knew—so she just kept telling me. I realized that this was the wrong time and subject to begin an interaction. I let her continue.

She had urged Jerry to get help from AA a year ago. "It helped for a little while, but then the drinking started again. At one point I thought I would lose my mind over his drinking. He got on the wrong track and in with the wrong crowd."

So far, they had given me the background of the problem. I didn't know it then but I would hear the same history many times—family denial of the alcoholism, enabling, irresponsible and dangerous activities of the addicted member, and a strict/lenient parent split. In fact, I would hear it so often in the next few months, I would erroneously believe that every chemically dependent family had the same patterns.

About 25 minutes had gone by, and I hadn't asked Jerry anything. He was squirming and restless, but somehow I ignored his discomfort. I also forgot to ask about his view of the problem.

Bev knocked on the door, and I left and stayed out of the room 15 minutes—much too long—during which the family made small talk ("Are they feeding you well here?"). Bev reminded me, among other things, that I was leaving Jerry out of the interview.

When I returned from the break, I included Jerry in the session by asking him to explain his drinking behavior to Sam. It was a dumb request and got the appropriate response from Jerry: "I don't understand it myself so how can I tell him why I don't stop after two or three drinks?" This prompted Sam to explain how his own drinking was different from Jerry's because Sam "always knew when to stop."

During Jerry and Sam's 10-minute interaction, I ignored Judy, who sat quietly and listened, mostly staring at the floor. I interrupted their conversation several times and gently accused Sam of "lecturing" Jerry. I tried unsuccessfully to get Jerry not to like it ("Yes, Sam is lecturing me, but it's okay."). My comments about his lecturing bothered Sam, but he took it well and agreed that he had that tendency.

This ragged interview was finally about over, and I set up another appointment. Throughout the session, my timing was poor, my questions were confusing, and I was pushing my own agenda on the family. But the family members apparently forgave me and complied with my requests as best they could. Later I would realize that most families, like this one, will cooperate in the first interview and do their best to help the helper.

Counseling Style

How we use ourselves as counselors is an important ingredient in counseling outcome. Our therapeutic styles, intimately tied to our personalities, will vary between counselors; a "right or wrong" way to interact with families is too simplistic. Perhaps the best we can do is to be aware of our developing style and whether or not it's taking us where we want to go.

Source: *DeskGallery Mega-Bundle*, Copyright 1995 by Dover Publications, Inc. Used with permission.

Asking Questions

Sometimes I ask questions to obtain important factual information. At other times, I use questions to make an important statement. For example, asking ''What happened when the two of you (spouses or partners) tried to reach a decision together about how to respond to your son?'' serves not only as a search for the facts but also as a way for me to make a statement, namely, ''It's good for parents to talk together about this.''

I can also use questions to explore my confusion during a session. Often, such questions stir up good information. ''Let me try to understand this. You both have your ways of helping your daughter, but sometimes these ways are different. Could she be confused about what you expect?'' Or, ''I'm puzzled; last week you were in close agreement about what plan to follow with your daughter. Can you help me understand why the plan failed?''

Punctuating Interactions

Because interactions between people are circular, each response creating a different reaction, which, in turn, prompts a different response, it doesn't matter too much which part of the behavioral cycle I enter, or punctuate. When one spouse is passively reacting to the other spouse's dominance, I can intervene in the sequence by making a comment to either spouse. To the passive spouse: ''I notice that when your spouse becomes intense about this topic, you back off and give him/her more space.'' To the dominant spouse: ''Your spouse's silence makes you believe he/she agrees with what you say.'' Either way, I am trying to bring attention to a repetitive sequence that blocks change.

Sometimes an interaction between family members can be punctuated by directing remarks to the speaker, but sometimes commenting to the receiver, or even the listeners, is often more powerful. When one parent angrily says to the other parent, ''You're not home enough to see what goes on!'' I could ask, ''Did you hear what I heard—that your partner is asking for your support?'' Or, to their son or daughter, ''What do you suppose your parent means when he/she says that to your other parent?''

Using Verbs

Instead of, ''How did you *feel* when that happened?'' I often ask, ''What did you *do* when that happened?'' Family members establish their patterns with each other according to one another's observable behavior, not according to each other's internal feelings, which can only be inferred.

Rather than verbally exploring a member's feelings and thoughts, I try to create the actual behavior by saying, ''*Turn* to him and *tell* him about that.'' Rather than hearing about separate plans from the parents about how to deal with a problem child, more parental teamwork is prompted by saying, "*Decide* together now what you will *do* if he or she *does* that again." Instead of the verb "feel," I frequently use the verb "react." This word permits a more flexible response. "How did you *react* when...?" allows the client to respond not only with a feeling but also with a thought, with a behavior, or with all three. To family members who resist expressing feelings, this is sometimes a less threatening question than "How did you *feel*?"

Giving Credit and Responsibility

Some therapists use the pronoun "we" when speaking to families. Using "you," however, gives them credit where credit is due. "*You* did some nice work together on reaching that agreement" (not "*we* did") or "I will help *you* work out *your* plan together if that happens again." Using "you" gives the family the responsibility for its actions: "When *you* made that decision, it was scary, but *you* were able to make it stick" or "If *you* can stand together as parents, your daughter will be less confused about *your* intentions."

The family members do the hard work of change—they take the risks, they have the final responsibility, and they get the credit. All I do is talk and listen.

Matching the Family Mood

Matching the family mood (depressed, happy, cautious, nervous, concerned, etc.) is important in the initial session and also for a few minutes at the beginning of each session. As the session progresses, however, I usually want to present a different mood to offer other possibilities. If family members are using inappropriate laughter to hide their anxiety, I can become more serious in my affect and tone of voice. If family members are silent and inactive, I can slowly become more active and animated. If families show a lot of nervous energy, I can offer calm energy.

It's a matter of being sensitive to the flow of feelings in the session. When the air is heavy with painful emotion, it's time to slow down and feel compassion and empathy with the family's struggle, to just be with the people in the moment. It's not the time for me to charge ahead with my own agenda.

Giving Explanations

I sometimes explain too much. Too much explanation can kill discovery. If I set up a conversation between members that becomes intense and meaningful to them and then interrupt to "illuminate" or explain a certain point, I have interfered, not facilitated. The interaction would have been better without me. At tense moments, family members may let me intrude because it's a distraction from their uncomfortable (but important) feelings. I have to remember that I am more of a guide than a teacher.

In my attempt to share with a family the understanding I have, I sometimes talk too much. I need to remember three things: (1) What the family says is often (but not always) more relevant to them than what I say; (2) I must try to reduce the quantity and volume of my message so I can hear the family's message; and (3) If I usually do most of the talking, I'm working too hard and taking too much responsibility.

Using Family Metaphors

One father used metaphors and humor when talking about trying to get his son to work hard, to take a direction in his life, to overcome his laziness: "If he got paid for lying down, he'd get up and quit!

He ain't got his cap on straight.'' I can join with this man by using some of his metaphors: ''So you would like to help him learn how to wear his cap with responsibility and pride?''

To direct a co-dependent who is taking too much responsibility for the spouse's recovery from substance abuse, I might say, ''He has a disease, but you're not a nurse.'' To parents, I can emphasize the importance of their children attending sessions: ''Your children are the heartbeat of your family; they help keep it alive.'' To a member who just made a statement about another member's behavior being *his* problem, not the speaker's, I could quip, ''Are you saying there's a bad leak in *his* end of the boat?''

Using Proper Pacing

I often want positive change to happen quicker than I have a right to expect. Sometimes I can be too eager, active, pushy, or directive. Over the years, I have slowly come to realize that change in behavior can begin quickly but doesn't usually develop quickly. Something new takes getting used to. Like shopping for clothes, several garments are tried on until one fits and becomes part of the wardrobe.

I can get so wrapped up in my own therapeutic agenda that I become insensitive to the family's. That's why I need to pace myself, take the time to listen to the family's message, and adequately understand its concerns. Discovering a therapeutic direction to take is one thing; knowing how fast to pursue it is quite another. Hearing the same story many times can convince me that I know the situation well enough to step up the pace of counseling, but when my tempo is too fast, I miss some of the critical cues from the family along the way. I try to take periodic breaks from my therapeutic direction, let it lay still for a while, then get back to it later.

Creating Intensity

I can highlight important subjects to create intensity in the session. Using an ***Enactment*** can generate emphasis and block distracting side trips by putting the spotlight on an interaction between and among family members and leaving it there long enough to generate some heat. ***Segmenting*** also adds intensity. If I want to emphasize something to the parents, and if it seems appropriate, I can get the parents' permission for the children to leave the room. This not only narrows the field of concentration for both counselor and family, it also adds importance to the topic.

Repetition creates intensity and is often needed to exceed our apparent loss of hearing when we don't understand something or we don't want to hear it. Important messages from family members, or from me, need to be repeated, preferably with different words and with appropriate timing.

Keeping It Simple and Brief

I have to strive to make a clear statement and to keep it brief and simple. In my opinion, short sentences are better than long ones, and the best filling between sentences is a reasonable silence. Family members need time to understand and to find words for their feelings and thoughts, to consider, ponder, or just try to absorb what is happening . . . .

They need my pauses.

Counselor Mistakes

Mistakes are actions taken by a counselor, however small or large, that don't have beneficial results. In this definition, mistakes are measured by their effects, not whether the action seemed appropriate or proper at the time it was taken. The mistakes we make are the family's way of teaching us about them, like the time I tried to gain power over a dominant 22-year-old son by politely ignoring him and speaking mostly with his parents. He promptly fired me and took his parents home. Or another time when I referred to a mother as "strong" for her single-minded dedication to her two children and husband; without a word, she got up and walked out. She later said she was tired of being the "strong one" for the family (an obvious message to her husband).

I learn more from my mistakes than my successes, maybe because mistakes are startling and embarrassing; they get my attention. But mistakes are also threatening (am I incompetent?) and can be hard to admit. Maybe that's why, when things don't go well, we are prone to talk more about the dynamics in the family—rather than what *we* did—that contributed to the failure. I try not to beat myself up about my mistakes but to talk and think about them enough to glean their lessons and to give myself permission to make as many mistakes as it takes to learn.

Here is a partial list of common mistakes by my colleagues who are learning family work. (I've made most of them more than once.)

1. Pushing the family to a feeling level without first laying the groundwork of trust and safety
2. Not joining well enough with the family member who has the power to bring the family back
3. In anxious moments between the adults, shifting the focus to the children
4. Not being in the here and now and missing too much of the information in the room
5. Not being able to acknowledge and briefly apologize for a misunderstanding or mistake

6. Not finding a way to structure a chaotic family enough to get some work done
7. Stubbornly sticking to a therapeutic agenda even though it's not working
8. Assuming you "know" when you only suspect
9. Staying too long on a subject that isn't going anywhere
10. Not pointing out strengths in the family
11. Being too long-winded with praise
12. Not initially matching the family's pace; going too fast or too slow
13. Becoming overly engaged with the most talkative member
14. Talking too much in family sessions
15. Setting therapeutic goals that are too ambitious

Source: *DeskGallery Image Catalog*, Copyright 1994 by Dover Publications, Inc. Used with permission.

The premier mistake, which trumps all others, is to learn too little from our experiences with families. If you want to learn sparingly, follow the suggestions below.

How to Work With Families Without Learning a Thing

1. Don't think about your sessions once they're over.
2. When the family doesn't return, say, "They weren't ready," and go about your business.
3. Don't talk to supervisors and colleagues about your sessions.
4. Be totally reactive, rather than proactive, during family sessions.
5. Attend only to the talkative, accessible members.
6. Depend on the question, "How do you feel about . . . " to take the family to a deeper level.
7. Don't have goals, strategies, directions, or themes; every session is a new start.
8. Stay in your head rather than in the room with the family.
9. Refuse live or videotaped supervision of your family work.

Counselor Successes

Successes are harder than mistakes to write about because it's difficult to do without blowing one's own horn. I, like other family counselors, have had many successes. My work has been the most effective when I have joined well, when I read the family dynamics well enough to make an intervention that they could receive, and when my timing in small, specific interventions was generally on the mark.

One father in a family I had seen for about 10 sessions told me later that I saved his family. Knowing that I don't have the power to do that, I accepted his gratefulness. He told me, "My wife and I are communicating about our differences on our son's problem and are more together now; our son has finally learned how to accept limits, but with much fuss; our younger daughter is doing better in school, and we've given up the divorce talks we were having."

Source: *DeskGallery Image Catalog*, Copyright 1994 by Dover Publications, Inc. Used with permission.

Notice that everything he said were actions *they* had taken, based on strengths *they* had fueled by *their* desire to keep *their* family together. Nothing he mentioned was action I had taken. The family suffers through the problems, takes the risky step to ask for help, and does the hard work of change.

But I do deserve some credit. I stayed with them through the hard times; I looked ahead and tried to prepare them for some of their crises; I insisted on parental togetherness during the dangerous limit-setting phase with their teenage son; and I was patient. They did their job, and I did mine.

I feel the most successful in working with families when I:
1. Work more in the background, while the family and its issues are in the foreground
2. Move in ways that get the family to do its own work
3. Acknowledge and manage my own induction (discussed at the beginning of this chapter)
4. React professionally, rather than personally, to remarks they make about me or my work
5. Am mostly relaxed in my role as helper (it's just a role)
6. Go beyond when they expect me to quit
7. Manage to join with a family member I don't especially like
8. Am able to make a positive connection with a member who intimidates me
9. Facilitate something between them that is important to them and *new*
10. Can be open to their feedback and even ask for it, especially around termination time
11. Have the solid feeling that I've done my best in spite of a poor outcome
12. Am able to recognize family moments* and can stay out of their way

About the time I think I have family work down, a family (or session) comes along to get me back in touch with my humility. I'm slowly learning that humility is appropriate, regardless of my length of experience, and that success is not dependent on being successful all the time. If I care about what I'm doing and stay open to learning, I can trust the outcome.

---

* A "family moment" is when the family is in the emotional grip of something that seems small and unimportant to the counselor but is fueled by a history the counselor knows nothing about. The trick is to sense when this is happening and to avoid interrupting (for clarification) until the moment has been felt by the family.

Counselor Self-Disclosure

It's the counselor's personal and ethical decision about how to self-disclose to clients. I do it when they ask me a question that I consider relevant to my qualifications to help them or when I believe that my self-disclosure may create a little bond, bridge, or commonality.

I believe in protecting our personal lives from the casual curiosity of our clients, but not to the extent of remaining unnecessarily anonymous to them. When I am talking to a Vietnam veteran, I let him know I am one, too, and we even swap the little bits of information veterans share. If a family member has a life-threatening illness, somewhere in the conversation they find out I am a cancer survivor. If a client is in grief over the loss of a parent, I let them know I've been through similar grief, or if the client grew up with an alcoholic parent, I tell them that I did, too. If I had children, I would mention it. These commonalties are connecting links and add to the relationship.

I was doing a consult with a family with strong religious values. As soon as I sat down, the father asked, "And what church do you attend?" In that context, I considered that a relevant question, so I answered, "I grew up a Baptist." If I am trying to help a family and someone asks me if I'm married, I answer (divorced). If they ask if I have children, I also think that's relevant, so I answer (no). (If appropriate, I may acknowledge that working with families and having no children is a handicap, and it makes me listen harder.)

Counselors Anonymous

Many counselors learned—in graduate school, I guess—not to answer personal questions from clients, except with another question: "Why do you ask?" or "How is that related to what we are doing?" or some such. From the clients' viewpoints, I can see that being a tad frustrating; they are revealing themselves, but they don't know to whom. Is this counselor a perfect human, without the problems the rest of us have to face? Does he or she know anything about this problem from personal experience, or does this person just study other people? Also, counseling is new to most families, and they don't know the rules. Often, they fall back on what's appropriate in social discourse by asking questions to orient them to the person they're talking to.

Of course, there are valid reasons not to reveal information about ourselves to clients. One reason is when we get this funny feeling that the client is asking about us for some manipulative purpose that is not clear at the moment. It just doesn't feel right. When that happens, rather than answering with a question, I want to say, "This is more about you than me. If I have personal information which may help, I will share it." In my experience, this is rarely necessary.

I imagine our secrecy is, in part, a leftover from Freud's notion that the helper should maintain a blank slate for the patient to project on. That makes sense if the management of client transference is a core ingredient in your treatment approach. But that's not the case in all approaches to helping, and certainly not in a systems-based model of family work.

Counseling is a decidedly human and personal enterprise. I favor being human, consistent with keeping my professional and personal boundaries intact.

Induction Worksheet

Counselors are inducted when they have lost their objectivity due to their own personal history, experiences, emotions, beliefs, or values. We may become so involved with the clients and with our own subjective reactions to the family that we distort the situation in front of us. Some induction is inevitable—even desirable—but too much will harm or destroy effective helping.

The following questions are helpful in uncovering our out-of-awareness feelings, which may be interfering with our work with clients. (Space is included for your notes.)

Our personal histories can induct us.

1. Do you have experiences in your family of origin that have been triggered on more than one occasion by a client, couple, or family?

2. In working with clients, are you occasionally reminded of significant past experiences you have had in your life?

Our current experiences can induct us.

1. What experiences are you having in your current life (divorce, significant loss, and so on) that have the potential to change the way you view your clients or their situations?

2. Does a particular client or family remind you of other clients you have recently had an intense experience with (positive or negative)?

Our strong beliefs can induct us.

1. What is one of your dearly held assumptions about what makes counseling work?

2. Name one value or belief you hold that is sometimes in conflict with the clients you serve.

Whose Family Stuff Is It?

Everywhere I go, I take myself, including my history and my family of origin influences. Sometimes, my past experiences distort my perceptions of the family in counseling in front of me and can impair my ability to help them. I can mix in my stuff with their stuff, like the time I became irritated (professionally, of course) with a wife in a couples session because I perceived her as being too passive with her dominant husband. I later realized that I was playing out my anger at my mother because she allowed my father to be so dominant in their relationship. Or the time I was inducted by a large, powerful father who cracked a joke every time things got a little tense, and I laughed with them through two sessions. This unconscious reaction was triggered by my own response as a young boy to a large, powerful family friend who was always joking, with everyone around him respectfully laughing.

We all have emotions from the past that are triggered by the present. But when it happens to us in the therapy enterprise, it can reduce our objectivity to near zero and can complicate our work with the family—*our* stuff becomes more compelling than *their* stuff. It's especially troublesome when it's outside our awareness, which it usually is. Without awareness, our distortions, our projections onto others of how we felt as a child, and our transference of feelings about past people onto present people can play themselves out unimpeded.

When we notice one or more of the following, it's time to reflect about ourselves:
- We are unusually irritated, frustrated, saddened, engrossed, or in some way consistently hypnotized by the family.
- We feel sorry for one member and try to protect him or her from the rest of the family.
- We feel emotionally triggered (especially through anger or fear) by someone.
- We stay with our intervention doggedly, beyond when we should have tried something else.

To get to what's really bothering us, these questions can help:
- Do any of the family members remind me of anyone I have known? Who?
- Can I think of a situation in my history that is similar to the situation of this family?
- Why do I so strongly identify with this particular child in the family, feeling his or her pain almost like it was my own?

~~~~

During family sessions, when we (as counselors) become inducted by our own histories, we usually get stuck: no matter how hard we try, nothing seems to be effective with the family. Because of the strong out-of-awareness pull of these inductions, it is essential to have someone like a colleague or supervisor to talk with about being stuck. Of course, the colleague doesn't usually know our detailed history, so he or she may not be aware of where our behaviors are coming from. But with the use of the foregoing questions, our explorations with a trusted colleague can lead to a better understanding of how our own stuff is mixing with the client family's stuff and making it difficult to move forward in the counseling.

In the earlier examples of my own induction, my colleague suggested I focus more on the husband's role in maintaining the dominant/passive marriage relationship: ''Go back and forth between them, but talk mostly to the husband about how he responds to his wife to keep the cycle going.'' In the case of the jovial joke-maker, my supervisor suggested I use the word ''serious'' at least four times during the session in referring to the family problem and that I do not laugh when the family laughed. I did this, and we finally got down to the serious business of the teenage son's dangerous behavior.

Use of Self

In counseling, we use our "self" as an instrument of communication—our facial expressions, movements, gestures, voice, etc. These behaviors fall into two types: the first type are the behaviors that are under our conscious control; the second type are those that are an integral part of our personalities—who we are—and are best left alone. Below are a few of the first type.

Source: *DeskGallery Mega-Bundle*, Copyright 1995 by Dover Publications, Inc. Used with permission.

Centrality

This is the degree to which the counselor is the center of attention during a family session. When, for example, I talk to each member and he or she talks to me, I am central; when the members are talking to each other while I listen, I am non-central. Of course, both are necessary. A natural progression is to start with a family in a more central role in the first session or two and to move into a less central role in later sessions, becoming less an interviewer and more a facilitator.

Rule of 20/20

If a counselor leans forward in his or her chair 20 degrees or more for 20 minutes or more during a 1-hour session, he or she is probably working too hard. This silly little ''rule'' (which I invented to make a point) doesn't say never lean; it says don't lean too much or too often. Constant leaning into clients invades their space, tries too hard to do them good, and sticks us in a highly central role, too much a part of the family mix. A consistent leaner can easily tumble into the swirling vortex created by the family's needs, showing us once again a family's uncanny power to neutralize an outside influence by swallowing it.

Eye Statements

We make statements with our eyes—a squint can communicate thoughtful attention, benevolent skepticism, empathy, or an indirect challenge to what you are hearing. Raising your eyebrows can communicate surprise, humor, delight, or amazement. I have no idea what raised eyebrows *with* a squint means, but it feels powerful.

Voice

Like the eyes, the voice—strident or soothing, slow or fast, gentle or firm—is a strong communicator; it qualifies your message. In fact, keeping your message about the same but just changing the tone and tempo of your voice can make an important difference in the message you send.

Movement

We can lean forward or back in our chair to communicate. We can exchange chairs with someone for a strategic purpose, move our chair closer to someone for emphasis, or even get up and stand or sit in another part of the room (''I'll get our of your way while you discuss that.''). These intentional uses of closeness and distance augment the counselor's message.

Timing

The right moments to speak or not speak, stay back or step forward, introduce an observation or insight, or use a technique are all matters of timing. Good timing requires us to be in the ''feel and flow'' with the family and is one of the most advanced skills in counseling. It slowly evolves, along with our confidence, and takes years to develop.

Counselor Centrality

	(Circle the number that applies to you.)						

1. I break uncomfortable silences during sessions.

   Agree   Disagree
   1   2   3   4   5   6   7

2. I often give family members help in answering my questions.

   Agree   Disagree
   1   2   3   4   5   6   7

3. I lean forward in my chair for a third or more of the session.

   Agree   Disagree
   1   2   3   4   5   6   7

4. If two members are talking to each other, I often interrupt to offer guidance.

   Agree   Disagree
   1   2   3   4   5   6   7

5. For most sessions, I talk more than the family members.

   Agree   Disagree
   1   2   3   4   5   6   7

6. It usually is up to me to determine the topic to be talked about.

   Agree   Disagree
   1   2   3   4   5   6   7

7. I talk to each member more than the members talk to each other.

   Agree   Disagree
   1   2   3   4   5   6   7

8. The proper role for a family counselor most of the time is:

Guide on the Side   **Sage on the Stage**

10	9	8	7	6	5	4	3	2	1

Results

Total your numbers for the eight scales above and mark your score along the line below.

Central   **Non-Central**

44	40	36	32	28	24	20	16	12

Your total score measures counselor *centrality*, which refers to the degree to which you are the communication switchboard in the room: The majority of the communication during the session goes through you rather than between family members. Whether centrality is good or bad depends on how it fits your style and personality and how it fits the family. I have noticed, however, that family counselors tend to become less central with experience. If you want to modify your degree of centrality during family sessions, put an arrow in the direction along the above continuum you want to move (to the right or left).

Colleague Consultation

If the family counselor is already receiving supervision for family cases, peer collaboration can provide important additional learning. I call this collaboration "colleague consultation"; it describes the informal conversations between peers about their cases.

Source: *DeskGallery Image Catalog*, Copyright 1994 by Dover Publications, Inc. Used with permission.

Colleague consultation has several advantages:

1. In team-oriented family work, such as intensive in-home services, much dialogue goes on between colleagues about their cases, especially when these team members see the family together. The peers share their observations with each other; one notes something in the session the other one missed; different perspectives on the family problems and members are discussed; and clinical impressions are revealed. These ''processing'' conversations are rich with learning. In my opinion, more can be learned from after-the-session talks than in the session itself.

2. Telling the details about your sessions to someone has intrinsic value—just describing your observations and experiences makes you more objective and insightful. Sometimes we don't put pieces together or realize what we think until we hear ourselves talk.

3. We can sometimes be more honest and straightforward with a colleague than with a supervisor who has an obligation to evaluate us.

4. Colleague consultation is especially helpful if the colleagues are being trained together or at least have gone to a workshop together and are learning the same model of family work. The colleague becomes the ''insider,'' familiar with the jargon and concepts. The supervisor may not have this advantage.

Tips for colleague consultation:

1. The relationship between the colleagues is two-way; that is, they offer each other sounding boards and suggestions at different times and on different cases.

2. When a case is discussed, *Mapping* is useful as a focal point.

3. Since this is not formal supervision, the counselor is free to use, or not use, any suggestions offered by the colleague.

4. Colleagues should do some live family work together. *Colleague Teamwork* offers several ideas. Colleagues sharing observations about the session (who said what to whom and how) is a fundamental input into learning counseling work.

5. The counselors' supervisors should approve of the colleague consultation.

Supervising Family Work

Supervision, unlike colleague consultation, implies that the supervisor has a higher status, and is presumably more experienced, than the supervisee (learner). In my experience as a supervisor, I have collected a few observations and guidelines.

Characteristics of early learners of family work:

a. Talking too much and trying too hard. This is a natural result of nervousness and lack of confidence. The novice makes up in conscientiousness what he or she lacks in experience. Much supervision is helping the learner to "not work so hard," to be less active and central in the family session.

b. Difficulty discriminating between information that is important and that which is interesting but not essential to the goals of counseling. The learner needs to be able to separate the wheat from the chaff and to make bread from the wheat.

c. Lack of confidence. Confidence comes with knowledge and repetitive experience. You can't help the learner shape his or her behavior with families if his or her behavior with families is not occurring. Insist that the learner get as much in-the-room time with families as possible. Use mostly live, videotaped, or audiotaped supervision. The most common form of supervision—the supervisee describing a case to a supervisor—is helpful but, in my opinion, is also the least effective.

d. Awkward timing. The right thing done at the wrong time is the wrong thing. Timing is one of the last skills the supervisee learns; good timing takes experience and discipline.

Supervision guidelines:

1. The supervisory relationship is primary; if the relationship has difficulty (competition, resentment, tension), the supervision doesn't work well. Primarily, it's the responsibility of the supervisor to keep it healthy and viable.

2. During feedback the supervisor should be

   Supportive: Find opportunities to point out what the learner has done well with a family and their strengths as a counselor.

   Specific: Illustrate your feedback and suggestions with examples, preferably from the details of the case you're supervising.

   Valuable: Don't withhold feedback because it's difficult to give. Be careful when and how you say it, but be honest about what improvements are needed.

3. Introduce concepts, principles, and guidelines about family work into the discussion of a particular case, but wait until the supervisee has "told her story" about the family and her experiences with it. Until then, she is not free to listen to abstractions or theory.

4. Learning something complex takes time. You will be repeating yourself to the learner many times, hopefully in different situations and with different words. Be patient.

5. Support and build on learners' strengths. Help them do better what you believe they are capable of doing. Supervisees' *potential*, more than their performance, is your source of energy. Keep the faith.

Review Lists for Family Counselors

These lists allow you to review information quickly. They apply to a wide variety of settings in which family work is done. I did not attempt to construct each list from the most important to the least important items.

Source: *DeskGallery Mega-Bundle*, Copyright 1995 by Dover Publications, Inc. Used with permission.

1. **Nine important reminders for a family counselor:**
   - Put safety of family members first.
   - Join before you challenge.
   - Search for strengths in the family.
   - Use *Positive Reframing.*
   - Engineer successes for the family during the sessions.
   - Stay relevant to the family's concerns.
   - Don't do what you can get a family member to do.
   - Work with colleague support.
   - Expect success.

2. **Five common strengths of "hopeless" families who accept counseling:**
   - They're here.
   - They care about preserving the family.
   - The parents sincerely want the best for their children.
   - Someone in the family is concerned about the problem and wants to do something about it.
   - Like all of us, they do the best they can.

3. **Four common traps for family counselors:**
   - Focusing on individual dynamics instead of the family system
   - Getting bogged down in induction
   - Switching the presenting problem or the problem person too soon
   - Working without the support of colleagues

4. **Four effective ways to recruit families for counseling:**
   - Convince the management of your agency to support a firm recruiting policy.
   - To the caller who makes the initial appointment, say "The way we work is to see everyone living in the home in the first session to get a clearer idea of the problem."
   - Leave an empty chair in the circle for the missing member in a session.
   - Make an audiotape of the session and give it to the person(s) present to take to whoever is missing in the session. (Get permission before taping.)

5. **The two most unexplored and untreated contributors to family problems:**
   - Substance abuse
   - Unacknowledged conflict between the parents or parent figures

6. **Six good ways to learn how to do family counseling:**
   - Live, supervised sessions with families
   - Live, unsupervised sessions with families
   - Viewing videotaped sessions with colleagues
   - Discussing sessions with colleagues

- Reading
- Workshops

7. **Four common strengths of beginning family counselors:**
    - A genuine desire to help
    - A fluid use of counseling skills
    - Enthusiasm to learn
    - An understanding of the phrase ''The willingness to do creates the ability to do.''

8. **Four common weaknesses of beginning family counselors:**
    - They see a collection of individuals instead of a collection of interacting relationships.
    - They work too hard by talking too much.
    - They settle for the ''eclectic'' model of family counseling, without the benefit of a coherent model.
    - They lack confidence. (Confidence is acquired through experience and learning.)

9. **Four common problematic family structures:**
    - ''Hidden'' conflict between the parents.
    - One parent is too close with one or more children; the other parent is too distant.
    - A single parent who is a ''friend'' to their children (enmeshed).
    - A blended family in which the mixture of loyalties is not understood by the parents.

10. **Four characteristics of all systems, including families:**
    - Organization
    - Interaction
    - Interdependence
    - Stability

11. **Four advantages of a systems orientation to family treatment:**
    - It helps our understanding of why people act the way they do.
    - It reminds us that change in one part of the system may affect the whole.
    - It erases the notion of blame since everyone, in varying ways and degrees, is contributing to the family equation.
    - It reminds us to think of an individual's behavior in a broad, interpersonal context.

12. **The single most helpful tool for a systems orientation to family work:**
    - Mapping

13. **Ten settings in which family counseling is useful:**
    - Mental health centers
    - Social work agencies
    - Private practice
    - Substance abuse agencies
    - Child care agencies
    - All inpatient settings
    - All outpatient settings
    - Schools
    - Youth service agencies
    - Counseling centers

14. **Six reasons to use family work instead of individual counseling:**
    - Everyone in the home affects, and is affected by, the problem.
    - The family usually has a more lasting influence on the identified patient than the counselor does.
    - It offers more options for change.
    - If a changed identified patient returns to an unchanged family, the gains are hard to maintain.
    - It's briefer than individual counseling and more cost effective.
    - It's more exciting than individual counseling.

15. **Four reasons family counseling is not more widely used:**
    - Most counselors have been trained in individual counseling in school.
    - Most helping agencies are individually oriented, making it cumbersome to document (and justify) family interviews for an identified patient.
    - Management support for family counseling is often inadequate.
    - Little or no training and supervision in family counseling is provided.

16. **Five important books in my family counselor education:**
    - *Problem Solving Therapy* by Jay Haley
    - *Family Therapy Techniques* by Salvadore Minuchin and Charles Fishman
    - *Foundations of Family Therapy* by Lynn Hoffman
    - *Lives of a Cell* by Lewis Thomas
    - *Treating Chemically Dependent Families* by John T. Edwards

17. **Four reasons for family resistance:**
    - Resistance to change is built into any system, including a family. It's normal.
    - Newness is awkward and uncomfortable for the family.
    - People have a natural inclination to keep trying to make the old way work.
    - Denial and resistance are used to defend against uncomfortable feelings and change.

18. **Six ways to "join" with a family:**
    - Listen.
    - Try to understand.
    - Accept their respective views of the problem.
    - Use the words and metaphors they use.
    - Maintain benevolent control of the session.
    - Learn how to challenge constructively (making a point without making an enemy).

Source: *DeskGallery Image Catalog*, Copyright 1994 by Dover Publications, Inc. Used with permission.

19. **Four reasons why counselors like to do family counseling:**
    - It's effective for a wide range of problems.
    - It makes a counselor feel more useful, since it is powerful and more people are being treated.
    - It's a good way to build colleague cohesion.
    - Family counseling is very interesting work.

20. **Five ways to feel competent as a family counselor:**
    - Have at least 100 family sessions with at least 20 different families.
    - Attend several days of family skills workshops.
    - Read three books; study two of them.

- Find one or more colleagues to learn with.
- Share with colleagues what you are learning.

21. **Four useful sayings in family counseling:**
    - "If a child is taller than a parent, he or she is standing on someone's shoulders." (Anonymous)
    - "Lead because you follow." (Minuchin)
    - "Think conceptually; act concretely." (Edwards)
    - "A family counselor who makes no mistakes is doing something wrong." (Edwards)

22. **Six definitions of "induction." The counselor has**
    - Lost his or her objectivity.
    - Been emotionally controlled by the family.
    - Been sucked in.
    - Been organized by the family's patterns.
    - Been boxed in and neutralized.
    - Been made powerless as a catalyst for change.

23. **Five ways to know when you're inducted. You**
    - Like the family (or one member) too much.
    - Dislike the family (or one member) too much.
    - Talk more than anyone in the room.
    - Get stuck and stay stuck.
    - Lean toward the family for more than one-third of the session.

24. **Five ways to become un-inducted:**
    - Ask yourself, "What is similar in this family to my own family?"
    - Talk to a colleague about the family issues, especially how they relate to your own family.
    - Talk less during the next session. Use *Enactments* instead.
    - Move your chair back one or two feet during the next session.
    - Use active techniques to put the family on center stage (*Sculpting*, *Drawings*, etc.).

25. **The single most difficult subsystem of a family to work with:**
    - The enmeshed parent-child dyad

26. **The most common subsystem worked with in "family" counseling:**
    - The enmeshed parent-child dyad

Questions and Answers

Questions

1. What should a "typical" family provide for its children?
2. What is the primary goal of the first session?
3. What should I do if the presenting problem is obviously a "red herring," meant to distract me from the real problem?
4. How do I handle strong resistance?
5. How do I get both parents (in a two-parent household) to attend sessions?
6. How do I persuade stubborn family members to see the obvious truth?
7. In the first family interview for a child problem, I find out the parent is an alcoholic. How do I switch the focus to his/her drinking?
8. How do I guide family members into my way of seeing the situation?
9. Should I try to control an overactive, misbehaving child during a session?
10. How do I get silent teenagers to talk?
11. In blended families, should I encourage equal partnership between the biological parent and the stepparent in managing the kids?
12. How do I get the family to return for the next interview?
13. How do I work with families that have no strengths and little concern for each other?
14. What should I do if they drop out of counseling?
15. If I realize I made a mistake with a family, should I acknowledge it?
16. But wouldn't this admission detract from my status as the counselor?
17. Do I side with the member who is obviously right against the one who is obviously wrong?
18. Suppose I can't get the family to change?

Answers

1. Roots and wings.
2. To have a second session.
3. Go fishing.
4. Practice the art of graceful yielding.
5. Get permission from the participating parent to talk with the missing parent by phone.
6. Never try to win an argument you can afford to lose.
7. You don't, unless you are practicing one-session family counseling.
8. Lead by following.
9. Only if you plan to move in with the family.
10. Give them permission to remain silent, and tell them they will learn something by listening to you talk with their parents.
11. Only if you believe that therapy is thicker than blood.
12. Give them something to return for.
13. Don't worry about it; you won't see such families.
14. Call the parent(s) and ask them to help you correct your misunderstanding.
15. Yes, and (if appropriate) apologize.
16. Yes, if the family believes that counselors are perfect people.
17. Please remember that the question is not who is "right" but what helps.
18. Change yourself.

CHAPTER 4
TECHNIQUES

Introduction

If you perform any activity enough times, its execution becomes smoother and more economical. Sooner or later, it evolves into a technique and acquires a name. Family therapists, including myself, have been doing this for years and have developed useful techniques with families to achieve a particular purpose during a session. They are the "tools of the trade," easily transferred from one professional to another. (In the following pages, techniques are listed alphabetically.)

The advantage of techniques is that they provide a structure, a little set of rules for the counselor and/or family members to follow, often unbalancing the family's normal interaction just enough to expose underlying feelings and issues. I have used *Alter Ego, Colleague Teamwork, Guardrail, New Talk, Sculpting,* and other techniques in this section many times to trigger a much-needed shift in a session. Techniques also save time, an important factor in brief models of family work.

Over half of the techniques in this section are original—I tried something experimental in a session that worked, so I tried it again with another family. If it achieved something worthwhile a second time, I gave it a name and wrote it up as a handout for my workshops. If it continued to be useful, it eventually ended up in this book. The other techniques in this section I learned through reading or "borrowed" from colleague therapists or from workshops. I have tried them all in family sessions—some many times—and I'm confident of their utility. But however useful they are, nothing I've found will work every time with every family. During a particular session, if a technique isn't working or is too difficult for the family, it's best to simply drop it and change the conversation.

It's helpful to remember two caveats about techniques. First, techniques tend to impart a mechanical flavor to the work, especially if they are used too frequently. Some structure is good, but too much dampens the family's expression. Second, the counselor can become so wrapped up in doing the technique correctly that he or she misses the important, subtle messages and body language from the family members.

To learn any technique in this book (or elsewhere), I suggest you do it three times with different families. Then add personal touches and make it yours. Once learned, techniques can promote confidence by adding to your options, your range of skills.

Techniques and skills are the craft of our profession; they are the building blocks in the art of family work. (Anyone who has labored to learn the skills and techniques of a complex art form—playing a musical instrument, painting, dancing, writing, and others—will know what I mean.) Over time, when family techniques and skills become familiar and comfortable, our "feel" for the work emerges, and we are free to be more relaxed and personable, less self-conscious, free to enjoy the work, and confident that we can somehow manage whatever happens. We have learned our techniques well enough to put them in the background. Then we enter another stage in our professional growth—learning to be more compassionate family counselors rather than better technicians.

Alter Ego

Definition

The counselor sits behind a family member and speaks for him or her.

Purpose

1. To create more intensity of feeling in the room.
2. To help the family deal with an important issue that is being avoided.
3. To allow the counselor to explore his or her ideas and hunches about how one or more members are feeling or thinking.

Procedure and Examples

1. Instructions: "I want to try something that may appear silly, but bear with me. I would like to talk for Christina. Christina, may I sit behind you and let the family pretend that you are talking instead of me? If I say anything you disagree with or want to change, please correct me."
2. With Christina's permission, put a chair behind her (or sit on the floor) *out of direct eye contact with the family*. This creates the illusion that Christina, not the counselor, is talking.
3. From behind Christina, start the conversation by picking up on a current topic or by saying, "You may want to begin by asking Christina some questions about how she is thinking or feeling. I will answer for her."

Comments

1. Before trying this technique, wait until some rapport and trust are established between you and the family (about the third interview).
2. You are not just role-playing the family member (that is, saying only what he or she would say). The power of this technique is that it allows you to gently bring up topics or feelings that the member would not say.
3. As the Alter Ego, start in a non-threatening way. Don't get deep into feelings and hot issues until the family adjusts to the game. Usually, about 10 minutes is long enough to be the Alter Ego for a family member.
4. Don't go too fast. Leave pauses and gaps to allow the family to absorb what's being said.
5. Variation: You can speak for a few minutes for one member, then shift to another member. Before speaking for anyone, get his or her permission. Also, repeat the instructions, "Please correct anything I say that is wrong."
6. Variation: Ask a colleague to join you for a session. After allowing 20–30 minutes for the colleague to get to know the family, each counselor can be the Alter Ego of a different family member simultaneously. Again, don't go too fast.

Brief Network Intervention (BNI)

Definition

An intervention in which the client, his or her significant others, and relevant professionals are brought together in a meeting to "help the client avoid a serious mistake or future harm."

One of the assumptions underlying the family systems approach is that symptoms are behavioral reactions within the context of family and significant others in a client's life. To change or remove problems may require changing the network behaviors that maintain the problems (inconsistencies, enabling, double messages, etc.). In a BNI, the client's behavior, family, significant others, *and* the professional helpers are all targets for change. The meeting represents a crisis for the entire network and can stimulate new ways of handling a problem.

Purpose

To block a specific future behavior by the client, such as dropping out of school, running away from home, losing a job, violating probation, or driving while impaired.

Procedure

Call a meeting of the client and the people who are involved in the client's life. Invite anyone who has some influence on the client: family, extended family, roommates, friends, and any involved professional (school counselor, probation officer, etc.). Because of the number of people involved, you can request help from an adult family member in contacting the family participants while you contact the professionals. You may want to inform the professionals in advance about the purpose and goal of the meeting. If the professional does not agree with the direction or intent of the intervention, his or her opinions would be respected and considered, but he or she would not be invited to attend. This screening assures an organized and agreed-upon direction during the meeting. Allow an hour and a half for the session.

Once everyone is assembled, the family counselor acts as moderator and coordinator, beginning with asking everyone to state their involvement with the client or family. Then clarify the goal: to help prevent the client from making a serious mistake, one that would very likely cause harm to him- or herself or to someone else. Keep the meeting focused on the goal, coordinate input from those present, summarize, clarify, and move the group toward a specific plan of action. How will each person react if the client engages in the destructive behavior? What can be done to prevent it?

Example

Denny, a 16-year-old son in a blended family, was in outpatient treatment for drug abuse and on probation for stealing. The BNI was held because Denny was on the verge of being expelled from treatment for poor attendance. Present in the session were Denny, his mother and stepfather, the natural father (who traveled several hundred miles to attend), a younger stepsibling, the family counselor, group therapist, supervisor of the treatment program, and Denny's probation officer.

It soon became evident to the client, and to everyone else, that unsuccessful completion of treatment would have far-reaching consequences for the young man. The mother and stepfather refused to allow Denny to remain at home without substance abuse treatment; the natural father did not offer refuge for the boy if he left the program; the family counselor and program supervisor said they would recommend inpatient placement with another absence; the probation officer would refer the case back to the judge if the client violated probation by leaving treatment.

Denny was squirming during the session. His escape from treatment was blocked by the tight cooperation of his family and professional network. But he also learned of everyone's concern for his welfare, especially that of his natural father, who he thought didn't care. Denny saw that his family and several professionals were taking the time and trouble to attend this meeting and state their limits on his behavior. What he had done casually—not coming to treatment—now became a serious matter. He decided to stay in treatment, which he successfully completed several weeks later.

Comments

A BNI has several advantages over a conjoint family session:

1. It increases the teamwork of the client's network by requiring coordination between the client's significant others and the involved professionals.
2. It shows concern for the client's welfare; people are taking this extra step to prevent harm to him or her.
3. The client learns that he or she cannot "divide and conquer" all the people involved.
4. It presents a clear direction for the client, family, and professional staff.

A BNI is a therapeutically arranged crisis. It takes advantage of the well-known phenomenon that the breakdown of rigid patterns of behavior is more likely during a crisis than during periods of stability. This technique can be used with any potentially harmful behavior where strong leverage and influence are needed quickly and for a specific purpose. Besides preventing someone from leaving treatment prematurely, I have used it for a runaway teenager (including the parents into whose home the son escaped), to avoid hospital commitment of an adult, to prevent an adolescent from going to jail, for a single mother to regain custody of her children, and for the dangerous behavior of a teenage girl who was reacting to her parents' divorce.

The meetings usually turn into a curious mixture of love and concern on the one hand and a "show of force" on the other. These special sessions create a sense of urgency—certain behaviors will be met with serious consequences. Not all these meetings accomplish their purpose, but something productive usually happens. During these interventions, change is in the air. Whatever the outcome of the session, the network and family feel the pressure to find new solutions; they cannot continue to deal with this problem in exactly the same way.

Chair Work

In family sessions, a chair is the one consistent prop available to counselors. We might as well use chairs for therapeutic purposes.

1. **Circle Up.** For family sessions, a circle of chairs is best. Sofas and loveseats may create undesirable seating arrangements (for example, enmeshed mother-child sitting together, while father is ''excluded''). Tables, desks, or other obstructions create barriers between members; a conference table promotes a ''conference'' more than an intimate exchange.

2. **Empty Chair.** Leave an empty chair in the circle for the family member who failed to show for that session. Refer to that member frequently during the session (''What do you suppose Paul would say if I asked him the same question?'' ''Where was Paul when that happened?''). Or, if a person in or out of the family is mentioned several times, pull up an empty chair in the circle for him or her. The chair gives something to refer to, and provides a reminder that the circle is broken.

3. **Talk to the Chair.** If a family member needs to have an important conversation with a person not present, practice the conversation by pulling up an empty chair: ''Pretend Margaret is sitting there. Tell her what you need to say while we listen.''

4. **Get Closer.** Use your chair to communicate with one or more members by pulling your chair near them to make a point, support, challenge, listen more intently, or protect your conversation from intrusion by other members. You can return your chair to the original spot after the intervention has been made.

5. **Slide Back.** You can facilitate an interaction between two or more members by sliding your chair back a few inches when you want to create an enactment between the members. ''Talk to Lakisha about that while I listen.'' Shifting your chair back signals that you are an outsider to the conversation.

6. **Take Sides.** In a conversation between two members, you can temporarily ''take sides'' by moving your chair next to one of the members to offer support, suggestions, etc. in a conversation with the other member. Get the person's permission before doing this, keep it brief (5–10 minutes), and, if appropriate, do the same with the other member later.

7. **Split the Difference.** If someone leaves the room (by request), you may need to move your chair to balance. For example, you may get the parents' permission for their children to leave while you talk with the parents. The children's vacated chairs could leave you sitting closer to one parent than the other. Move your chair to split the difference between the parents.

8. **Change Chairs.** Get two family members to swap chairs. This could get a child ''out of the middle'' between two parents, put the adults closer together to facilitate you working with them, or break up the distracting side conversations between siblings.

9. **Fill the Chair.** Get up, stand behind your chair, and ask the family, ''Name someone who should be sitting here. Who is missing?'' Talk about why that person's presence is necessary, and ask who can get him or her to the next session.

Circular Questions

Definition

Source: *DeskGallery Mega-Bundle*, Copyright 1995 by Dover Publications, Inc. Used with permission.

Questions directed to a family member about *other* members.

Purpose

The purpose is to
1. Give the counselor a quick overview of the family structure or to test a hypothesis about the family.
2. Give the family members information about other members' perceptions of relationships.
3. Encourage members to begin thinking of the family as an interacting unit rather than as individuals acting independently.

Procedure and Examples

1. Instructions: "To get to know you better as a family, I would like to ask you several questions about each other. This will give us a clearer idea of how everyone is thinking. If I ask anything you would prefer not to answer, please say so."
2. In the following sample questions, assume the counselor is in a session with a mother, father, and teenage son and daughter.
   a. To mother: "Which of your children do you believe is most worried about this problem, your son or your daughter? When you and your husband have a disagreement, who reacts to it the most, your son or your daughter?"
   b. To father: "If your wife and daughter should have an argument, how does it affect your son?" "Who do you think reacts more to your daughter's moods, your wife or your son?"
   c. To son: "If your mother is upset, who would notice first, your sister or your father?" "When you and your sister have an argument, what does your mother do? Your father?"
   d. To daughter: "Which is the stricter parent, your mother or father?" "If your brother comes in late, who would talk to him first?"

Comments

1. Answers to the questions often trigger conversations between members. Pursue these if they seem productive.
2. You may check out answers with other members ("Do you agree with that?").
3. Questions do not have to be evenly distributed among family members.
4. This technique works because most people will comment on relationships if they are not directly involved. Concerning others, we all have some "armchair psychologist" in us.

Colleague Teamwork

Most family counselors need support, feedback, sharing, and someone to talk to when the going gets difficult or confusing. I have worked with families for periods of time entirely alone, and for other periods with one or more close colleagues. The first way is the road to burnout; the second is dynamic and uplifting, is better therapy for the family, and sparks more learning for the counselor.

1. **Colleague Consult**

    One counselor works with the family alone but talks to the colleague before and after one or more sessions. By describing the family and its process, counselors can clarify their own thinking and add to their objectivity. It works better if colleagues do this for each other.

2. **Temporary Co-Therapist**

    With the parents' permission, ask a colleague to join you for one session with the family. Introduce the colleague and explain to the family, ''We sometimes work together to get a second opinion of how we can be the most help to your family.'' Plan beforehand how the two of you will work together—how active each will be, who will lead the session, the goals, etc.

3. **Reflecting Colleague**

    With the family's permission, a colleague is brought in and introduced to the family: ''The way we sometimes work is to use two heads instead of one. To get another viewpoint, I asked Juanita to sit with us for a while. Occasionally, she and I may talk together.''

    Two or three times during the session, the counselor and colleague talk to each other in front of the family. The colleague ''reflects'' back to the counselor what he or she sees, hears, thinks, and feels about the family's struggles, strengths, patterns, and processes. The counselor and colleague have a dialogue about the family. Anything is permissible, even gentle challenges, as long as it shows respect for the family and its situation. It's best to keep it short—three minutes or less. Families usually show great interest in these conversations.

4. **"Expert" Colleague**

    Introduce the colleague as one ''who is experienced at talking with children (or adolescents) about this problem.'' With the parents' permission, the identified patient child goes with the colleague for an assessment interview. This privacy allows the family and the young person to speak more freely, adding new information. After a 20–30 minute session with the child alone, the expert colleague can return to the session and discuss his or her findings with the parents.

5. **Student Colleague**

Introduce the colleague as one who is "learning to work with families and can also be helpful to the family." During the session, the colleague asks the counselor "naive" questions. Examples:

- "This parent seems willing to try that, but do you think the other parent is willing?"

- What will happen if the son is treated one way by one parent and a different way by the other parent?'

- "How will the parents' plan with their son affect the other two children?"

The counselor answers the questions, talking with the colleague while the family listens.

Drawings

Drawings by family members can give important information to the counselor and to the family. They reveal the part of each person's feelings, thoughts, and attitudes that are difficult to put into words; many clients will draw what they are unable or afraid to say.

Drawings are especially useful with children who need a nonverbal way to express themselves. More complex and flexible than words, drawings get at the richness of our inner experience. And they provide a concrete object to focus on, to study, to revise, to accept or reject.

Below are several drawings to use with families. After experimenting with these, you can create some unique drawing exercises to fit a particular family.

Source: *DeskGallery Image Catalog*, Copyright 1994 by Dover Publications, Inc. Used with permission.

Circle Method*

1. Give each person a pencil and a sheet of paper on which you have drawn a large circle.

2. Instructions: "Place your family on the paper. You can put them inside or outside the circle, you can put them close together or far apart, and you can draw them large or small. Please indicate each person with a circle (that is, don't draw the person's face or body)."

3. Family members should not see each other's pictures while they are drawing.

4. When they finish, ask each person to place his or her picture on the floor or hold it so everyone can see the drawing. Then ask the family, "What do you see?" The family will discuss the drawing.

5. The counselor can also make observations about each drawing, ask questions, and prompt discussion. *Do not make interpretations*; just make comments about the figures on the paper ("I notice that you put yourself closest to your grandmother and your sister closest to your mother."). After each observation, pause for a reply, if the person wants to give one.

6. When the discussions are over, ask the members if you can keep their drawings. Put name, age, and date on each drawing and file them in the client's chart for later reference.

7. Variation: After they finish drawing: "Now turn the page over and draw it the way you *want* it to be." (The differences in the two drawings could be taken as a general "contract" between the family and the counselor, that is, what family members want). Discussion follows, as before.

Family Drawing

1. The family sits on the floor (or uses a table) to draw.

2. Provide one large sheet of blank paper (preferably newsprint size).

3. Instructions (to the whole family): "Draw a picture."

4. Observe the process: how they decide what to do, who takes charge, who accommodates whom, who talks the most/least, etc.

---

* This exercise was originated by Susan M. Thrower, ACSW, et al., in "The Family Circle Method for Integrating Family Systems Concepts in Family Medicine," 1982, *The Journal of Family Practice*, *15*, pp. 451–457.

5. When they finish, discuss the drawing. Prompt the discussion by making observations about the picture they drew or about how they went about creating it ("I noticed that three of you contributed to one picture and one drew a separate picture," etc.).

Relationship Drawing

1. This is usually more appropriate with dyads: spouses, parent-child, or couples.
2. Instructions: "Draw your relationship with each other."
3. They may include other people in their drawing.
4. When they finish, ask them to swap pictures; then ask each person, "What do you see?" Encourage them to talk to each other about the drawings.

Open House

1. This is more appropriate for younger children (age 5–12) than for adolescents or adults. It can be done during a separate interview with the children or given to them as a task while the counselor talks with the parents. The drawing gives information about the family's home life.
2. Instructions: "Pretend that you take the roof off your house and look down into the rooms. Draw the rooms in your house. Put your family in the house doing something. It's 8:00 o'clock at night."
3. When they finish, encourage the children to show (and explain) their picture to their parents.

Draw-a-Dream

1. This is more appropriate with children (age 12 or younger) and should be done without the parents being present. The purpose is to reveal some of the underlying fears of the child.
2. Draw a rough sketch of a child sleeping in bed. Above it place a large cartoon balloon (for the drawing).
3. Instructions: "This is a little girl (boy) sleeping in bed. She is having a bad dream. Draw the bad dream the little girl is having."
4. When the child finishes the drawing, ask him or her to explain the dream and the figures in the drawing. Let the child make up a story about the drawing, or just talk about it in any way he or she will.
5. Get the child's permission for his or her parents to see the picture and for you to talk to the parents about it.

Family Mapping

Mapping is the technique of using symbols to draw the counselor's impressions of the family relationship patterns—who is close or distant, who is aligned with whom, who has the apparent power and influence in the family, and who is in conflict with whom. It is different from a family genogram: A genogram is a multi-generational and factual picture of the family system, giving basic social information (divorces, deaths, etc.). A map is subjective rather than factual and gives little social history. A map includes more information than a genogram about current relationships between members.

The purposes of a map are to

1. Organize and display our impressions of a family structure.
2. Help us maintain a systems focus for the counseling.
3. Indicate a broad goal for counseling with the family.

Here are the symbols I use and what they mean:

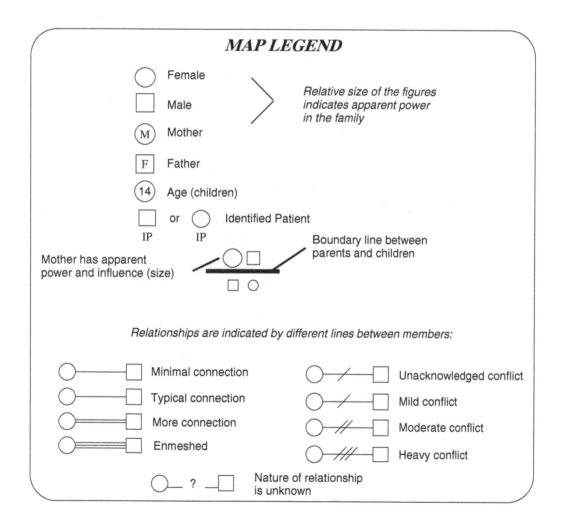

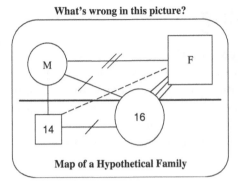

What's wrong in this picture?

Map of a Hypothetical Family

The map to the right shows conflict between the parents and a large difference in size (apparent power) between them. The older child is larger than the mother and is placed partly above the parent-child boundary, indicating too much power and influence. The father and daughter are overinvolved (enmeshed), and the daughter is in conflict with her mother and brother. The father-son bond is weak. (This map, as the one below, is for the purpose of illustration only; many alternative family structures are possible, but the *symbols* representing closeness/distance, conflict, and power are the same.)

Assuming the daughter is the identified patient, the following are examples of systemic goals for counseling (while the focus is on solving the presenting problems):

1. Help the parents reach agreements concerning their limits on the daughter's behavior. If the parents are more in agreement, the father-daughter closeness will decrease. This will place the daughter in a less powerful position in the family, especially in relation to the mother.

2. Explore the father-son relationship, creating conversations between them during the sessions. If father and son become more communicative, it will also decrease the father-daughter enmeshment.

3. Likewise, explore the mother-daughter relationship. If they become better able to communicate, the daughter-father closeness will be diminished.

A map helps us clarify what we currently believe about the family organization and what may be contributing to the presenting problem. However, it's important to keep in mind that a map is not a fact; it is simply our opinion. It's a current working hypothesis about relationships and is subject to change as we learn more about the family.

What does an "Ideal" family look like?

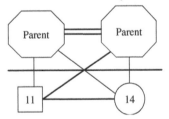

Mapping an "ideal" family reveals our assumptions about how family relationships function best. The map to the left shows the following (the symbol shape of the parents is altered to avoid a heterosexual bias):

1. The parental bond is the strongest in the family.
2. Parents are of equal size.
3. Children are below the parent-child boundary.
4. Children are smaller than parents.
5. The older child is slightly larger than the younger (a little more power).
6. The map has no conflict lines.

Obviously, not many families look like the above figure, certainly not all the time. It's a model, an ideal; it gives a standard to aim for in counseling.

Family Questions in Individual Counseling

These questions are useful if you are doing individual counseling with a client and want to bring in his or her family. The first step is to talk with the client about his or her family relationships; this makes it relevant to invite them to an interview. The questions would be worked into the conversation at appropriate times.

Define the family system.

1. ''To be helpful to you, it's important that we know who else is involved.''
2. ''Who lives in your home?''
3. ''How close to you do your parents live? How often do you see them?''
4. ''Do you have brothers or sisters?'' ''How often do you see them?''
5. If the client is divorced or separated, how often does he or she see the former spouse and children (if it's a non-custodial parent)?
6. Ask about grandparents and other extended family the client has contact with (uncles, aunts, cousins, etc.).
7. ''When you need someone to talk with outside the family, who do you go to?''

Inquire about family relationships.

1. Introductory comment: ''We have found that family members are usually aware of a problem one member is having.''
2. ''Since you live with (name members), how are they involved in the problem? What is their reaction?'' (Find out this information about each person in the home.)
3. ''How do you and your spouse generally get along? What does he or she do when the problem is happening?''
4. ''Tell me about your relationship with your mother and father.'' (Ask this whether the client lives with them or not.)
5. If appropriate, ask how long it has been since the client has lived with his or her parents. ''Do they provide any support for you now (money, car, food, etc.)?''

Miscellaneous family questions:

1. ''Tell me about (family member's) attitude toward the problem?''
2. ''Has (family member) ever complained about the problem?''
3. ''Has your relationship with (family member) changed in the past year or so?''
4. ''If you picked someone in your family to be here talking with us now, who would it be?''
5. ''Who was involved in your decision to seek help?''
6. ''Has (family member) ever encouraged you to seek help before?''
7. ''Is anyone afraid of someone in the family getting hurt?''

Make the family appointment.

If the client approves of family members being involved in the counseling, ask him or her to invite them to a session.

Guardrail

Definition and Purpose

The parents are asked to hold hands to show their child ''where the line is''—what limits on the child's behavior the parents will stand together to enforce. The purpose is to bring parents together as a team and to show parental unity.

Introductory Comments to the Parents

''When you join together, support each other, and continue to work as a team, it provides clear limits to your son/daughter. It's like a strong guardrail lining a tall bridge you're crossing in a car—you hope you never touch the rail or even go near it, but it's comforting to have it there. You know it will keep you from going over the side, even if there was an accident.''

Procedure

''To make this point, I want to ask you to do something. Hold each other's hand (one hand, not both). To make the guardrail even stronger, move your hand up each other's arm and clasp the other's forearm.'' (Illustrate by clasping your forearms with opposite hands.) While you are joined this way, your son (daughter) sees his boundaries and limits. Your son knows that if he goes beyond the limits you have set, you will take action together. This is the kind of mutual support you will need from each other to set clear limits for your child. One of you may temporarily weaken, but as long as the other is holding firm, the guardrail is in place.''

Examples

To the son/daughter: ''Will you push the guardrail to test its strength? Push on it to get its feel.'' (When this is done, the guardrail will give a little, but remain in place.) ''The guardrail is flexible, but it's also strong and solid.''

   If it's not too uncomfortable for them, the parents should maintain the guardrail while you ask other questions:

- ''How can your son be sure the guardrail is in place?''
- ''How can he get past the guardrail—go under or over it without you knowing?''
- ''What would make one of you loosen your grip?''
- ''Who is likely to loosen their grip first?''

Comments

This exercise fixes the idea of parental togetherness and teamwork in setting safe limits for their child. It will also bring out differences between the parents regarding the strict/lenient split on how to respond to their son or daughter. If other children are present, this exercise gives a visual example of parental unity and is a prevention message to the other children who may be tempted to try some of their sibling's rebellious activities.

   If the parents acknowledge differences or conflicts between each other on how to respond to their son or daughter, have a private conversation with the parents about how they want to handle these differences so that they can provide their children with clear and consistent directions.

The MIGS Sheet

As family counseling concepts and techniques are learned, how do we put them together to form an integrated whole, a model? My attempt at integration is expressed in the MIGS Sheet. MIGS stands for **Mapping, Issues, Goals,** and **Strategies.** In my opinion, these are the four essential pieces of information needed to conduct counseling with any family with any presenting problem. I use the MIGS Sheet to add direction and focus to family sessions, an important consideration in a brief model of therapy.

I also use the MIGS Sheet as a training tool; it helps to structure and discipline our thinking and to form the habit of attending primarily to that information which can be used. Without structure, trainees tend to collect myriad interesting bits of information about a family that have no organizing purpose, like Christmas tree ornaments with no tree to hang them on.

"Who is involved in the family drama (the *Map*)?" is a productive question because it expands our view of the broader social context of the problem. "What are the main concerns of the family (*Issues*)?" is another good question—within it lies the family's motivation to look at itself. "What am I trying to do with this family (*Goals*)?" keeps our attention on action rather

Source: *DeskGallery Image Catalog*, Copyright 1994 by Dover Publications, Inc. Used with permission.

than on random exploration with families. And finally, "How do I accomplish these goals (*Strategies*)?" is often a neglected piece of the puzzle. Goals may fail, not because they are unrealistic, but because the specific steps to accomplish them are not thought through.

The following pages contain a sample MIGS Sheet, along with instructions for its use. I have also included a blank MIGS Sheet (which you may duplicate).

MIGS Sheet Instructions

You can obtain most of the information on the MIGS Sheet in the first session with the family and modify the information as the sessions progress. The sheet should be briefly reviewed before and after each session. Does the counseling have a destination? Is it on track? To facilitate making changes on the form, it's best to use pencil rather than ink.

Map (see Family Mapping). Mapping is a visual display of your impressions of how a family is organized: who is close to whom, who is in conflict, etc. Make the map as broad as possible, including anyone who you believe is a player in the problem drama or who may be a resource in solving the problem. Good questions to ask are:

1. "Who lives in your home?"
2. To parents: "Where are your parents and siblings? Do they have contact with anyone in your family?"
3. "Besides those living in your home, who else knows about the problem?"
4. To an adolescent identified patient: "Who is your best friend? How often do you see him/her?"
5. To parents: "If you talked to someone outside your household, who would it be."

Don't hesitate to put extended family members, friends, neighbors, a minister, probation officer, DSS worker, or other professionals on the map. A good map gives a broad network focus to the family counseling.

Issues. These are the problems identified by the family members *and* the problems or potential problems perceived by the counselor. State them briefly: ''School truancy.'' ''Our son won't mind us.'' ''Rule out substance abuse by the identified patient.'' ''Possible violence between mother and father.''

''Family Strengths and Resources.'' What does the family do right? What in the family life is working well? Who (on the map) seems to be a healthful influence? What resources, professional or otherwise, have benefited the family in the past? What resources could help them now?

Therapeutic Theme. This is the broadest possible statement about what *structural* or *relationship* changes you're trying to accomplish in the family to help them overcome their current problems and prevent future ones. Example: ''To strengthen the single mother alliance with other adults in her life, to give her the support needed to set appropriate limits on the identified patient child.'' Different topics will be explored during the sessions that do not relate directly to the theme. However, each session should, in some way, support the therapeutic theme. If not, the theme should be changed.

Goals. Most goals should relate to the therapeutic theme. In the earlier example theme, what should I *do* to strengthen the single mother alliance with other adults? Could I invite an adult close to the mother to the next session? As the counseling progresses, goals that have been accomplished or are no longer active can be removed.

Strategies. These are the concrete steps to accomplish each goal. In the example, *how* do I choose the adult to invite, and who should invite him or her? The strategies, like the goals they implement, should be changed, added to, or deleted as the work progresses. The strategies should be current and active.

Notes. For any notes you want to make, including relevant information that doesn't fit other categories.

''Counselor's Use of Self'' includes any changes in your approach, style, or process you want or need to make. Examples: ''Take a firmer stand in stopping the interruptions by the identified patient.'' ''Join better with the stepfather.'' ''Become less central in the sessions.''

MIGS Sheet (Sample)

Map-Issues-Goals-Strategies

Map	**Issues**
(Family relationships)	(Family concerns *plus* problems you see)

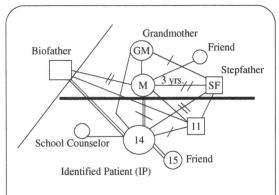

Note: All figures do not have to be connected by lines.

Circles = females; squares = males. Size of figures indicates apparent power of member. Number in figure = ages of children. IP = Identified Patient

Closeness/Communication:	**Conflict:**
.... Minimal	┬─ Moderate
─── Moderate	┬╫ Heavy
═══ Close	┬╱ Hidden conflict
─ ?─ Nature of relationship unknown	

Issues

1. Parents worried about IP being expelled from school for fighting and classroom behavior.
2. All are worried about violence between IP and angry stepfather.
3. IP is too powerful in the family because of M's closeness with IP and IP's alliance with biofather.
4. Open disagreements between M and step-father, esp. around IP.
5. Possible drug use by IP and friend.

Family Strengths & Resources:

Mother and biofather very concerned about IP.

GM's ideas for daughter and granddaughter are good.

GM could help to interrupt M's enabling of IP.

M - SF marriage appears solid in spite of problems.

Therapeutic Theme (one-sentence summary that guides the work with this family): While keeping the presenting problems of the IP in focus, clarify and strengthen the adult alliance to parent the IP child and the non-IP child.

Goals **(What to do)**	**Strategies** **(How to do it)**
1. Put M and SF in charge during the sessions, while keeping M in a more central parenting role than the SF.	Help M/SF reach agreements together concerning rules for the IP. If IP interrupts, ask M to deal with the interruptions.
2. Help IP negotiate with parents her reasonable requests, while giving full decision-making power to the parents.	To IP: "I will help you talk to your parents about what you want from them. Ask them for something you want. I will respect the decisions of your parents."
3. Ask the parents' permission for an individual interview with the IP.	In this interview, explore the IP's use of alcohol or other drugs. If found, explore with parents.
4. Uncover and resolve adult disagreements about parenting the IP: Stepfather/M disagreements, biofather/M , and GM/M.	Ask M's permission for biofather to attend a session (without the stepfather). Also explore GM attending a session.
5. Direct the parents' attention to the effects of the family issues on the son.	Define the son as one who acts good to avoid more problems in the family.

Family Name _____

MIGS Sheet

Map-Issues-Goals-Strategies

Map   **Issues**

(Family relationships) (Family concerns *plus* problems you see)

1.

2.

3.

4.

5.

6.

Note: All figures do not have to be connected by lines.

Circles = females; squares = males. Size of figures indicates apparent power of member. Number in figure = ages of children. IP = Identified Patient

Family Strengths & Resources:

Closeness/Communication: **Conflict:**

.... Minimal   —⁄— Moderate

——— Moderate   —⁄⁄— Heavy

=== Enmeshed   ——— Hidden conflict

     — ?— Nature of relationship unknown

Therapeutic Theme (a summary that guides the work with this family):

MIGS Sheet

Goals (What to do)	Strategies (How to do it)
1.	
2.	
3.	
4.	
5.	

Notes

	Counselor's Use of Self

New Talk

Definition and Purpose

The counselor asks a family member to say something to another member that he or she has never said to the person before. The purpose of this exercise is to break through to a new level of honesty in the family or to get beyond "analysis paralysis" of a particular issue. If a member makes a new and important disclosure, it can be explored. The importance of the topic depends on the emotion attached to it, not its content.

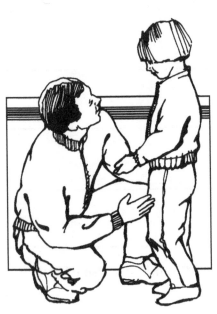

Source: *DeskGallery Image Catalog*, Copyright 1994 by Dover Publications, Inc. Used with permission.

Procedure

1. Instructions (to a member): "Will you take a small risk and try something with me? Say something to Susan that she hasn't heard you say to her before. Anything's OK as long as it's new."

2. Sit to the side of or behind the talking member. This is to remove the temptation for the member to draw you into the conversation. It is also a good position from which to lend support if the request is difficult for him or her.

3. After the talking member says something, ask the receiving member if it was old or new: "Have you heard this before from him?" If they have ever heard it before, ask the talking member to try again.

4. The receiving member responds any way he or she chooses.

5. You may want to reverse the roles by getting the receiving member to do the same thing with the talking member. If he or she doesn't want to, let it go.

Comments

1. This technique is especially useful for advice-giving parents who repeatedly tell their son or daughter the same things. This conversation, although well intentioned, is not beneficial because it has been repeated so many times.

2. Variation: If the member says only negative things to the family member, ask him or her to add something positive.

3. Variation: During a conversation between two members—father and daughter, for example—ask the other parent, "What do you see happening between your spouse and daughter?" Then set up the New Talk between father and daughter. After it is completed, ask the other parent again, "Now what did you see?" Through this, the family becomes more aware of its own communication process.

4. Variation: Ask each member to do the exercise, one at a time: "Pick someone in your family and say something that you haven't said to him or her before. Anything is okay, as long as it's new.

Paradox

Paradox is a therapeutic technique that induces change through joining, rather than opposing, the client's resistance and symptoms. To be effective with paradox, a counselor needs a solid foundation in the principles of paradoxical therapy and must be comfortable with being highly directive in making interventions. Included here are a few of the milder paradoxical strategies that I have tried. As a memory aid, they all start with "P." If you want to learn more about this technique, begin with a good book on the subject, such as *Paradoxical Psychotherapy* (1982) by Gerald R. Weeks and Luciano L'Abate (see Recommended Readings).

1. **Permission**

    Giving permission *not* to engage in a feared behavior. I have used this for families with poor therapy attendance (the ''feared'' behavior) to build motivation for treatment: ''This may sound strange, but I don't think you've had enough time to fully understand the problem. Let's meet again in 3–4 weeks; maybe it will be clearer then.''

2. **Postponement**

    The client family members are encouraged to delay making a decision they are ambivalent about. I have used this to weaken the ''yes, but'' reactions. Parent: ''I know we've got to do something soon, but it looks like we are damned with anything we do.'' Counselor: ''Maybe you should go slow with this one; the best decisions take time.''

3. **Prohibition**

    Forbidding clients from engaging in an activity that they are not engaging in. In couples therapy, where lack of communication is a problem, I frequently prohibit them from talking together in any meaningful way between sessions: ''It would be best if you didn't try to talk about this topic outside this room—it will just end in an argument. Save it until the next time we meet, and I will help you talk about it.''

4. **Prediction**

    Predicting a ''relapse'' for a client who is planning one. I give a standard prediction to parents who are making a plan together to set more appropriate limits on their problem child's behavior: ''When you carry out the plan, be prepared for your son to pull a surprise on you. It will be something you haven't seen before.'' This would normally be said with the child present.

5. **Prescription**

    The counselor advocates the continuation of the symptom, only this time under the counselor's control. If there is a sullen, uncommunicative teenager (identified patient) in a session, I may say to the parents, ''Your daughter may be silent in order to protect the family from arguing.'' To the teenager: ''If you can just listen, maybe you can learn something from me talking with your parents.''

Parent's Childhood

Source: *DeskGallery Mega-Bundle*, Copyright 1995 by Dover Publications, Inc. Used with permission.

Definition

The counselor asks the parents, one at a time, to talk about his or her family of origin, parents, and childhood.

Purpose

1. To give the children a sense of family history and to better understand that their parents were also children.
2. To give talking parents and their spouse a clearer idea of how their personal histories in their families of origin have influenced their roles as parents and spouses in their present family.

Procedure

1. Ask each parent (or the single parent) to talk with you about his or her family of origin. "I want to know what it was like for you growing up in your own families. It will give your family a better understanding of your history. They can listen while we talk."
2. If necessary, move your chair or change the seating arrangements to accommodate your one-on-one conversation with the parent.
3. The goal of the conversation is to explore the emotional influences in the parent's childhood and the origins of his or her style and beliefs around parenting and marriage. Any questions that bring out this information are appropriate.

Examples

1. Begin by asking the parent to define his or her family of origin: "Who was in your home when you were growing up?"
2. "What is one of your early memories about your family?"
3. "Which parent was more strict and which was more lenient? How were you disciplined as a child? Did this change when you became a teenager?"
4. "What was your mother and father's parenting style? How did they handle disagreements between each other? How did they handle family emotions such as anger?"
5. "All parents make mistakes with children. As you look back, what mistakes do you believe your parents made with you?"
6. "How was your parents' relationship different from the one you have now with your wife/husband/partner?" (This question brings the conversation more into the present and will often reveal important information and create dialogue between the parents.)

Comments

1. This technique works best when at least one of the children is old enough (8+) to attend to the conversation. It can also be used, however, when only the parent(s) are present.
2. The primary job of the spouse and children is to listen to the dialogue between parent and counselor; this may be the first time the family has ever heard the spouse/parent talk to an outsider about his or her own family-of-origin experiences. Allow occasional questions or comments from the others, but return the focus to the exercise.
3. Anecdotes and side stories can be important. They help fill in details of the family story.
4. If the parent grew up as a child of an alcoholic or addict and the current presenting problem involves substance abuse, explore the parent's emotional reactions and coping strategies as a child and their beliefs about the causes and cures for chemical dependency.

Reflecting Team

Family members often listen better when they are not being talked to. This technique, developed mostly by Tom Andersen and his colleagues, takes advantage of this phenomenon. I have used it a number of times with good results. Reference: *The Reflecting Team* (1991), edited by Tom Andersen (see Recommended Readings).

Definition and Purpose

A procedure whereby two or more colleagues observe the counselor and family during part of a family session and then talk to each other about what they saw and heard. The family and counselor listen to this conversation between the colleagues, then talk to each other about what they heard. The purpose is to introduce new observations to the family members about their patterns and processes.

Procedure

The counselor explains to the family: ''We often function as a team in our work with families. With your permission, I would like for my team to observe us for a little while (from inside the room or through a one-way mirror) and then talk to each other about what they think. We will listen to their conversation and then discuss what we heard.''

Examples of observations by the reflecting team (assume a single father who is permissive with his problematic teenage daughter; a younger son is also present):

a. ''The father is doing an admirable job in a difficult situation—raising two children while working full time. He obviously loves his children and will do anything for them.''

b. ''Maybe the daughter's anger at father is really fear. She may be afraid that he will not stand firm when he really needs to.''

c. ''I hope the son is not getting the message that to get father's attention, you have to act up. The son is not a problem for him, but I wonder if the son feels too much pressure to be good because of the problems between dad and daughter.''

Comments

1. The reflecting team consists of at least two colleagues. Talk with them before the family arrives, so the team is aware of the family picture. You may want the team to emphasize certain themes or points, since you know what you are trying to accomplish with the reflecting team technique.

2. Begin the team conversation by pointing out the family's strengths and successes.

3. While the team is talking together, the counselor stays with the family and observes the family's reactions to the conversation (signs of agreement, disagreement, confusion).

4. If the reflecting team stays in the therapy room, the counselor helps the family resist the temptation to break into the conversation between the reflecting team members (with questions, objections, denial, clarification). The counselor reminds the family members that they will get a chance to talk when the team finishes.

5. When the team finishes ''reflecting'' on the family (about 10 minutes), the counselor begins the discussion by making an open-ended comment to the family like ''What did you hear?'' The team listens. When this is over and the family leaves, the team and counselor talk about what happened.

Reframing

There are two types of Reframing:
Problem Reframing
and
Positive Reframing

Problem Reframing

Definition

A redefinition of the presenting problem that shifts the perspective from an *individual* to a *family* level.

Purpose

To slightly alter the family's framing of the problem, thus allowing a more flexible, family-based solution.

Examples

Presenting Problem	Reframe	Implied Action
"Our child gets into trouble and won't do what we say."	"Under-responsible behavior"	*Parents* teach him more responsibility.
"He won't talk to me or reveal how he feels."	"You want better communication with him."	Work on communication together.
"Our teenager is rebellious and runs with a bad crowd."	"She's doing her own thinking without the benefit of the parents' experience."	How to get her to accept the parents' help.

In the above examples, the presenting problem is that one person is behaving poorly; he or she has a deficit or flaw that needs correcting. The problem is within the skin of the individual in the family. This is not an interactional or systemic view of the difficulty. If this individual ''frame'' of the problem goes unchallenged, the family does not need to be present; individual counseling would be the proper treatment. The counselor's job is to find a way to include more than one person in the definition, to place the problem (or solution) in a *relationship* context. This accesses the systemic mode of working with the family.

To use an analogy, the counselor takes the family's picture of the problem at face value, reframes it, providing a different perspective on the same picture, and hands it back to the family. This slight redefinition may help to gain the cooperation of the family members in solving the problem. It also includes everyone as part of the action, making family counseling more relevant to them. A good problem reframe does not spread out the blame to encompass everyone but rather makes everyone a part of the solution.

Positive Reframing
Definition and Purpose

A way of thinking that assumes that for every negative thought, action, or feeling, there is a positive intention or characteristic of the person being expressed. Positive reframes are used to build positive relationships with clients.

Examples

Statement	Reframe
(Client says)	**(Counselor says to the client)**
"He never listens to me."	"It's clear that you want better communication with him."
"If people would just leave me alone, I would be all right."	"You like to do your own thinking and take care of yourself."
"I'm going to leave treatment, and nobody can stop me!"	"Once you make up your mind, you're very determined."
"There's nothing wrong with me. *They* have the problem."	"I like the way you are exploring exactly where the problem lies."
"No matter how hard I try, I can't do better."	"Trying hard and doing better are obviously things you value."
"He's so stupid. He can't do anything right."	"So, intelligent action is important to you."

Comments

1. A positive reframe is different from a reflection or interpretation:
   A **reflection** gets at the here-and-now *feelings* behind the words.
   An **interpretation** gets at the deeper *meanings* behind action or feelings.
   A **positive reframe** gets at the positive *intention* or personal *trait* being expressed.
2. Springboard: A question can be added to the reframe to shift to a more productive, hopeful subject. ("I can see that you want a closer relationship with her. *What seems to work the best?*")
3. Variations:
   1. Reframe one person's statement to another person (not to the speaker).
   2. Reframe the interaction (argument, etc.) between two or more people.
   3. Reframe behaviors (silence, overactivity, etc.) instead of words.
4. Points:
   1. State it affirmatively ("It's clear to me that....")
   2. Say only what you believe.
   3. Use it sparingly (about three times in an hour is enough).

Practice With Positive Reframing

To be fluid with positive reframing takes repetition and practice. Below are examples of negative statements and suggested reframes.

1. "I have no friends, I'm lonely, and life is miserable."
   Positive reframe (PR): Relationships are obviously important to you.

2. "Why shouldn't I use drugs? All my friends do."
   PR: It's clear that your friends are important to you.

3. "My parents treat me like I'm a child."
   PR: I see that you want your parents to understand that you are maturing and want to be treated that way.

4. "Coming here to these groups is a waste of time."
   PR: Clearly you want to get something out of the time you invest.

5. "I've said before that I would stop drinking, but this time I mean it!"
   PR: I can see that your credibility is valuable to you.

6. "If I do something they don't like, they just give me another lecture."
   PR: You want more of a two-way conversation with your parents.

7. "Every time something goes wrong, they blame me!"
   PR: You have a strong sense of fairness and don't want to be blamed for something you believe is not your fault.

8. "You don't believe me. Why should I talk to you?"
   PR: Obviously, trust in a relationship is important to you.

9. "You counselors are always trying to get inside my head!"
   PR: I can see that you value your privacy.

Can you think of a positive reframe for each of these process behaviors?

- Silence
- Overtalking
- Externalizing
- Blame
- Excessive squirming
- Storytelling "Yes, but ..."

Relabeling

Definition

The use of begin words, phrases, definitions, and metaphors to facilitate counseling.

Purpose

To allow certain negative behaviors to be referred to without using disparaging labels.

At a workshop I attended, Salvadore Minuchin played a videotape of a family in which the mother dominated the session. She corrected everyone, interrupting her spouse and children to provide more detail, ''clarification,'' or to reveal hidden motives.

Minuchin turned off the tape and asked for a word or phrase that described the mother. ''She's a lawn mower!'' a workshop participant answered. ''No, no,'' Minuchin replied. ''She's a deep-sea diver!'' Minuchin's relabeled description of the mother could be used explicitly with the family in a session to refer to the mother's behavior whenever it occurred; the student's couldn't.

Examples

Here are some common terms used by family members to describe other members during family sessions (expletives deleted) and my attempt at more neutral or benevolent substitutions.

Client Label	Counselor Relabel
"nagging"	"conscientious"
"jealous"	"passionate, loyal, devoted"
"overreacts"	"sensitive"
"sloppy"	"casual"
"aloof"	"rational; objective"
"flighty"	"spontaneous"
"too strict"	"protective"

Comments

There is a troublesome little four-letter word that can cause problems in working with overinvolved parent-child situations. The word is ''help.'' Some young people's symptoms are the result of overly conscientious parents helping too much (enabling, spoiling). Urging these Parents of the Year Nominees to ''*not* help their child so much'' makes no sense to them. They look at you funny, like you've lost your mind. Counselors need to stay with the idea of *help* but try to give it a new meaning. Here are some re-definitions I have used in these enmeshed, enabling family situations. ''Help'' is

> Allowing your children to learn from natural consequences.
> Teaching them responsibility for their own actions.
> Giving them strong incentive to change.
> Loving them enough to let them skin their knees.
> Preparing them to be on their own.

Safe Rebellion

Definition

Parents allow the child to "rebel" by expressing disapproval of a certain behavior but *not* trying to change it.

Purpose

To ease tensions between parent(s) and child. Many parents believe that adolescents do peculiar things—dress funny, wear their hair in odd ways, have sloppy personal habits, or use strange language. The amount of anger and conflict, however, can be out of proportion to the importance of the behavior involved. The underlying issue becomes one of control.

Procedure

Usually, this intervention is set up without the children being present. First, make some basic statements about normal adolescent development to the parents. Explain the adolescent's need to rebel, to establish autonomy, to discover who he or she is. These traits, although hard on parents, are normal and expected.

Then ask the parents to choose one "rebellious" thing their adolescent does that the parents have unsuccessfully tried to correct but that does not affect the health and safety of anyone in the home, such as his or her choice of music, clothes, or language. If two parents are involved, they should talk to each other and agree on one behavior.

Once the behavior is chosen, the counselor sets the rules for the intervention: parents are to continue expressing disapproval and annoyance at the adolescent's behavior but *make no attempt to change it*. If the opportunity arises, each parent, or the involved parent, is to make several negative comments during the coming weeks to the adolescent about the target behavior ("You're wearing *that* out in public?") but *not* try to correct it.

Examples

A single mother brought her 14-year-old daughter, Amy, to counseling, complaining of her uncooperative behavior at home. The mother was distraught after several months of unsuccessful efforts to correct her daughter's personal hygiene, choice of clothes, and friends. The typical parental moves of granting and removing privileges had not worked. While Amy waited in the reception area, the counselor explained that some form of rebellion is normal during adolescence and that Amy was trying to establish her own identity. The mother was asked to choose something about Amy's habits, behavior, or activities that the mother would be willing to let go of. She picked the way Amy kept her room—disorganized, dirty clothes everywhere, stale food under the bed—which had been a point of conflict for the past year.

The counselor then set the task: the mother was to continue what she had been doing—expressing disgust and disbelief as she passed by Amy's room—at least twice during the coming week. The only difference was that this time, she was not to try to get Amy to clean her room. The mother agreed to take action only if the mess created too many roaches or rats or if "something moldy and green" began growing into the hallway.

Within two weeks, the mother reported that she had carried out the task: "Amy is still no angel, but things are better between us." Amy added, "We don't fight as much."

Comments

The parent regains control of the war by letting the adolescent win the battle. Everyone in the home benefits by the easing of tensions around one of the conflict topics in the family. The counseling moves along, bolstered by the parent's success in making a decision, taking action, and getting results.

Sculpting and Movement

Physical movement in the sessions creates energy, for both family and counselor. These exercises can be done at any time after the initial interview and will add interest—and maybe a breakthrough—in the session.

Sculpting

Definition

The physical arrangement of family members that represents the sculptor's picture of relationships in a family at a particular time.

Purpose

Physical movement creates energy and variety in the session and can sometimes create a breakthrough in the awareness level of family members.

Procedure

Say to one member, "Imagine that you are a sculptor and that your family is made of clay. Make a sculpture of your family. You can place each person anywhere, in any position (illustrate by touching and moving the sculptor as you explain). Go ahead and be the sculptor. I want to see how your family looks to you."

Examples

When the family is sculpted, ask several questions:
1. (to sculptor, if necessary): "Put yourself in the picture."
2. (of each person): "What's it like for you in this picture?"
3. (of each): "Does the picture surprise you?"

Optionals

1. (to sculptor): "Now show me how you would *like* it to be."
2. (to a highly verbal family): "Let's do this without talking."
3. "Give your picture a title."

Comments

1. Move chairs out of the way before starting. Everybody is standing.
2. In some families, it is best to ask a child to be the first sculptor; he or she is more willing to "play" and will provide a warm-up for the adults.
3. Model physical touching by touching the sculptor while explaining the procedure; be animated and active.
4. Everyone gets a turn.
5. Use objects (chairs, etc.) to represent absent people.
6. Allow time for discussion after everyone has had their turn. Make objective comments about their sculpts and get their reaction ("Father was the only one not touching anyone; the daughter was looking away from the family," etc.).

Show Me

1. Instructions (to one member or to the whole family): *Show* us the problem (or situation). What is each person doing or saying? I want to see how the problem (situation) *looks*.''
2. When the family is placed in the problem situation (examples of questions):
   a. ''What is each person doing?''
   b. ''Give each person some words to say.''

Most/Least

1. Instructions (to one member): ''Arrange your family in a line according to who is most and least worried about the situation. This part of the room will be the most worried and that part the least. Let' s do this without talking.''

   <u>Other content:</u>
   who *talks* the most/least   who is *strict* the most/least
   who *protects* others the most/least   others that fit the family situation

2. When they are in place, talk about what they created.

Change the Distance

1. Stand and move away from the family while giving instructions.
2. Instructions (while couple or family is sitting): ''I want to ask you to do something that may appear silly, but bear with me. Change the distance between you.'' (If they ask for clarification, just repeat the instructions.)
3. After they move, make observations about who moved closer or moved farther away, who moved first and last, small behaviors (gestures, glances, etc.). By making observations, the counselor is creating metaphors about family relationships by using their movements.

Examples

''I noticed that everyone waited for the mother to move, then positioned themselves according to where she went.''

''Father is the only one who stayed firm where he was.''

''When one person moved, everyone had to shift.''

Place Yourself

1. When two or more members are talking to each other on a relevant topic, turn to another member and say, ''*Place* yourself in this conversation. *Show* me where you are in this.''
2. You're looking for a physical movement, for the member to actually *place* him- or herself in the conversation.
3. Talk about what happened. The member could take sides by moving next to one of the talking members, moving in between them, or moving away from both members, or he or she may even leave the room. Anything that happens is a statement about relationships. (As a bonus, this technique can also interrupt stuck, repetitive interactions between two talking members.)

Sibling Talk

Definition

During a family session, two or more siblings talk to each other about a specific topic while the parents listen.

Source: *DeskGallery Mega-Bundle*, Copyright 1995 by Dover Publications, Inc. Used with permission.

Purpose

To emphasize the importance and integrity of the sibling relationships, to draw appropriate family boundaries, or to highlight the influence of the family problems on the children.

Procedure

1. Ask the parents' permission for their sons/daughters to talk together on a particular topic (specify): "Is it O.K. if I ask Kishana and Antonio about how Kishana coming home late last weekend affected Antonio? Let's see if Antonio was worried about his (younger) sister." Getting the parents' permission underscores their leadership role and supports the natural hierarchy of the family. For adult siblings, getting the parents' permission is not necessary.

2. Help the siblings get started in their conversation by making comments or by asking questions: "Tell your sister how you saw the situation we're talking about. What did you think about it?" The counselor can also make clarifying comments, help them stay on an important subject, positively reframe, or offer other support. However, the counselor, like the parents, should not intrude as long as the siblings are productively engaged with each other.

3. For teenage or older siblings, the instructions can be more general: "Talk to each other about how your relationship has changed over the past year ("since the problem started, since the incident happened," etc.). Any talk between the siblings is permissible as long as it is not an old argument (a new argument is fine) or superficial conversation they have often. If they get too far off the subject, direct them back to the central question ("As a result of all that, how has your relationship changed?").

Examples

1. Brothers, aged 17 and 19, talked about how they became estranged in the past three years because of the younger brother's drug use, which forced the older brother to side with their parents.

2. A 16-year-old sister tearfully apologized to her 11-year-old brother for being a poor role model for him during her parent-defying behaviors at home and at school.

3. An adult sister talked with her adult brother about her long-held resentment of his closer relationship with their parents.

Comments

1. It is important for the parent(s)—especially if one or both are over-involved with the children—to stay out of the conversation. If they have difficulty staying out, or they allow themselves to be pulled into the dialogue, remind everyone that the siblings are able to deal with this issue on their own. Gently redirect the conversation back to the children.

2. This technique works best when the siblings have a benign or close relationship. It does not work well when they are in open conflict, since any dialogue between them leads to a repetitive argument. In this case, *New Talk* would be a better choice.

Strategic Child Assessment

Definition and Purpose

Source: *DeskGallery Mega-Bundle*, Copyright 1995 by Dover Publications, Inc. Used with permission.

A technique for the assessment of the identified patient child for the purpose of engaging the parents in counseling with their child.

Procedure

The parent who makes the first contact is asked to bring in everyone in the home so that the counselor can get a complete picture of the child's problem. When they arrive, a first family interview is conducted. During the interview, if the parents are overly focused on the child's problems to the exclusion of everything else, and it appears that at least one of the parents will resist *family* treatment, the counselor can increase motivation for the next family appointment by asking both parents to bring the child to the second interview for an individual assessment of him or her and a discussion of the results. Complying with the medical model, the clinician agrees to examine the patient.

A guiding principle is for the individual assessment to be relevant to the parents' view of the child's problems. If the problem is that the child is performing below his or her ability level in school, the counselor tailors the assessment interview to school information. If the presenting problem is sibling fighting, the siblings are given an "interpersonal assessment" to determine the reasons for the conflict. If the parents complain that their teenager won't obey them, a private interview with the adolescent is scheduled to "get at the reasons for his/her behavior."

Examples

In the discussion with the parents about the assessment results, frame the problem in a way that includes the necessity for the family to accompany the child in counseling. For the school problem, for example, the counselor might say, "My assessment shows that your son is having difficulty concentrating in school even though he certainly has the intelligence to do good work. Can the two of you (parents) think of a way to find out what may be interfering?" For the sibling fighting: "After my interpersonal assessment of your son and daughter, it appears they can't decide who in the family is supposed to be in charge. Can you, as parents, help them clarify this?" For the adolescent who won't obey the parents: "During my assessment I found some confusion and doubt in your daughter. She doesn't fully understand that you, as her parents, will stand together to present clear limits to her behavior. What can the two of you do to help her with this?"

Comments

Parents do not usually think systemically about their child's problems. Their view is that the child is behaving poorly and should be treated ("Fix my kid."). The Strategic Child Assessment accommodates this view by seeing the child alone for an individual assessment and then by *framing the problem to the parents in a way that motivates the parents to continue in counseling with their child*. This makes family counseling relevant to the parents. The assessment techniques and the way the information is presented to the parents will be different in each case, since every child assessment is tailored to the parents' view of the situation.

Strategic Predictions

Definition and Purpose

The counselor predicts the course of the child's symptoms for parents who naively believe the problem is solved. This technique is appropriate for parents who present a child who has gotten into trouble because of substance use.

Procedure

If you see that the family members won't stay in counseling because they believe that the child has completely quit using alcohol/drugs, let them go and make them aware of some possible future behaviors their child may exhibit. This gives the parents specific substance-related behaviors to look for and—if some of the predictions are accurate—improves the counselor's credibility, thereby increasing the chances that the family will return to counseling when necessary.

Examples

Kevin (age 15) was referred by his school for using marijuana and drinking beer on school property. Because of the information revealed in the individual drug assessment with Kevin and the secretive way he acted during the family sessions with his parents, the counselor knew that he was more heavily involved with drugs than his parents were ready to admit.

The family sessions continued for three meetings, during which Kevin stayed out of trouble. The parents were no longer worried and wanted to stop counseling. During the third session, the counselor privately told the parents, "You seem to suspect that the problem with Kevin's alcohol and drug use is over. Certainly, we all hope so. But just in case, here are some things to watch out for in the next few weeks." (Jot down the predictions, and give them to the parents.)

1. "You may notice Kevin *becoming secretive* when asked about his friends."
2. "He may have trouble *meeting his curfew*, especially on weekends."
3. "You may notice Kevin having *mood changes* and reactions that don't fit the situation."
4. "Kevin may have *unexplained money problems*."
5. "Kevin may continue his *lack of interest in school*, with absences and poor grades."
6. "He may angrily *accuse you of not trusting him* and of being too suspicious."
7. "I cannot say that any of these things will happen, but with your son's safety at stake, it's worth watching closely for a while. If any of these signs do appear in the next few weeks, please call me, and together we'll explore it more."

Comments

1. Some parents minimize the seriousness of their adolescent's alcohol or other drug problems and see no need to continue family sessions once the young person shows improvement.
2. Offer the predictions as behaviors to be alert for, not stern warnings about what *will* happen.
3. In most cases, make the statements to the parents without the young person being present. The exception is when you want the predictions to have a paradoxical effect—the teenager is determined not to do what you said they might do.
4. Use a time frame for the predictions, anchored to some future event or calendar date (about 4–8 weeks in the future): "Before mid August, you may notice . . . ." "Between now and Thanksgiving, you may find . . . ." "By her sixteenth birthday, . . . " "Before the first frost of winter, . . . "

Toybox

Source: *DeskGallery Image Catalog*,
Copyright 1994 by Dover Publications,
Inc. Used with permission.

Definition

The counselor's creative use of objects, props, and toys to communicate with a family.

Purpose

A form of metaphor that is a natural for family counseling is the use of concrete things—objects and props—to help convey meaning. They are natural because they are already being used in the counseling room: the counselor's notepad or chart, the client's coat, pocketbook in the lap, cup of coffee, hat, dark glasses, etc. All these things communicate about the person, or the person's message, in some way.

Procedure

The general idea is to stimulate action in the room with some type of object. If the therapist and family are dealing with an important phone call someone needs to make, the therapist can go get a phone book (or better, a phone). If a spouse complains of her partner's hiding behind the newspaper at breakfast, the therapist can get a paper for the partner to hold while the spouse is asked to ''show us what you would like to do in this situation.''

Examples

1. During a couples session, the wife meekly complained how her spouse did not help her with the responsibilities of the house and children, leaving her ''holding the bag.'' The counselor picked up a plastic bag that happened to be in the corner of the room and handed it to the wife. The wife became more agitated as she sat there holding the bag while they talked. Within a few minutes, this nonassertive lady flung the bag to the floor and exclaimed, ''I will not do this!'' This unusual behavior got her spouse's attention, allowing them to address her strong resentments.
2. A family was in counseling for a problematic teenage son. After several sessions, the son ran away from home. The parents seemed surprisingly unconcerned. To add significance to the event and to prompt action by the parents, we held a ritualized ''funeral'' during the next session by placing a wilted gardenia in a vase in the room and eulogized the ''lost'' son who was gone, dismembered from the family ''before he had a chance to blossom.'' The penetrating odor of the gardenia helped to anchor that session in the parents' consciousness. After the interview, they found out where the son had gone and got him back; counseling proceeded from there.

Comments

Props can trigger a shift in the mood or intensity of a session and can add immediacy to a therapeutic move; something in the room can be more compelling than something on the mind. Sometimes the air in the room needs to be lighter, sometimes heavier. To achieve either of these, the therapist's playful objects (the ''toybox'') can be brought—with unbalancing impact—into the family counseling room.

Worried Child

Definition

With the facilitation of the counselor, one or more children express their concerns and worries to the parent *about* the parent.

Purpose

This intervention is for a family with a child identified patient whose parent abuses mood-altering substances, including prescription medication. (It can also be used when the parent is the identified patient and has an addiction problem.) It's a relatively mild form of intervention for chemical dependence because it is kept within the immediate family, and only the child or children are doing the "confronting" of the parent. A child's pain, however, can be the final straw in the parent's crumbling defense system.

Source: *DeskGallery Image Catalog*, Copyright 1994 by Dover Publications, Inc. Used with permission.

Procedure

1. Have an assessment session with the child alone. Among other things, ask the child questions about activities in the home, especially on evenings and weekends. If the child mentions alcohol or other drug use by a family member, explore it. Be sure to get specific information (who, what, where, when). You may also want to use drawings—such as **Draw-a-Dream** and the **Circle Method**—to show the parent after the assessment.

2. Have a private conversation with the parent(s) about your assessment findings. Your diagnosis, however, should be uncertain, the only certainty being that something powerful and emotional is preoccupying the child and affecting his or her behavior. Speculate with the parent(s) about what is producing such anger, hostility, disregard for parental authority, school problems, or whatever forms the problems take.

3. After some exploration with the parent, offer your best guess about the cause of the problems: He or she is "worried" about the parent. Explore with the parent any guesses he or she has about why the child is worried. If the parent mentions the substance use, briefly explore it (what drugs, how often, where, etc.). At this point, however, it is important not to entirely switch the focus to the parent's substance abuse, since that would change the problem (and patient) brought to therapy. Keep the focus on the child and his or her problems and emotional state. Your goal is to gently and repetitively support the idea that the child may be upset and worried about the parent (which the child usually is). Get the parent's permission to help the parent and child have a conversation about what is bothering the child.

4. If the parent agrees, arrange the appointment and help the child talk about his or her worries, especially around the substance use. You may need to patiently prompt the child, using the specific information the child revealed to you. ("Will you tell your mom about not being able to sleep until you hear her come in at night?")

Comments

This is a difficult issue in family counseling. If a child is the identified patient and the counselor directly addresses the parent's substance abuse, it will often elicit the parent's anger and denial and may result in the parent removing the child from treatment altogether. It's a dilemma. In these cases, it is often best to "speak through the child."

Sometimes, this intervention will result in the adult talking with you about getting a substance abuse assessment from a qualified professional. At the very least, it will interfere with the parents' denial about how his or her drinking or drug use is affecting the children.

Summary of Systemic Techniques

I have classified the techniques in this book according to their level of difficulty. But don't be intimidated by the classification: If a counselor has joined well and works with sensitivity and respect, even an inexperienced counselor can use all of these to help the family. Page numbers for the techniques are in parentheses.

Basic

Drawings: Paper and pencil representations of the family members' perceptions (115–116).

Enactments: Getting two or more members to talk to each other about one of their real-life issues (44).

Family Mapping: Drawing the counselor's impressions of family relationships through use of symbols (117–118).

Family Questions: Questions asked by the counselor to explore family relationships (119).

Joining: Building a foundation of rapport and trust with family members (47).

MIGS Sheet: Using four vital areas of information—Mapping, Issues, Goals, and Strategies—this form develops for the counselor an informal treatment plan for the family (121–125).

Recruiting: Getting family members to the first interview (37–39).

Sculpting: A family member (the sculptor) arranges other members in physical postures to represent how he/she sees the family (135–136).

Segmenting: Working with a portion of the family at a time (44).

Task: A between-session activity for the family (44).

Intermediate

Chair Work: Various ways to use chairs in a session to communicate with the family (111).

Circular Questions: One member is asked about relationships between *other* members (112).

Guardrail: Parents join hands to form a limit-setting boundary for their problem child (120).

New Talk: A family member says something to another member that he or she hasn't said before (126).

Parent's Childhood: A parent tells about his or her family experiences as a child (128).

Reframing: Offering a new perception to a problem or to a negative statement (130–132).

Relabeling: The counselor's use of benign words to represent how a family member describes another member (133).

Safe Rebellion: A parent allows his or her child to rebel in safe ways while the parent "protests." (134).

Sibling Talk: Siblings talk to each other while parents listen (137).

Strategic Child Assessment: The child is "diagnosed" to involve the parents in the treatment (138).

Strategic Predictions: Parents are advised about behaviors their child may exhibit in the future (139).

Toybox: Using objects and props to anchor a point during a session (140).

Worried Child: After preparing the child alone, helping the child tell his or her concerns to the parents (141).

Advanced

Alter Ego: The counselor sits behind a member and talks for him or her (108).

Brief Network Intervention: Family, extended family, and professionals solve a problem together (109–110).

Colleague Teamwork: Various ways for colleagues to work as a team in helping families (113–114).

Paradox: Several techniques for going with, rather than opposing, resistance (127).

Reflecting Team: A colleague team discusses the family while the family listens (129).

CHAPTER 5
MULTIPLE FAMILY GROUPS

Introduction

Multiple Family Group (MFG) is a collection of families, including the identified patient, who meet together with one or two counselors to share experiences, to give and receive support, and to acquire insight and new behaviors in a safe environment. The purposes of the group can be for education and discussion, for sharing and support, for more intensive therapy, or for some blend of these. Learning occurs in each individual, between families, between individual members of different families, and between members of the same family. This approach is well suited for treating families with a problem adolescent or any other problem that gives the families a common focus, such as a family member with a medical or psychiatric condition or a child with an attention deficit disorder. The shared experiences of the families are the bond.

Perhaps the most common use of MFG in the mental health setting is for adolescent problems. Therefore, for language consistency, this section will assume the MFG is convened around problem adolescents—for substance abuse, oppositional behavior, legal problems, and so forth. Regardless of the problem the families have in common, the ideas, techniques, and procedures in this section will apply.

As a therapeutic modality, MFG has several advantages. First, it combines the power of group process with the therapeutic power of family counseling; it's a nice blend of the two. Second, because of the shared experiences of the participants, the group members do much of the therapeutic work; the therapist can observe more and participate less. Third, with discouraged families, the MFG setting offers not only support but also hope. Each family sees that other families have similar problems and are able to cope with them. Finally, MFG is an economical approach, since more clients are receiving treatment with less staff time than with individual counseling, group therapy, or one-family sessions.

It's important to note that many of the ideas, interventions, and techniques in this book can be adapted for use in a MFG. For example, if you want to use a technique—such as *Enactments, Circular Questions,* or *Sculpting*—with a particular family, it can be accomplished just as easily in the MFG as it is in a one-family session. When an exercise is done with one family and observed by the group, every member in the group benefits. The therapeutic effect is even greater when the therapist facilitates group discussions (observations, opinions, interpretations) with all group members after the exercise is completed. During these discussions, all group members are gaining multiple perspectives and ideas about their own family situation.

Readers can use this section to set up a new MFG in their inpatient or outpatient treatment setting or to add ideas and techniques to an existing MFG. After a little experimentation, you can decide what is best suited to your caseload and treatment program.

Suggested Procedures for Multiple Family Groups

1. The room should be large enough to allow space to move around (for *Sculpting* and other activities). Moveable chairs are preferred.

2. One-and-a-half to two hours is a good length for MFG. I recommend a frequency of once per week.

3. The maximum number of families for a manageable group is 6–7, ideally 4–5 families. The maximum number of participants is about 20, ideally about 15. For groups whose primary purpose is education and support rather than more intensive therapy, the numbers could be higher, perhaps 8–10 families, with a total of 25–30 participants.

4. For purposes of MFG, a family is everyone who lives in the home of the identified patient or who does not live in the home but who is concerned about and involved with the problem, such as grandparents, other extended family, or close friends of the family.

5. In two-parent households, it's important to have *both* parents attend.

6. Normally, age 8 should be the youngest child in the group; below this age children usually do not have sufficient attention span for the meeting. A separate group for younger children can be established to run concurrently with MFG. This has the added advantage of providing child care while the parents and older children are attending the MFG.

7. Include time for social mixing to allow participants to get to know each other in an informal way. A 15-minute break for this purpose can be provided midway in a one-and-a-half or two-hour group. An opportunity for casual interaction is important for the comfort and cohesion of the group.

8. Preferably, two counselors are assigned to each group.* They should decide how they work together. Most counselors function best when their two roles are complementary rather than identical. Complementary roles—when both counselors contribute to the goals of the group but not in exactly the same way—add power and interest to the group, as when one counselor leads the general activities of the group and the other brings up information and issues pertinent to specific clients and families. Or, counselors can alternate sessions in taking the leadership role. Identical roles (co-leadership) can cause confusion about moment-to-moment direction in the group, like two people trying to steer the same car.

9. I recommend an open group that runs continuously and takes referrals continuously. This helps ensure a full group and prevents a waiting list. If the group is too large for a particular session (35+), it can be split, with each counselor taking half of the group for all or a portion of the scheduled time. This allows each family more time to participate.

Family Recruitment for Multiple Family Groups

1. The earlier in the treatment program the family is recruited, the more successful recruitment will be. Families are more willing to comply when they are invited to participate at the very beginning of their child's treatment instead of days or weeks after their adolescent is admitted.

2. The parents should attend the intake session with their adolescent. While the adolescent is having his or her individual assessment with the intake worker, parental recruitment can be done by the MFG counselor, who talks with the parents about joining the MFG.

---

* Other treatment staff members can be present, either for training purposes or to learn about their client in their family setting. They would also participate in the after-session staff discussions. They would not, however, participate in leading the group.

3. The MFG should be presented as an integral part of the adolescent's treatment, not as a separate service for family members. When talking with the parents, emphasize the importance of the parents and others in the home being included for the benefit of the adolescent. A good phrase to use is, "The way we work is to include the parents and other involved family members in helping your son/daughter to correct the problems he/she is having. Your son/daughter needs your help." The MFG component of treatment can then be explained.

Clinical Tips

1. Arrange a circle of chairs before the group arrives. Members of each family sit together in the group. (Allowing adolescents to sit together, rather than with their respective families, is a bad idea.)

2. At the beginning of each group session, go around the circle, with everyone saying their first name and their relationship to the identified client.

3. As a memory aid in large groups, write down their names in the order they are sitting as they identify themselves at the beginning of the session. Get on a first-name basis. Know the first names of every person in the room, and call them by name frequently (refer to your names notes when necessary). This helps the group learn everyone's name. Within the group, anonymity works against cohesion, since members are more reluctant to talk to someone in the group whose name they don't know.

4. Ways of beginning a session:
   - "I want to hear everyone's main concern in their family tonight." Beginning at your left or right, ask, for example, "Joe, what is your major concern in your family?" Within each family, ask the parents before asking children or other family members. This keeps the parents in the leadership role and provides a model for their children on how to respond to questions about the family. (Tip: If you want every family in the group to respond to a question you have posed, it is quicker to go around the circle than to ask for volunteers.)
   - "I want to find out how the problem has affected each family." Beginning at your left or right, ask, for example, "Margie, how has your son's problem affected you? How has it affected your family as a whole?"
   - For groups that have had several meetings together, you could begin the group by asking simply, "What's important to someone tonight?"
   - Groups could also be started with a brief presentation by the facilitator on a particular topic or by offering a topic for discussion (trust, expression of feelings in families, etc.).

5. For a session in which there are new members, let them introduce themselves and talk about their family situation and what led to placing their child in treatment. Family members become a part of the group only after they have taken the risk of sharing with the group about themselves. Everyone in the new family should speak.

6. Sometime during the first or second session for the new families, determine how each new parent is thinking about his or her child's problems. Some parents minimize the problem or attribute the teenager's behavior to various causes, such as bad peers or bad luck. Leave parental denial alone until the parents have attended 2–3 sessions, giving them the opportunity to change their own minds if they need to. Parents also need time to become connected within the group before they will receive direct feedback from the group members about their denial.

7. At times, the facilitator is central to the group communication, allowing the members to speak directly to him or her; at other times, the facilitator becomes non-central, encouraging the members to speak directly to each other. In well-functioning groups, the facilitator is non-central much of the time.

Therapeutic Activities

In addition to group and family skills, counselors need a few specific approaches to use with families in MFGs. (Also, a counselor can use any technique in this book with *one* family while other families observe.) Here are several activities that are especially suited to MFGs.

Fishbowling

A fishbowl is a therapeutic activity conducted with a portion of the group who sit inside the circle while the remaining group members observe. It could consist of a role-play, work with one family, or an experiential exercise. The purpose is to spotlight a particular topic, to do a few minutes of counseling with one family, to conduct a role-play, to demonstrate a communication skill, or to provide some other therapeutic experience for the group. The facilitator sets up the exercise and invites the participants to move their chairs to the center of the circle. The facilitator may or may not join them in the center, depending on the nature of the activity.

Examples

To demonstrate a communication exercise, such as assertiveness or active listening.

To role-play a typical family situation, such as the parents talking with the adolescent the morning after the teenager violated curfew.

To work on an important topic or recent event in one family.

Note: When any activity with a subset of the group is completed, open the discussion to the entire MFG, inviting everyone's observations and comments.

Inner/Outer Circle

This exercise divides the group into two subgroups, which form two circles, one inside the other. Members of the inner circle have some sort of interaction with each other while those in the outer circle observe. After the activity, the facilitator opens the discussion to the outer circle, asking for observations and comments. Members of the inner circle may also want to comment on what happened. After this, the circles reverse, with the outer circle becoming the inner, and the activity is repeated. The purpose is to focus on an issue that is shared by many of the families or to promote better understanding between the subgroups in families (parents in the inner circle, children in the outer, for example).

Example. Invite family members (except for the identified patient) to sit in the inner circle and talk together on a particular topic while the identified patients from each family observe from the outer circle. The topic could be started with a question such as, ''Let's talk together about how you and your family have been affected by the problem of your family member (the adolescent). Have you been scared, angry, confused, or what? What's it been like for you?''

After 15–30 minutes of talk, the outer circle is invited to comment on what the inner group talked about. After this discussion, the circles trade places, and the new inner circle is prompted to talk about the same topic: ''What's it been like from your side?'' When members of this group finish, the outer circle members make comments or ask questions, as before.

Trust Exercise

In a MFG convened around substance-abusing adolescents, the family's lack of trust in the adolescent's abstinence is an almost universal issue for families. It can be a sensitive and volatile topic that becomes the centerpiece for family arguments. Because of its delicate nature, lack of trust is difficult to talk about in families, giving it the power to generate anger and resentments and even to trigger a relapse back into drugs by the adolescent.

To emphasize the importance of the trust issue, and to make the point that it is a normal and expected issue, the facilitator prompts group discussion on the topic through comments and questions: "I have noticed how often the issue of trust comes up in families who worry about their teenager. How long should it take before the family begins to trust the adolescent to stay alcohol and drug free? Does lack of trust go on forever?"

After some comments and discussion by the family members, the facilitator sets up the exercise: "Are you (the adolescent) willing to give your family permission *not* to trust you for a while, as you and the family adjust to your new life?" The facilitator then asks each adolescent (one at a time) to turn to his or her family members and say to them, "I give you permission not to trust me for six months around the issue of my drug or alcohol use." Some of the adolescents may refuse to give this permission, which generates active group discussion and differing opinions. Even if the adolescent refuses, the importance of the trust issue has been highlighted.

Who's Missing?

The entire family—everyone living in the home of the identified patient plus other members who are not in the home but who are involved—is rarely present for every session. If these missing members are not mentioned in the group, the family members and the facilitator are minimizing their importance in the total family picture. In a two-parent household, for example, a parent who does not attend MFG or any type of education or treatment may actively resist change in the family.

To emphasize missing members, the facilitator can ask each family, "Who's missing? Who do you believe should be here?" The missing member(s) can be briefly talked about: "What does he/she think about the problem? Why should he/she be here?"

I recommend that these questions be asked of each family member whenever the opportunity arises. Talking about the essential missing members (such as a parent living in the home) keeps them in everyone's thinking about the family situation and builds motivation for the family to persuade the missing member(s) to attend.

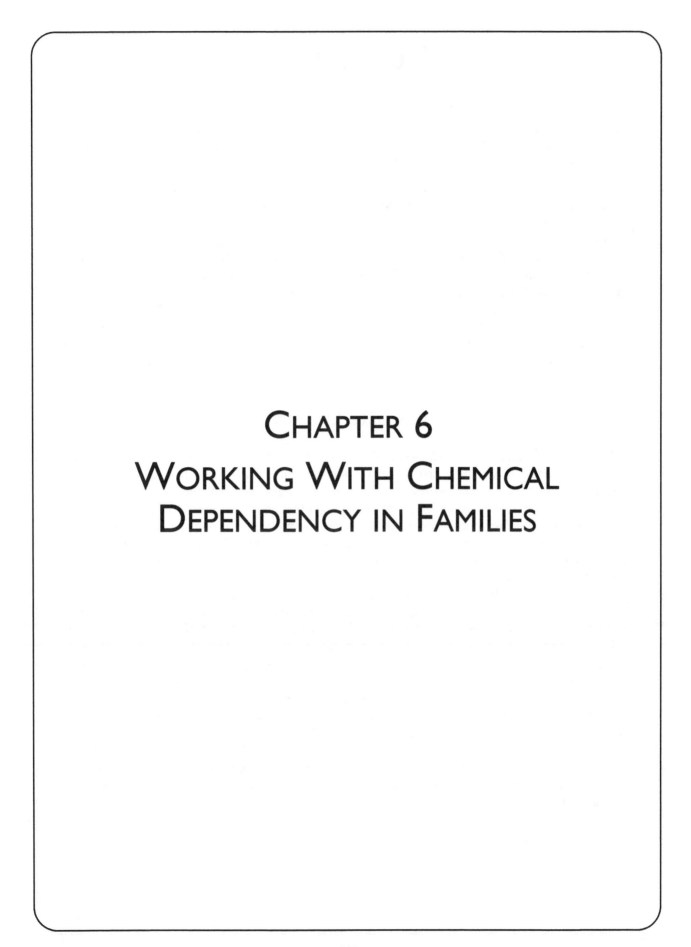

CHAPTER 6
WORKING WITH CHEMICAL DEPENDENCY IN FAMILIES

Introduction

Please note: Almost all the ideas, methods, and techniques in this entire book are appropriate for counseling chemically dependent (CD) families. I make this topic a separate section only because a little specialty knowledge should be added when working with CD problems in families.

This section contains basic information about chemical dependency—the definition, the drugs, the identification of the problem in a family, the disease concept, treatment, relapse, recovery, and so forth—for counselors who want to learn more about this disorder. It also includes a section on the common patterns in CD families and treatment suggestions for each pattern.

Many helping professionals are treating the effects of CD problems, even though the initial presenting problem does not include alcohol or other drug use. Family violence, abuse and neglect of children, individual anxiety and depression, and the problem behaviors of teenagers are just a few of the problems related to chemical dependency, either in the presenting client or in his or her family. A reasonable estimate is that more than 50 percent of couples, families, or individuals who seek counseling for *any* reason have a CD problem in themselves or at least one family member. In some highly stressed populations, the proportion is closer to three-fourths. With this prevalence, all family professionals need a basic understanding of this disorder.

The Debate Lingers . . .

A philosophical difference can still be detected when mental health and substance abuse professionals get together. What do you treat first: the psychological causes of the chemical addiction or the addiction itself? Mental health professionals argue that unless you treat the root causes for the chemical dependency, such as anxiety, depression, and other emotional problems, abstaining from the chemicals won't last long because the causes of the problem will still be active. Substance abuse professionals argue that chemical dependency is a disease in itself—chronic, progressive, and fatal—and cannot be viewed as a symptom of some other disorder. In fact, substance use is a *cause* of anxiety and depression as much as a result.

Clinicians who are doing the work eventually learn that treating the psychological causes of the addiction while the addiction rages is mostly futile. It's like doing relaxation therapy with someone on amphetamines. The person is in a chemically altered state that directly interferes with any attempt to change his or her moods and behavior. For CD problems, the addiction itself becomes the primary and life-threatening problem. When sobriety becomes stable, the CD person is free to look deeper into the psychological and self-defeating behaviors that result in his or her abuse of substances. The best insights from clients often come during abstinence and recovery, not while their addiction is active.

I have a personal interest in working with chemically dependent families, perhaps because I grew up in one. In fact, I've written a book on the subject—*Treating Chemically Dependent Families: A Practical Systems Approach for Professionals* (1990), now published by Hazelden. Not surprisingly, I recommend my book, which is packed with practical ideas, methods, and techniques for working with CD families. Other excellent books on the subject are listed in the Recommended Readings at the end of the book.

A Working Definition of Chemical Dependency

If a person continues to use alcohol or other mood-altering drugs in spite of persistent negative consequences from their use, the person is chemically dependent.

Advantages of this simplified definition

1. It is problem-based. It focuses on the effects the drug has on the life of the user and other people in the user's life.
2. It is a "great leveler" in that it does not take into account the type of drug, amount of drug, or frequency of use. These factors are not part of this working definition of chemical dependency but will become relevant in the person's substance abuse treatment program.
3. It gives family professionals a focus to our involvement with the user and his or her social network. What we are most concerned about is the problems caused by the use: legal, financial, employment, familial, medical, behavioral, emotional, etc.
4. Since our focus is problem based, we are not as concerned about labels such as "alcoholic," "drug addict," "coke head," etc.
5. A problem-centered approach interferes with denial by making a direct connection between substance use and client/family problems.

Points and example

1. It is not a family professional's responsibility to officially diagnose addiction problems; this is usually done by addiction specialists. It is our responsibility to explore how the substance use precedes or accompanies family problems.
2. For example, a family professional is gathering information about a mother reported for maltreating her child. The worker interviews this mother's mother (the child's grandmother). The worker would be setting up vague labeling language—and language the grandmother may resist—by asking the grandmother, "How does being an *addict* affect your daughter's ability to parent her child?"
3. By contrast, the worker would be influencing the grandmother to provide more useful information by asking a problem-centered question like, "Can you tell me if your daughter sometimes does things that cause you concern about your grandchild's well-being or safety?" Behavioral information is what an agency needs if it is to determine a person's ability to parent.
4. We don't want labeling language ("alcoholic," "addict," etc.) to create unnecessary defensiveness and denial in our clients and families. The problem *is* what the problem *does*.

Drugs of Abuse

Here are some, but not all, of the drugs on which dependency can develop.

Name	Street Names	Methods of Use	Signs of Use
Alcohol and Sedatives Valium, Xanax, Seconal, Librium, Ativan, Amytal, and others	Barbiturates: barbs, reds, yellow jackets, rainbows Tranquilizers: Tranqs, roaches, greens, whites	Taken orally	Increased sleep, slurred speech, confusion, impaired coordination, lowered inhibitions
Marijuana	Pot, Reefer, Grass, Weed, Dope, Herb, Hash, Joint	Smoked in pipes or hand-rolled cigarettes; added to foods and eaten	Red eyes, dry mouth, increased appetite Paraphernalia: rolling paper, pipes, bags, roach clips
Cocaine	Coke, "C," Speedball (when mixed with heroin), Crack, Snow, Charles, Rock	Usually snorted through a small tube (a "quill") and absorbed through the mucous membrane. *Crack* is a pure form, is less expensive, and is smoked.	Runny nose, tremors, irritability, depression
Narcotics Opium, morphine, codeine, heroin, Percodan, Dilaudid, and others	Junk, Smack, Horse, Hop, White Lady, Footballs, "D's"	Usually mixed with water and injected just under the skin ("skin popping") or directly into a vein ("mainlining")	Needle marks on arms, hands, knees, and abdomen; constricted pupils; drowsiness; itchy, moist skin
Inhalants	Aerosol products such as paints and hairsprays, gasoline, Freon, butane, glue, and many others	Inhaled	Odor of chemical on clothes and breath; intoxication
Stimulants Benzedrine, Dexedrine, Ritalin, Methamphetamine, and others	Bennies, Splash, Speed, Uppers, Meth, Crystal, Black Beauties, Crank, Ice	Pills taken orally; crystal forms are inhaled or mixed with water and injected. Methamphetamine (Ice) is smokable.	Dilated pupils, trembling hands, perspiring, weight loss, needle marks

Chemical Dependency

Former vs. Current Assumptions

Former Assumptions (Italicized words defined in the Glossary)	Current Assumptions
1. Parental chemical dependency (CD) is a collateral factor in child maltreatment.	Parental CD is a *causative* factor in child maltreatment.
2. Identification of *CD* depends on the amount, type, and frequency of alcohol/drug use.	Identification of CD depends on the consequences of the use to the user and to his/her family and significant others.
3. *CD* is an individual disorder.	CD is an individual, family, community, and cultural disorder.
4. Motivation for recovery must originate from within the *CD* person.	Motivation for the CD person's recovery usually originates from those around him/her.
5. The family counselor is responsible for motivating the *CD member* for treatment.	The counselor is responsible for energizing the *network* to motivate the member for treatment.
6. *Network interventions* are useless until the CD member hits bottom.	Network interventions are used to raise the bottom.
7. *Abstinence* and *recovery* are essentially the same.	They are different. Abstinence is getting sober; recovery is getting well.
8. *Enabling* is in the family and social group of the user.	Enabling can also include professional service providers and the courts.
9. *Relapse* is a failure in treatment.	Relapse is a therapeutic opportunity.
10. Family and network interventions require more time, effort, and money.	Network interventions save time, effort, money, and human suffering.

The Disease Concept

What are the reasons for calling chemical dependency (CD) a disease?

1. The World Health Organization defines a disease as a ''pathological condition resulting in impairment in the mental or physical functioning of an individual.'' Under this definition, CD certainly qualifies.

2. The main reason for calling it a disease lies in four of the disorder's characteristics: primary, chronic, progressive, and fatal.

   a. **Primary** means it isn't the symptom of some other disorder. CD is a disorder in itself.

   b. **Chronic** means that once you have it, you always have it.

   c. **Progressive** means that it tends to get worse over time.

   d. **Fatal** means CD can kill the person through accident, suicide, homicide, or biological deterioration.

What are the clinical advantages for using the disease concept?

1. The disease concept—which is taught to clients and families in most treatment centers and is endorsed by Alcoholics Anonymous and the American Medical Association—reduces the shame and stigma associated with the disorder.

2. If the individual and family see CD as disease, they are less likely to view it as weakness of character, personality flaw, irresponsibility, immaturity, or moral failing.

3. ''Disease'' implies that there's a treatment for it.

4. ''Disease'' implies that the disorder is serious and is beyond the will power of the user.

5. ''Disease'' gives the client and family something to manage. Like the diseases of diabetes or hypertension, chemical addictions can be successfully managed but not cured. The main form of management for chemical dependency is a program of abstinence and recovery.

If it's an individual disorder, why work with the family?

1. Because it's also a *family* illness; everyone is affected and is forced into an unhealthy role.

2. Involving the family motivates the CD member to recover.

3. By the time a family reaches the treatment stage, all members have been emotionally damaged by the ordeal. They all need support to begin to recover.

4. The family's reaction to the CD could be helping to maintain it (enabling).

5. Treating the family could prevent problems in its children, especially younger ones.

6. All members need education about the disease, which could help the family react to the CD member in a different way.

7. When sobriety begins, the family needs help in learning to readjust its patterns of interacting. Ironically, the family needs to learn how to live without the problem.

8. Having everyone meet together around this problem can be a new and unbalancing experience in itself. The family cannot deal with the CD problem in quite the same way they did before. Examples: the ''family secret'' is out; counseling helps alleviate shame and guilt; they learn about co-dependency, enabling, whole-family involvement, etc.

Indirect Signs of Chemical Dependency

Indirect signs of chemical dependency are important to family professionals, since these signs are ''red flags'' that an alcohol or other drug problem may be in the home, even though it is not the presenting problem. Since we would rarely observe an individual actually drinking or drugging, indirect signs are all we have. Addictions spawn many child and family problems, and if some of the signs below are present, substance dependency should be ruled out or confirmed.

While meeting with the client and family, reviewing a case, reading the client's chart, or listening to other professionals discuss the case, be alert for items on the lists. Any one sign by itself does not necessarily indicate a substance problem. But if I noticed two or three, I would wonder.

Behavioral and Social Signs	Physical Signs
1. Conflicts; domestic violence 2. History of child abuse/neglect 3. Driving while intoxicated 4. Smell of alcohol on breath 5. Recurrent job problems; unemployment 6. Suicide gestures/thoughts/attempts 7. Depression; difficulty concentrating 8. Irritability; agitation; mood swings 9. Memory lapses; memory blackouts 10. Missed appointments 11. Intense family drama; family chaos 12. Prostitution or promiscuity 13. Stealing 14. Urgent money problems	1. Tracks (sequential purplish bumps along veins from needle use) 2. Hand tremors; shakes 3. Bloodshot eyes 4. Dilated or constricted pupils counter to appropriate lighting 5. Puffy face 6. Sores, bruises, abrasions 7. Excessive dryness or wetness of the skin 8. Nose problems such as bleeding, running, irritation (like a cold) 9. Sudden weight changes, especially weight loss 10. Erratic eating and sleeping patterns

Identification of Chemical Dependency in a Family

The following questions can help you identify chemical dependency in a family. It is not usually necessary to ask all the questions; be selective, depending on the family circumstances. Questions can be asked when the whole family is present or in one-on-one conversations with family members (usually, the non-CD members) during *Segmenting*.

An affirmative answer to one of these questions should be cause for concern. The questions are appropriate if an individual and/or family is in CD treatment but the CD member is still in denial or if a family is in counseling for problems *other* than CD but the substance use of a member may be contributing to the problems.

1. Is the person drinking or using drugs more now than in the past?
2. Is anyone afraid to be around the person when he or she is drinking or using other drugs?
3. Has the person ever forgotten or denied things that happened during a using episode?
4. Do you worry about the person's drinking or other drug use?
5. Does the person refuse to discuss his or her drinking or other drug use?
6. Has the person broken promises to control or stop his or her use?
7. Has the person ever lied about his or her use or tried to hide it from you?
8. Have you ever been embarrassed by the person's drinking or other drug use?
9. Have you ever made excuses for the way the person behaved while intoxicated?
10. Are many of the person's friends drinkers or do they use other drugs?
11. Does the person make excuses for or try to justify his using?
12. Have you ever helped the person to "cover up" for a drinking or using episode?
13. Does the person's behavior change noticeably when he or she using?
14. Are you afraid to ride with the person after he or she has been drinking or using?
15. Has anyone else talked to you about the person's using behavior?
16. Do any of the following problems seem to be related to the person's substance use: financial difficulties, job or school problems, medical problems, parenting problems?

Note: The above questions were adapted from Vernon Johnson's *Everything You Need to Know about Chemical Dependence* (1990) (see Recommended Readings).

Questions for Family Assessment of Chemical Dependency

The following questions are suggested to screen for drug and alcohol problems during the family assessment if the presenting problems *do not* include substance abuse. To make this series of questions less threatening, I have embedded several non-substance (but related) questions.

1. Does anyone in your home use prescription medication? If so, what?
2. Has anyone had a serious medical condition in the past five years?
3. Who in your family uses alcohol or other drugs?
4. Has anyone in the family tried non-prescription drugs such as marijuana, cocaine, etc.
5. Has anyone been hospitalized in the past five years? If so, what was the reason?
6. Has anyone in the family received a Driving While Impaired (DWI) conviction?
7. Has anyone in the family quit drinking or using drugs? How long ago?

Treatment of Chemical Dependency

Types of Treatment

1. Outpatient in public or private treatment centers. The major treatment modality is usually group and/or individual sessions, which meet a total of 1–4 hours per week. Some programs have an active family component, which includes orientation and education, sometimes Multiple Family Groups, and sometimes individual family sessions.

2. Inpatient in public or private centers. Typical stays are 2–4 weeks. Most are based on the AA 12-step model. Patients usually receive group, individual, and family treatment.

3. Intensive Outpatient. These programs are relatively new in the treatment field and show good promise. The patient comes to the treatment center 4–5 times per week after work and receives group, family, and other forms of therapy until 8:00–9:00 at night. These programs avoid the life-disrupting effects of inpatient stays.

4. Alcoholics Anonymous (AA), Narcotics Anonymous (NA), and related self-help groups. These meetings are usually started during treatment and serve as continuing care for recovery, from a few months to several decades after treatment.

Goals for Family Treatment of Chemical Dependency

1. To increase motivation for recovery. Fear of loss of the family, the fatigue around the conflicts caused by the CD, and the guilt associated with how the substance use is affecting the family are all motivations for the CD member to recover. This motivation is brought to life when the family is present.

2. To convey the whole-family message. The entire family—not just the CD member—is affected by chemical dependency. The family organizes around the illness, and all members develop unhealthy survival behaviors. Family counseling helps the members to understand the whole-family idea, to come to terms with their feelings, and to begin recovery individually and as a family.

3. To change family patterns that work against recovery. Enabling, chronic conflicts, taking sides, enmeshment or disengagement (too close or distant), and deep-seated anger are some of the family "hangovers" after the CD member becomes abstinent. Counseling offers help in recognizing and changing these habitual patterns.

4. To prepare the family for what to expect in early recovery. Families usually believe that when the drinking or drug use stop, family problems stop. They are often surprised at the troubling issues that pop up during recovery.

5. To encourage family members' own long-term support. Regardless of what the CD member chooses to do, each family member has the opportunity to seek help for him- or herself. Al-Anon, Nar-Anon, and Alateen are the primary groups for family and friends.

Ways to Work With Families During CD Treatment

1. Conjoint: Everyone in the home meets together for sessions with the counselor.
2. Multiple Family Groups: Several families, including their CD members, meet together.
3. Family Members Groups: Several families, excluding their CD members, meet together.
4. Spouse Groups: Spouses of the CD members.
5. Couples Groups: CD members and their spouse or partner comprise the couples.
6. Children's Groups (two ages: 6–11 and 12 and older): For children of CD parents.
7. ACOA Groups: For Adult Children of Alcoholics.
8. Family Orientation and Education Groups: For films, lectures, discussions.

Recovery

In the chemical dependency lingo, *treatment* and *recovery* are not the same.

Treatment is ...	Recovery is ...
Getting sober	Getting well
A professional service	A way of life
Breaking through denial	Practicing honesty
Short-term (or intermittent)	Life-long
Often involuntary	Always voluntary
Getting started	Getting real
Structure-oriented	Process-oriented
An inconvenient step	A leap of faith

Recovery is a philosophy of living that has four essential components:

1. **Acceptance**

    By accepting the fact of his or her addiction and disease, the person is guarding against the denial once again entering his or her life, the way it did when the person was using. The Serenity Prayer goes:

    > God, grant me the serenity to accept the things I cannot change,
    > The courage to change the things I can,
    > And the wisdom to know the difference.

2. **Honesty**

    To continue using alcohol or other drugs despite problems, a chemically dependent person has to be ingenious in his or her dishonesty, lies, and denial to protect his or her use. During active addiction, the person forgets about truth in favor of the most convenient lie or self-deception. In recovery, a person must be willing to be painstakingly honest with themselves, and with others, to survive the addiction.

3. **Open-mindedness**

    Open-mindedness does not get most people into treatment and recovery; desperation does. They were trapped and had nowhere else to go. Open-mindedness, which tends to grow with each passing sober week, means not saying ''no'' to the changes required in recovery.

4. **Willingness**

    Recovery requires a willingness to invest energy and work. If you put nothing in, you get nothing out. The gains made in recovery are in direct proportion to how hard the person is trying to recover.

Stages of Recovery

Cocaine Addiction*

Many patients have encountered the following stages in their efforts to stop cocaine use. The explanation of these stages is often met by patients with a sense of relief: they validate the patient's experience, increase the credibility of the counselor, and provide a strong rationale for extended treatment involvement. It is possible that these stages are based on the biological recovery of the brain following cocaine abstinence. This information was adapted from *Cocaine: Recovery Issues*, by Rawson, Obert, and McCann (1991) (see Recommended Readings).

1. **Withdrawal Stage (first 2 weeks)**

    During withdrawal, clients are disoriented, depressed, and very fatigued. They feel out of control, do not understand what is happening to them, and require explicit direction during this period.

2. **Honeymoon Stage (2–7 weeks)**

    Cravings are reduced, mood improves, energy increases, confidence and optimism return. The client may feel that the problem is over. Since energy is high, a client often acts in scattered, inefficient ways. Stopping recovery activities or returning to alcohol (which the client used with cocaine) may occur because the client sees no obvious need for continued education and treatment.

3. **The Wall (7–16 weeks)**

    This period is perhaps the major hurdle in cocaine recovery. Relapse risk increases as clients experience a return of low energy, little pleasure in life, difficulty concentrating, irritability, loss of sex drive, and insomnia. Clients often believe that these conditions will persist indefinitely.

    A major theme during this period: "If this is how I'm going to feel as a sober person, it's not worth the work." The only strategy that appears to help relieve the symptoms reliably is exercise. Patients who exercise at least 20 minutes per day, 3–5 times per week report fewer symptoms.

4. **Adjustment Stage (16–24 weeks)**

    Clients may feel a great sense of accomplishment at having completed the Wall Stage. They may have a sense that finally everything is returning to normal. Clients who successfully deal with this stage begin to adjust to the lifestyle and relationship changes that began in previous stages.

5. **Resolution Stage (24 weeks–indefinite)**

    Completion of the six-month period signals a shift from learning new skills to monitoring for relapse signs, maintaining a balanced lifestyle, and developing new areas of interest. For some clients, individual or relationship issues may emerge that require therapeutic attention.

---

* In my opinion, these stages can be used to understand recovery from all types of drugs, including alcohol.

Recovery Plan

Recovery from CD is a life-long adventure and will be different for each individual and family. All recovery plans, however, need to consider the following six areas of intervention.

Intervention	CD Member	Family	Duration
1. Detox	If needed	Not applicable	3–5 days
2. Treatment	One or more: Inpatient Outpatient Intensive Outpatient Follow-up care	Family should be involved in treatment: education and discussion groups, individual family sessions, Multiple Family Groups.	2–10 weeks
3. Self-Help Groups	Alcoholics Anonymous (AA) Narcotics Anonymous (NA) Codependents Anonymous (CODA)	Al-Anon Nar-Anon Alateen CODA	At least 12 months
4. Social Support	AA/NA Family Extended family Friends Job; Church	Family Al-Anon/Nar-Anon Extended family Friends Job; School; Church	Indefinite
5. Relapse Management	Can be handled by treatment program, follow-up care, self-help group, or all three. Relapses are common; they can be used for therapeutic purposes.	Family needs a relapse plan: 1. Spotting a relapse before it happens 2. Safety plan for family 3. Setting consequences and limits	Indefinite
6. Lifestyle	1. Changing "playgrounds and playmates" 2. Neighborhood (drug-infested?) 3. Housing: May need to change 4. Job: Go to work, keep present job, find a new job	1. Family dynamics will change (learning to live without the problem). 2. Family may have more together time. 3. Family routine will change.	6–12 months

Families in Early Recovery

Although families react to recovery in unique ways, the following problems often occur in the first year or so of recovery. Talking about them openly with family members sends the message that these problems are *normal*. Also, with prior knowledge, family members will feel less unsettled if they happen to them.

1. **The family's lack of trust that the CD member will stay clean and sober**

   Family members will usually be suspicious of any of the CD member's behavior that resembles the old using pattern: spending much time away from home, coming home late, exhibiting a certain mood, or even using a certain look or tone of voice. If the CD member has unsuccessfully tried to stay clean before, the family doubts that this time will be different.

2. **Walking on eggshells**

   This is the family "tiptoeing" around the CD member, not wanting to cause the person's anger, frustration, or any negative emotion that may drive him or her to the drug.

3. **Floating on Cloud Nine**

   This is the client and family's "flight into health," a sort of rebound from the crises, turmoil, and sickness of the past. The recovering CD member is often euphoric and may say things like, "I feel better than I have in years, and I'm through with drugs/drinking forever!" In the person's mind, the problem is over; a recovery program for the CD member and the rest of the family does not seem necessary.

4. **"Stinking Thinking"**

   The CD member (or even the family members) can start to believe that he or she has the problem under control and can now drink/use in moderation: "I will never let it be the problem it was before." Or, "My drug was cocaine so it's OK to drink. I never had a problem with alcohol." (This is called "changing seats on the Titanic.")

5. **Relapse**

   Chemical dependency is a primary, progressive, chronic, and relapsing disease. Relapse may or may not occur, but if it does, it doesn't mean that the member has given up recovery.

For any of these issues in family recovery, it is advisable to

1. Gently educate the family about each of them, even if they believe it won't happen to them.

2. Describe each issue as a normal, natural occurrence in recovering families.

3. Include as many family members as possible when the issues are discussed.

4. Encourage the family, with the CD member's participation, to develop a plan to handle any of these issues ("If this happens, what will you do?").

As the family professional, you must believe fully in the necessity of the CD member being actively involved in an ongoing recovery program (like AA, NA, or treatment aftercare). Dropping recovery activities before at least a year of abstinence is often a sign of impending relapse.

Relapse

Relapse is a return to using alcohol or other drugs after a period of intentional abstinence. Relapse can be one using episode or last for days or weeks. If the professional helper or family member is aware of the dynamics of relapse, he or she can usually detect signs of an impending relapse before it occurs. The relapse process often begins with one or more of the following:

1. **Set-ups**
   - Going into high-risk situations like bars or familiar hangouts where most of the person's drinking or drugging was done.
   - Going back to old using friends and not making new, non-using friends.
   - Letting everyday problems intensify, and suddenly being unable to cope with the stress of daily living.
   - Avoiding support systems, such as a drug treatment program, AA/NA, or other supportive relationships.

2. **Feeling cured after a few weeks of abstinence**
   - Denying that he or she has a disease and claiming that his or her use is now under control.
   - Arguing that everybody should leave the person alone since he or she is now sober and clean.

3. **Desire to test control**
   - Social use of alcohol or other drugs. (The person may be able to do this a few times, but loss of control will most likely return.)
   - Switching from drug of choice to another drug (for example, cocaine to alcohol, alcohol to marijuana, street drugs to prescription drugs).

4. **Negative moods**
   - Angry, impatient, and critical of others.
   - Bored, restless, argumentative.
   - Withdrawal from others; isolating into loneliness.

5. **Exhaustion**
   - Falling into old patterns of skipping meals, sleeping less, or overworking and not taking care of oneself physically.

Myths About Relapse

- A sign of poor motivation
- A sign of treatment failure
- Unpredictable and unavoidable
- Occurs only when clients use their drug of choice
- Absence of relapse guarantees successful recovery
- Erases or nullifies positive recovery changes made so far
- An instantaneous event that occurs only when the client actually takes drugs/drinks again

Common Patterns in Chemically Dependent Families

The maps on the following pages are typical family structures in which a member is chemically dependent. They are generic *types*; a particular family will only approximate the examples given. They illustrate a systemic *way of thinking* about family patterns and how to strategically intervene in them. These patterns are used with permission from *Treating Chemically Families* by John T. Edwards (Hazelden, 1990).

The five patterns are:

Two-Parent Families:	*CD Father*
	CD Adolescent
	Good Kid/Bad Kid
Single-Parent Families:	*CD Mother*
	CD Adolescent

The following points apply to these maps:

1. See the ***Mapping*** technique for an explanation of the map symbols. ''IP'' in the maps is the Identified Patient (the CD member).

2. Since these maps are hypothetical family types and not actual cases, the ages of the children (in their circles or squares) have been omitted. In mapping an actual case, children's ages would be included.

3. These mapped examples assume that the IP is drug-free and in separate treatment (outpatient or inpatient, usually accompanied by AA or NA) and that the family is in early recovery. Family counseling is supplementing the primary treatment of the IP. If the IP is still actively using, the first priority (as in all CD family cases) is to use the family sessions to motivate the member to enter primary treatment.

4. Regarding gender, each pattern reflects the most common family constellations. For example, the majority of single-parent families are headed by mothers; the majority of two-parent families are heterosexual. Obviously, chemical dependents and co-dependents can be male as well as female and gay and transgendered as well as straight. For single fathers and gay couples (regardless of gender), the suggested strategies also apply.

5. Maps can't show everything. A picture cannot give important information such as:

    a. The severity of the alcohol or other drug problem and the strength of the CD member's desire to recover.

    b. Race, cultural, and community attitudes and values, especially around the use of legal or illegal drugs.

    c. The personalities of the family members, the amount of family denial and resistance, and the strength of the members' desire to preserve the family.

    d. Extended family influence, especially the parents' families of origin.

Two Parent–CD Parent

General Goal

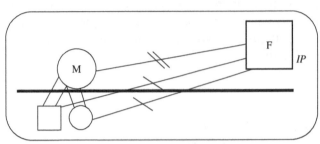

Two-Parent–CD Parent

To help the family accept the recovering parent into role-appropriate membership in the family. My mapped example depicts the father as the using parent. The principles are the same if the mother is the using member or if the parents are same sex (lesbian or gay).

Suggested Strategies

1. This is perhaps the most common pattern in CD families when a parent is the using member. The survival structure is in place: ''us against him (or her).'' The parents are in open conflict; this affects the children more negatively than most parents realize.

2. Once the using parent is in recovery, encourage the couple to slowly begin making joint decisions about parenting. They need to work together to allow the using parent to adjust to his or her ''new role.''

3. Pay close attention to the non-using parent (in earlier example, the mother). He or she has been the overly responsible member and is likely to have the greatest stress load in the family. When the using parent stays sober for a few weeks and becomes stronger and more reliable, the non-using parent may show more weakness.

   a. Resentment by the non-using parent is usually centered around his or her anger at the using parent for abandoning the family: ''You were never here for the kids. You don't even know them. You can't just march back in and take over as if nothing happened.''

   b. The non-using parent is in the central position. When that parent begins to set appropriate limits in the spouse relationship (especially around drinking or drug use), he or she will need support.

   c. Explore the non-using parent's support system—parents, siblings, extended family, friends. Al-Anon referral is especially important, or any other support group.

4. After a few weeks or months of sobriety, a new relationship needs to start developing between the recovering parent and children. (Don't rush this change, however. As Alcoholics Anonymous would say, ''Easy Does It.'') To begin exploring relationships between the using parent and the children, manage the non-using parent's influence carefully. The non-using partner is not likely to trust the recovering parent in a new parenting role and may sabotage any changes between him or her and the children. This possibility could be acknowledged by the counselor in the family sessions: it's a *normal* reaction by families to this situation.

5. Explore the recovering parent's support system. Who is he or she likely to go to, outside the home, for emotional support during early recovery? The recovering parent's continued sobriety is the highest priority in counseling.

6. Discuss, and normalize, the family's lack of trust in the parent's sobriety. In early recovery, the family may be ''walking on eggshells,'' worried that he or she will relapse.

Two-Parent—CD Adolescent

General Goal

To decrease the son's power by reducing the father-son overinvolvement. The less inappropriate power the parents give to the son, the less likely enabling will continue. My mapped example depicts the son as the using member. If the user is a daughter or if the parents are same sex (gay or lesbian), the principles are the same.

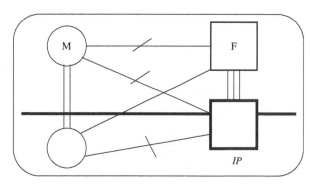

Two-Parent–CD Adolescent

Suggested Strategies

1. During the sessions, clearly support the parents as heads of the family while treating the son as an adolescent who must live by the parents' rules. Because of the son's power in the family, this should be done carefully; he may have enough influence to stop the sessions.

2. Be alert to the father becoming the adolescent's treatment "sponsor," taking too much responsibility for the son's recovery program. The responsibility for abstinence and recovery should be kept squarely on the son.

3. Four ways to make the father-son distance more appropriate are
   a. Bring mother and father together around their concern for the son's recovery.
   b. Using the ***Enactment*** technique, pair the father-daughter and mother-son in separate conversations. This unbalances the two camps by "crisscrossing" each parent with the more distant child.
   c. Work on the mother-son relationship. If it improves, father and son will become less overinvolved (enmeshed). This may also interrupt the father's enabling and gives the mother, the stricter parent, more influence with the son.
   d. In limit-setting talk from parents to son, encourage the father to take the lead. This strict talk from the more lenient parent shows the son that something different is happening.

4. Meetings with the two parents together without the children are usually necessary. The purpose is to help them negotiate their agreements regarding how they should react as a parental team. What will they do together to present a clear and consistent direction for the son's recovery? What will they do if the son ignores their limits? What is their relapse plan? What will happen if one parent stays firm on the agreements and the other weakens? How can they convince the son that they are serious about changes?

5. Spread the parental concern to the non-IP child (in the mapped example, the daughter). Explain the "stair-stepping" phenomenon to parents: that sometimes, when the older child becomes drug-free, the younger teenager moves up to take the sibling's place in the exciting and daring world of drug use. To avoid this, the daughter needs to see the strict limits imposed by the parents on the son; she is then less likely to follow in his footsteps. Focusing on the daughter takes some of the heat and pressure off the son. It can also increase the motivation of the parents to work out their parenting relationship toward the IP child to avoid going through this family crisis again with their other child. Repeating all this with another child is a horrifying idea to most parents.

"Good" Kid/"Bad" Kid

General Goal

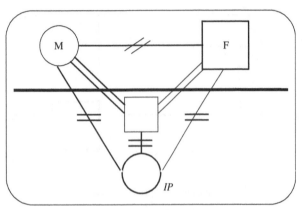

"Good" Kid / "Bad" Kid

To help the family bring to the surface and resolve the underlying tension and conflict in the family that is partly the cause and partly the result of maintaining the IP as a scapegoat. Of course, the strategies are the same if the scapegoated child is a son and if the parents are gay.

Suggested Strategies

1. In general, it is not a good idea for the counselor to try to protect a scapegoated member of a family, especially if he or she is a child. If the counselor sides with the child, it often redoubles the family's attack on him or her.

2. Since the daughter feels that the rest of the family has ganged up against her, find out who her allies are: an extended family member, a friend, or another adult outside the home. These "advocates" for the daughter could be discussed in the session and, if appropriate, invited to a session. The group or individual treatment counselor for the adolescent could also serve this purpose by attending one or more family sessions.

3. When the daughter enters treatment and becomes drug-free, encourage the parents to give her some privacy and breathing room. This privacy is necessary for adolescents in general but also because of the daughter's anger at the family.

4. Sensitize the parents against making comparison statements about the two children. Explain that even though the daughter may have brought this on herself by her behavior, statements by the parents comparing the siblings ("Why can't you be like your brother!") are often more painful to her than she will admit. (Oddly enough, such statements may also be uncomfortable for the "good" kid.) Ask the parents to remind each other not to use such statements in case one of them forgets.

5. About the third session, begin to spread the concern to the "good" kid, especially if he is younger than the IP. Explain that his attempts to be "perfect" are his way of helping the parents, but it puts him under stress. This discussion distributes some of the focus and helps the IP feel that the whole family, not just she, is being looked at. This talk about the "good" kid also undermines the aura of perfection surrounding him and dilutes the stark contrast between the children. It alerts the parents to the burden being carried by *both* children.

6. Anticipate open or implied "blackmail" by the IP kid: "If you're too hard on me you're causing me to return to drugs." Parents will need each other's support to avoid this trap.

7. After several sessions, gently shift the focus to the parents to see if they will explore their relationship as spouses or partners, possibly revealing some of the buried anger and tension between them that has been transferred to the scapegoated child. The children should not be present for this talk. A good introduction for this shift: "A problem like your daughter's can cause a lot of stress on a relationship. How has it affected yours?"

CD Single Parent

General Goal

To work closely with the single parent, offering him or her support for recovery, both within his or her extended family or social network and in self-help recovery groups. The parent's *adult* support is necessary to help the parent avoid burdening the children too much with emotional issues during early recovery. (In this example, the single parent is the mother. If the single parent is a father, the goals and strategies are the same.)

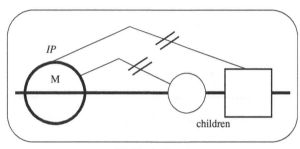

CD Single Parent

Suggested Strategies

1. In the this map, the mother vacillates between being a parent, when she's sober, and being a child to her children when she is incompetent and sick with her alcohol or other drug use. Conversely, the children must vacillate between being children and being protector and caretaker for their mother.

2. If the mother becomes serious about recovery, she will need close support for an extended period. During and after treatment, she will need a tight connection with AA, NA, or another self-help group, plus any other support groups available in the community. The family also needs other support—extended family, friends, etc.—to assist in child care while she works her recovery program.

3. Look beyond the parent-child relationships. Find out others who are involved—mother's parents or siblings, other extended family, friends, dating relationships, colleagues at work. You will be searching for the mother's sources of support for her early recovery. You may also discover those who are enabling the mother, since it is unlikely that she remained active in her addiction without being unwittingly enabled in some form.

4. Explore the involvements, if any, of the extended family (parents, siblings, biological father, close friends, and others). Will these relationships change now that the mother is clean and sober?

5. While the mother is successfully abstaining, support her competence and authority as a parent. The mother's authority will probably be resisted by the children, especially if they are older children or teenagers. There is too much anger and insecurity and too little trust for them to suddenly accept her authority as a parent.

6. Increase the mother's awareness of her children's *normal anger* in this situation and how they may undermine her attempts to regain control. The children may be accustomed to much freedom and won't take kindly to limit setting.

7. Depending on the relative ages of the children, prepare the mother for the possibility that the children may unite against her. The children have formed a close coalition for survival, and it may continue until they are convinced that she seriously intends to get well.

8. If appropriate, convince the mother that her children need separate counseling and support (children or teenage groups, for example) and a chance to vent their pent-up anger and fear. At first, they may need to do this away from the mother.

Single-Parent–CD Adolescent

General Goal

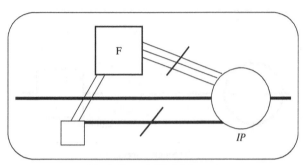

Single Parent–CD Adolescent

To help the parent find *adult* support for the many stresses experienced by single parents. Adult peer support decreases the parent's need to use his or her relationship with the children for emotional support and keeps the parental role more appropriate and consistent. (In this example, the single parent is a father. If the single parent is a mother, the goals and strategies are the same.)

Suggested Strategies

1. Encourage adult support for the father. This could come from professional sources such as the CD treatment center, other counseling, parent support groups, Al-Anon, Families Anonymous, or Parents without Partners. Additional adult support could come from more immediate sources: extended family, co-workers, friends, or dating relationships.

2. Discuss how the children would react if he started dating, since a single parent frequently underestimates how far the children will go to discourage him or her. For reasons of jealousy, protectiveness toward the parent, fear of loss, and resentment at someone taking the other parent's place, the new friend in the living room is not always welcomed by the children. If the single parent decides to date, he or she should be prepared to get a reaction from the children.

3. Peer support is also needed for the CD daughter. Encourage the father to allow the daughter to find new, non-using friends. Also discuss his rules on the daughter's dating, curfew, schoolwork, and so forth.

   Note: The above three strategies are designed to interrupt the father-daughter enmeshment by providing both of them *separate* sources of age-appropriate support and friendship. When the father and daughter develop other important friendships, their strong emotional need for each other is reduced, allowing a healthier parent-child relationship to develop.

4. Explore the biological mother's role, if any, in the family. Does she have contact with the children? Do the children visit her where she lives? Do the separated/divorced parents have agreements about the children's behavior during their visits in the mother's home?

5. Explore the son's role in the family, his emotional state, and his desires and concerns. By the third or fourth interview, the son should be as actively involved in the sessions as the daughter. Is the single parent sure the son doesn't feel neglected, with all the attention going to the daughter's problem? Is the father worried that the son may be the next to try drugs? Is the son trying so hard to be a ''good'' child that it causes him emotional difficulties the father doesn't know about? Again, the strategy is to interrupt the father-daughter overinvolvement by spreading the father's attention more equally between the children.

The Golden Years Trap

A grandmother recently said to me, ''I didn't know I would spend my golden years raising my daughter's children. But if I don't, what will happen to them?'' Her daughter had an addiction problem. In these days of epidemic drug problems in our country, this family pattern is common and deserves special attention.

Source: *DeskGallery Mega-Bundle*, Copyright 1995 by Dover Publications, Inc. Used with permission.

In these families, the grandmother is certainly to be commended for protecting the children and keeping the family together, but she is in a desperate trap: if she reveals the incompetence of the mother and her addiction, she could lose the children to the Department of Social Services (DSS). If she doesn't reveal the mother's addict lifestyle, she stays in her stressful situation and enables the addiction to continue. With the best of intentions, she is protecting the mother from the consequences of her drug use by making it possible for the mother to keep her children *and* her drugs.

Usually, the mother still has legal custody of the children but provides little or no financial support for them. She may or may not live with the grandmother and children and spends much time with drug-using friends. She may have had a number of sexual partners over the years, and her children often don't have a common father. She supports herself through welfare, friends, by prostitution, by selling drugs, or by intermittent work.

Because of the many negative influences of the addicted mother on the family, one or more children may develop behavioral and emotional symptoms, bringing the family to the attention of professionals.

This situation is toxic:

1. The children carry a chronic emotional wound; they have been rejected by both parents—the father who abandoned them and the mother who seems to prefer her drugs and friends to her children. The mother-children relationship is loaded with broken promises, guilt, anger, and mistrust.

2. The children are caught in the middle of the tension and conflict between grandmother and mother and between other family members and mother. Being in this angry crossfire makes children anxious, confused, and difficult to manage.

3. The mother's social life inevitably puts the children in poor company from time to time, even to the point of sexual, physical, and verbal abuse by the mother's irresponsible friends.

4. The children's biological and social legacy puts the children at high risk from birth. Often, one or more children were born with drugs in their blood and/or neurologically damaged in utero. Their genetic heritage is addiction, usually from both parents, and they are several times more likely to have their own drug problems when they reach adolescence than children born to non-addicted parents. Their social legacy is no more appealing: crime, unemployment, promiscuity, and a drug-using lifestyle. As the children mature, they often continue the multi-generational cycle—drugs, sex, premature babies born of premature parents.

5. Initially, the family has a code of secrecy. Although the grandmother is desperate for help, she must deny or minimize the mother's addiction for fear of the Department of Social Services taking custody of the grandchildren. The children are sworn to silence for the same reason. This protective secrecy makes it difficult to assess what's happening, and only when a relationship is established with the family will the ''secret everybody knows'' surface.

What to Do

Any professional who enters this situation will earn his or her pay, especially if he or she makes a serious attempt at family change. Every family is different, and each situation will present unique challenges and opportunities. Here are a few guidelines:

1. The cardinal rule is to do something on a *family* level. Do not try to "fix the (IP) kid," leaving the family situation unchanged.

2. The first step is to know all the players; you may need them as the case progresses. Who is involved and worried about the situation—any extended family (especially the mother's siblings), involved neighbors of the mother and grandmother, peripheral fathers or grandfathers, professionals and friends involved with the children, teachers, school counselors, and others. The players are rarely limited to just the grandmother, mother, and children, since this desperate situation usually attracts attention from other adults.

3. When possible, keep the mother involved at every step; treat her as a *mother*, not an addict. Our tendency is to exclude her as an uncaring parent, a "lost cause," but the chances for triggering her treatment and recovery are diminished if we don't have a relationship with her. The mother's guilt at what she's doing to her children is usually a strong motivator for abstinence and recovery.

4. Child abuse and neglect are common in these situations, especially if the grandparent is unable to supervise and parent the children. To create leverage for change, you may have to contact DSS (after a discussion with your supervisor and colleagues). In fact, most state laws *mandate* that you contact DSS with any suspicion of abuse or neglect of children. You don't need hard evidence or proof—suspicion is enough.

5. A DSS investigation will not necessarily result in improvement for the children. If abuse or neglect is substantiated, the children may be removed from the home, split up, and put in foster care; if abuse and neglect are not substantiated, the children remain in their unstable environment and their symptoms intensify. To avoid this, professional services (preferably in-home and for six months or longer) will be needed.

6. Removal of the children is an option, but this extreme action should be taken only after all other interventions fail.

7. Talk to the grandmother about pursuing legal custody of the children (most courts would grant her custody in this situation). Since she has the responsibility for the children, she also needs the authority that goes with it. It also may bring financial relief for her. Also, if the grandmother gets legal custody, she can at least have better control over the access of the mother to the children and protect them better. The mother, of course, will fight this intervention, as she suddenly becomes pressured to make a choice—the custody of her children or drugs, but not both.

8. The goal is substance abuse treatment for the mother, usually inpatient. Carefully create leverage and pressure on the addicted mother. If DSS is not involved, try to get the agency involved. DSS may be able to force a transfer of custody to the grandmother (if she will take custody). Also, use the social and emotional leverage of children and extended family (see next two items).

9. Use the technique ***Worried Child,*** which was created for this situation. This sets up a conversation between children and mother about how much the children are worried about her. It makes the connection between the mother's addiction and the children's distress.

10. Use the ***Brief Network Intervention.*** This is a broad meeting of family, extended family, friends, and professionals to take action to prevent future harm to one or more of the children. The identified patient child is usually a good choice for the target of the intervention. In attempting to prevent harm to the children, these meetings often turn into a therapeutic intervention on the mother's addiction, possibly leading to her treatment.

Adolescent Substance Abuse

Typical Steps in Family Treatment

1. Get the family in:
    1. Invite everyone in the home of the adolescent, plus others the parent(s) want to bring. Use the phrase, "*The way we work* is to see everybody in the home at least once to get a clearer picture of how we can help your son/daughter."
    2. Try to avoid seeing only the overinvolved parent and the problem teenager (leaving out other people in the home). This parent-child pair, if seen in counseling by themselves, does not usually give a clear picture of the family dynamics that may be contributing to the adolescent's problems.

2. Conduct the first interview:
    1. The first priority is to get the drinking/drug use stopped. Usually, inpatient or outpatient treatment for the adolescent user will be necessary.
    2. The second priority is orientation/education for the family members (especially the parents). This could be Al-Anon, Nar-Anon, Tough Love, family members groups in the treatment center, etc. (Some of this education will also occur in the family sessions.)
    3. If the teenager has a driver's license, talk to the parents about driving privileges. *Driving should be stopped until the parents (and counselor) are sure about sobriety.*
    4. If parental substance use is brought up (by anyone), don't switch the focus to the parent's use: "Let's put this on hold until (the adolescent) is out of danger."
        Reasons:
        a. The using parent might not return or might even stop the family sessions.
        b. If a parent is also an identified problem, it's difficult to create a unified parenting team to set appropriate limits on the adolescent.
        c. If the family had been ready to present the parent as the identified substance abuser, the parent, not the teenager, would be the identified patient.

3. Continue seeing the family (including the IP) through outpatient or inpatient treatment for the identified adolescent. Clinical tips:
    1. In a two-parent household, distinguish between the lenient and strict parent ("soft love" and "tough love"). One parent is usually stricter or more lenient than the other. After a couple of sessions with the family, ask the parents to identify which is which. If the parents won't distinguish, ask the children. This distinction identifies the potential parent enabler ("soft" parent); it also brings out the obstacles to parental togetherness to set firm limits.
    2. To add motivation for the parents, talk about how the teenager's substance use is affecting the other children in the home, especially younger ones. Is the using adolescent setting an example for younger siblings?
    3. Together, parents develop a plan (without the children present). After the plan is agreed to by the parents, the adolescent is brought in and the parents inform him or her of the agreements:
        a. Teenager's responsibilities and privileges at home, curfew, driving privileges, etc.
        b. How will they know if the adolescent is using again?
        c. What will they do if they discover that he or she is using again?
        d. Can the parents support each other—when one weakens, the other stays strong?

4. After several family sessions (if sobriety is stable):
    1. Tell the parents about some of the warning signs of alcohol/drug abuse to be alert for (see Adolescent Substance Use Checklist, which follows).
    2. Tell them you will call them in 2–3 weeks to see how things are going. (When you call, talk to both parents, if possible.) In the meantime, ask them to call for an appointment, if needed.

Adolescent Substance Use Checklist

The items on this list correspond to the behaviors of alcohol-/drug-using adolescents. The parent(s) complete the questionnaire, without the child. It can be used when you have reason to believe that substance use of the adolescent is contributing to his or her problem behaviors, but the parents are unaware of or denying the child's use. Do not reveal that this is a *substance abuse* assessment until you have discussed their completed assessment with them. (Three or more circled items are cause for concern for a substance problem.)

Instructions: Please circle the number of the item that describes the problem behavior of your son or daughter. The results will be discussed with your counselor.

1. Chronic lying.
2. Very rebellious and defiant.
3. Loss of overall motivation: grades fall, classes are cut, activities are given up.
4. Change in dress habits: punk or rock styles, tighter clothes, more jewelry.
5. Unexplainable mood swings.
6. Verbal and possible physical abuse of family members.
7. Language change: ''street'' language, more slang.
8. Solitary times in their room with cell phone.
9. Change in friends; reluctance to talk about new friends.
10. Illogical, hazy, or unrealistic thinking.
11. Depression; mental and physical deterioration; references to self-harm.
12. Late night phone calls; callers won't leave their names.
13. Lack of participation in family activities, including mealtimes.
14. Strong and angry denial of drug or alcohol use.
15. Regular use of Visine or Murine.
16. Sudden weight gain or loss.
17. Sleep disturbances: insomnia or severe difficulty arising in the morning.
18. Unexplained money problems.
19. Stealing money or items that can be converted to cash.

Co-Dependency

Definitions

Co-dependency is present when a person maintains an attachment to another person despite negative consequences from the relationship. This disorder was first noticed in the chemical dependency field when it became evident that many addicted people had someone around them who was as ''hooked'' on them as the addicted person was hooked on alcohol/drugs. The concept has now spread to include an adult who takes too much responsibility for a psychologically impaired or irresponsible person, sacrificing himself or herself for that person's well-being to the long-term detriment of both. Being needed gets confused with being loved.

The co-dependent person focuses on someone else's needs to the exclusion of their own needs. If co-dependency is present, not far behind will be *enabling*, which describes behaviors in a relationship that protect the using member from the natural consequences of his or her addiction to alcohol or other drugs. For example, a person who tolerates abusive behavior from substance-abusing partners, makes excuses for them, and repeatedly ''bails them out'' of jail or other difficult situations is an enabling co-dependent.

Discussion

The extreme forms of co-dependency can have fatal consequences. The co-dependent can remain in the abusive relationship until someone (including children) get hurt or killed. In fact, inpatient treatment centers have been established to treat co-dependence as a serious disorder in itself, not just a collateral problem in the primary treatment of the using person.

I have seen co-dependency so entrenched in an adult relationship that it was more resistant to change than the chemical dependency, partly due to the strong secondary gain for the co-dependent—being seen by others as loyal, sacrificing, unselfish, and strong. It can also continue into the recovery phase of using partners and prevent users from taking responsibility for themselves and their own sobriety.

Like most human dysfunctions, the developmental path to co-dependency has varied origins. We frequently find that codependents grew up with an addicted parent or in an otherwise dysfunctional family. Abuse and neglect are common. In adulthood, the co-dependent has a deep-seated need to be needed and readily finds the drug-addicted person who needs someone to help him or her with the consequences of excessive drug and alcohol use. These ''perfectly matched'' needs will, in the long run, usually cause suffering for both partners, along with family, children, and friends. If circumstances or volition end this destructive relationship, the co-dependent will tend to find another equally destructive partnership. The cycle doesn't end until the co-dependent seeks help and becomes aware of the ''here we go again'' pattern and its depressing effect on his or her life.

Treatment

The treatment for co-dependency is similar to that of the chemical dependent: individual, group, and family therapy. Co-Dependents Anonymous (CoDA), modeled after the 12-step recovery philosophy of Alcoholics Anonymous, is the long-term recovery group. Unfortunately, these groups don't exist in every community, but the co-dependent who is ready to seek help can usually find it through a therapeutic relationship with a professional. Most professionals will spot the disorder quickly and hopefully offer a loving hand in the client's difficult journey back to the self.

Couples Work for Chemical Dependency

These are bits of advice to myself when working with couples with a CD problem. The guidelines apply if the couple is married or unmarried, living together or separately.

1. Most of these guidelines assume that the using member of the couple is in separate, primary treatment for CD (inpatient, outpatient, intensive outpatient) and that the couples work is being done *in addition* to the primary treatment for the user. If the user has not yet entered substance abuse treatment, your goal is to patiently help him or her get there.

2. If the CD member denies that his or her use is a problem, proceed carefully. At the first mention of substance abuse, don't jump on it. Separate and primary treatment for the user is one of the top goals for the counseling, but rushing it can be a mistake.

    Reason: The non-using partner's main agenda is the user's substance abuse, and the user knows it. If the counselor is too quick to join the chorus, the user may psychologically retreat or drop out.

3. With a couple, one of whom is chemically dependent, you usually have two identified patients.

    Reason: Being in a committed relationship with a chemically dependent person creates its own emotional, cognitive, and behavioral problems. For the relationship to improve, both partners need to recover. The non-user's job is to come to couples/family counseling and to attend meetings (Al-Anon, Nar-Anon, Co-Dependents Anonymous) while the user devotes him-/herself to treatment and meetings (Alcoholics Anonymous, Narcotics Anonymous, Cocaine Anonymous, etc.).

4. A common therapeutic error is for the counselor to align with the non-using partner.

    Reason: The counselor siding with the non-using partner, however subtle or unintentional, can impair or destroy the couples' treatment; the user may drop out. (Maintaining impartiality is even more important if the counselor is the same sex as the non-using partner.) Also, in this situation, the counselor may feel the frustration and anger toward the user that the partner feels; the user is likely to perceive this and react to the counselor in the same defensive way he or she reacts to the partner.

5. If the non-user drinks or uses other non-prescription drugs in any amount, ask for a commitment to abstinence during the period of the partner's treatment.

    Reason: If he or she continues use, it's a bad influence on the user, and it may cause conflicts.

6. Try to keep the responsibility about treatment and recovery with the using member, where it belongs, not with the non-using partner.

    Reason: When the co-dependent becomes too "responsible" (active or pushy) with ideas about the partner's recovery, it can trigger a power struggle around the substance use. The user may be determined to show the co-dependent partner that he or she is not in charge. If the non-user comes on too strong, at some point the user's personal pride and ego may kick in, making the user's resistance and denial even stronger.

7. It's usually a good idea to have a separate interview with each partner.

    Reason: You may get important information that doesn't come out in the couples sessions: contemplation of divorce, a past or current affair, reports of violence or other immediate danger, etc. If something important does emerge, try to make it a part of the conversation with the couple together (with his/her permission).

8. Once rapport and trust have been established with the couple (third or fourth session), ask about their sexual relationship.

    Reason: Sexual functioning is a troublesome area for many couples in recovery.

9. Find the strengths, love, and areas of agreement in their relationship. Don't stay overly focused on the drinking/drugging, especially if the using member is consistently angry and defensive about the topic.

    Reason: If they don't express reasons they are still together, and reasons to go through the hard work of recovery, the whole enterprise seems hopeless.

10. If the couple has children, talk about them. Remember their names and mention each one often.

    Reasons: (1) Some of the hard work of couples change is done because of their children, and (2) If the user is a devoted parent, this focus on the children could amplify his or her main reason to recover (to keep the family intact).

11. Start a couples group for recovery.

    Reason: Couples in early recovery need to hear from others who are currently going through the same issues or have gotten through them. Couples can sometimes absorb information from other couples better than from the counselor.

12. Inform the couple about the normal obstacles they may experience in their transition to sobriety: ''Walking on Eggshells,'' ''Cloud Nine,'' temporary emotional detachment by one or both members, ''Stinking Thinking,'' relapse, and the almost universal lack of trust around the use of alcohol or other drugs (see Families in Early Recovery).

    Reason: If these early recovery issues are defined as ''normal''—which they are—they may cause less of a crisis if they occur.

If you are an individual counselor and don't typically do family or couples counseling:

13. If you are doing individual counseling for chemical dependency and the person is in a committed relationship, have at least one session with your client and his or her partner together.

    Reason: The recovery of the CD person will take place within the married or committed relationship. You need a firsthand view of what this relationship is like.

14. If you are treating a single person who is a parent, at least one session should include the children, regardless of age (infant to adult).

    Reason: The love and guilt parents feel for their children is one of the most powerful motivators for abstinence and recovery. The best way to acknowledge that these relationships are important for recovery is by seeing the family members together.

Working With Chemical Dependency in Families: 21 Guidelines

1. Separate ("primary") treatment for the CD member (in addition to family counseling) is the first priority. If the problem user is not in inpatient or outpatient treatment for chemical dependency, the goal of the family counselor is to use the emotional leverage of the family to help the CD member enter primary treatment.

2. Define the relevant players in the drama. Who is concerned about the member's use of substances? Do not limit yourself to those in the home, to family members, to those in the immediate area, or to those who have frequent contact with the using member.

3. View your intervention as a *family* and *network* intervention, not as a one-on-one therapeutic assault on the using member. Work with those in the addicted person's life who are affected by, and willing to deal with, the substance issue.

Source: *DeskGallery Image Catalog*, Copyright 1994 by Dover Publications, Inc. Used with permission.

4. Avoid labels like "alcoholic" and "addict," unless the family uses these words first. Instead, say "problem use," "issues around drinking/drug use," "concern for his/her drinking." These euphemistic phrases will reduce resistance in the early stages of intervention.

5. If possible, let the family members do their own confronting of the CD member. Do not take that responsibility for them unless you have little choice.

6. Do not let the using member stop the family therapy by not showing up for the sessions. If he or she refuses to attend, have the session with the family members who will come.

7. In families in early recovery, the family's lack of trust toward the CD member is almost always present. Prepare the family to expect this very normal reaction. It usually takes months of abstinence before the family begins to trust the CD member to stay drug- and alcohol-free.

8. For an adult, having useful work to do is important for recovery. I don't trust recovery if the person has an empty life. If the adult CD member is not productively engaged (paid employment, volunteer work, child raising), this should be fully explored. For a recovering adolescent, school is the productive work.

Source: *DeskGallery Image Catalog*, Copyright 1994 by Dover Publications, Inc. Used with permission.

9. Recovery in a family can have a domino effect. A recovering teenager, for example, can trigger the treatment of a substance-abusing parent and vice versa. A recovering partner or spouse can trigger the partner's treatment. In a relationship between two people, I don't give the relationship much hope if one is serious about recovery and the other continues to use heavily.

10. Dual CD spouses: Their treatment should be separate. If they try to recover exactly alike, they will often relapse alike. Explain your position on this, and encourage separate treatment programs and separate AA/NA meetings.

11. Children motivate parents. A using parent, for example, may not try to get well until his or her relationship with the children is seriously threatened (especially by removal of the children from the home). If the using member is an adolescent or young adult living at home, parents will often take action with the adolescent to protect other children in the home, especially younger ones.

12. Always keep children in the forefront. How does the member's use affect them? Are there safety issues for the children? Who in the family is worried about the children? Gently motivate these people to speak up about the parent's chemical use to protect the children.

13. Watch for signs of dealing drugs by the adolescent user. Dealing is even more serious than use. If you suspect dealing, have a private conversation with the parent(s), without the identified patient. Encourage them to pay close attention, including phone surveillance and room searches (preferably in the presence of the adolescent).

Source: *DeskGallery Image Catalog*, Copyright 1994 by Dover Publications, Inc. Used with permission.

14. If you can't interrupt the co-dependent enabler's behavior, try to involve more people in the sessions (parents and/or siblings of the co-dependent, for example). These extended family members may be aware that the co-dependent is an enabler, and they can be a strong influence for change.

15. Take a firm stand with parents who are casual about their teenager driving an automobile if the parents are not certain that he or she is drug- and alcohol-free. Parents should suspend automobile privileges until they are sure about their child's abstinence. (This is not a private family issue; it's a public health issue.)

16. Be alert for harmful chemical use by all teenagers in the family, regardless of who the identified patient is.

17. Stay problem-centered. What are the problems as perceived by the family? What family or individual problems can be linked to the substance use?

18. See intervention as a process, not an event. A person's experiences, especially emotional ones, are cumulative; it may take several attempts before treatment is successful.

19. Where necessary, use emotional, family, and/or legal leverage. Most successfully recovering people were, in some way, coerced into treatment.

20. Support the family strengths and assets. All families, including chemically dependent ones, do some things well.

21. Just before termination with families who get better, ask, "In our family meetings, what has been helpful?" This feedback accelerates our learning as family counselors.

Family Counseling for Chemical Dependency: Summary

1. Include all children living in the home, whether the IP is a parent or a child. The welfare of children is often the strongest motivation for family recovery.

2. Always consider the social context within which recovery will take place: extended family, friends, other professional helpers. The more people involved in the counseling or in the counselor's thinking about the case, the more influences are available for therapeutic change.

3. Emphasize separate self-help recovery groups (Al-Anon, Nar-Anon, Alateen) for the family members. Some of the healing is done in the family, and some is best done away from the family members. Recovery groups are their long-term support for crises, adjustments to the family sobriety, and the other inevitable problems that will arise.

4. Pursue therapeutic goals based on the structural characteristics of the family. This is not an "anything goes" type of counseling where every session is a new beginning. Pursuing a definite direction based on the clinician's view of the family will provide more information and feedback than undirected pursuit of random issues.

5. When the IP is a child, try to bring parents together in an alliance with each other around the child's problems. Work on the parental relationship *while keeping the presenting CD problem child in focus*. This approach has several rationales:

    a. The CD is primary; it is not a secondary or symptomatic problem, one that can be put aside until later. Primary and separate treatment for the CD member is the first priority.

    b. How the parents—acting together—respond to the problem is an important factor in whether or not the young person abstains from alcohol or other drugs. Parental unity and consistency give the IP child a clear and convincing message about abstinence.

    c. We can assume that the parents' relationship is under stress and needs help, partly as a result of the child's chemical problem. Supporting the parents, who have the most influence on the family functioning, is the best short- and long-term benefit for the family and for the CD child.

    d. Improving the parental partnership is also prevention work, especially if younger siblings are in the home. If parents pull together and react successfully to the IP child, they may prevent a similar problem if a younger child later takes his or her turn at alcohol or other drug use or at other destructive behavior.

6. With a parent IP, primary emphasis should still be on the spouse/parent relationship. The rationales for this approach are

    a. The parental relationship has the greatest effect on how the recovering parent and the family fare during recovery.

    b. The non-CD parent has either been highly stressed and needs help from his or her partner or spouse or needs to explore his or her own issues of power, control, and co-dependence.

7. In a single-parent or divorced household, adult support for the parent should be the primary focus. The improved functioning of this person, whether he or she is newly sober or has a recovering child, is important for the family recovery.

APPENDIX A
RESEARCH REFERENCES

Abikoff, H., Hechtman, L., Klein, R., Weiss, G., Fleiss, K., Etcovitch, J., . . . Pollack, S. (2004). Symptomatic improvement in children with ADHD treated with long-term methylphenidate and multimodal psychosocial treatment. *Journal of the American Academy of Child and Adolescent Psychiatry, 43,* 802–811.

Alexander, J., Sexton, T. L., & Robbins, M. S. (2000). The developmental status of family therapy in family psychology intervention science. In H. Liddle, D. Santisteban, R. Leavant, & J. Bray (Eds.), *Family psychology intervention science.* Washington, DC: America Psychological Association.

Banner, L., & Anderson, R. (2007). Integrated Sildenafil and cognitive-behavioral sex therapy for psychogenic erectile dysfunction: A pilot study. *Journal of Sexual Medicine, 4,* 1117–1125.

Barbato, A., & D'Avanzo, B. (2008). Efficacy of couple therapy as a treatment for depression: A meta-analysis. *Psychiatric Quarterly, 79*(2), 121–132.

Barrett, P., Farrell, L., Dadds, M., & Boutler, N. (2005). Cognitive-behavioral family treatment of childhood obsessive-compulsive disorder: Long-term follow-up and predictors of outcome. *Journal of the American Academy of Child and Adolescent Psychiatry, 44,* 1005–1014.

Bressi, C., Manenti, S., Frongia, P., Porcellana, M., & Invernizzi, G. (2008). Systemic family therapy in schizophrenia: A randomized clinical trial of effectiveness. *Psychotherapy and Psychosomatics, 77,* 43–49.

Brinkley, A., Cullen, R., & Carr, A. (2002). Prevention of adjustment problems in child with asthma. In A. Carr (Ed.), *Prevention: What works with children and adolescents? A critical review of psychological prevention programmes for children, adolescents and their families* (pp. 222–248). London, England: Routledge.

Byrne, M., Carr, A., & Clarke, M. (2004). The efficacy of couples based interventions for panic disorder with agoraphobia. *Journal of Family Therapy, 26,* 105–125.

Carr, A. (2009). The effectiveness of family therapy and systemic interventions for child-focused problems. *Journal of Family Therapy, 31,* 3–74.

Cohen, J., Mannarino, A., & Deblinger, E. (2006). *Treating trauma and traumatic grief in children and adolescents.* New York, NY: Guilford Press.

Cook-Darzens, S., Doyen, C., & Mouren, M. C. (2008). Family therapy in the treatment of adolescent anorexia nervosa: Current research evidence and its therapeutic implications. *Eating and Weight Disorders–Studies on Anorexia Bulimia and Obesity, 13*(4), 157–170.

Crane, D. R. (2008). The cost-effectiveness of family therapy: A summary and progress report. *Journal of Family Therapy, 30,* 399–410.

Deas, D., & Clark, A. (2009). Current state of treatment for alcohol and other drug use disorders in adolescents. *Alcohol Research and Health, 32*(1), 76–82.

Diamond, G., Reis, B., Diamond, G., Siqueland, L., & Isaacs, L. (2002). Attachment based family therapy for depressive adolescents: A treatment development study. *Journal of the American Academy of Child and Adolescent Psychiatry, 41,* 1190–1196.

Dowell, K. A., & Ogles, B. M. (2010). The effects of parent participation on child psychotherapy outcome: A meta-analytic review. *Journal of Clinical Child and Adolescent Psychology, 39*(2), 151–162.

Farrell, E., Cullen, R., & Carr, A. (2002). Prevention of adjustment problems in children with diabetes. In A. Carr (Ed.), *What works with children and adolescents? A critical review of psychological interventions with children, adolescents and their families* (pp. 249–266). London, England: Routledge.

Fristad, M., Goldberg-Arnold, J., & Gavazzi, S. (2002). Multifamily psychoeducation groups (MFPG) for families of children with bipolar disorder. *Bipolar Disorder, 4*, 254–262.

Hays, P. (2001). *Addressing cultural complexities in practice: A framework for clinicians and counselors*. Washington, DC: American Psychological Association.

Heyne, D., & King, N. (2004). Treatment of school refusal. In P. Barrett & T. Ollendick (Eds.), *Handbook of interventions that work with children and adolescents: Prevention and treatment* (pp. 243–272). Chichester, England: Wiley.

Hinshaw, S., Klein, R., & Abikoff, H. (2007). Childhood attention-deficit hyperactivity disorder: Nonpharmacological treatments and their combination with medication. In P. Nathan & J. Gorman (Eds.), *A guide to treatments that work* (3rd ed., pp. 3–28). New York: Oxford University Press.

Jelalian, E., & Saelens, B. (1999). Empirically supported treatments in pediatric psychology: Pediatric obesity. *Journal of Pediatric Psychology, 24*, 223–248.

Jensen, P., Arnold, L., Swanson, J., Vitiello, B., Abikoff, H., & Greenhill, L. (2007). 3-year follow-up on the NIMH MTA Study. *Journal of the American Academy of Child and Adolescent Psychiatry, 46*, 989–1002.

Kissane, D., & Bloch, S. (2002). *Family focused grief therapy: A model of family-centered care during palliative care and bereavement*. Buckingham, England: Open University Press.

Le Grange, D., & Eisler, I. (2008). Family interventions in adolescent anorexia nervosa. *Child and Adolescent Psychiatric Clinics of North America, 18*(1), 159–173.

Le Grange, D., Crosby, R., Rathouz, P., & Leventhal, B. (2007). A randomized controlled comparison of family-based treatment and supportive psychotherapy for adolescent bulimia nervosa. *Archives of General Psychiatry, 64*, 1049–1056.

Letourneau, E. J., Henggeler, S. W., Schewe, P. A., Borduin, C. M., McCart, M. R., & Chapman, J. E. (2009). Multisystemic therapy for juvenile sexual offenders: 1-year results from a randomized effectiveness trial. *Journal of Family Psychology, 23*(1), 89–102.

Lewinsohn, P., Clarke, G., Hops, H., & Andrews, J. (1990). Cognitive behavioral group treatment of depression in adolescents. *Behavior Therapy, 21*, 385–401.

Liddle, H. A. (2002). *Multidimensional family therapy for adolescent cannabis users, Cannabis Youth Treatment (CYT) series*. (Vol. 5). Rockville, MD: Center for Substance Abuse Treatment, Substance Abuse and Mental Health Services Administration.

Liddle, H. A., Rowe, C. L., Dakof, G. A., & Henderson, C. E. (2009). Multidimensional family therapy for young adolescent substance abuse: Twelve-month outcomes of a randomized controlled trial. *Journal of Counseling and Clinical Psychology, 77*(1), 12–25.

Martire, L., Lustig, A., Schultz, R., Miller, G., & Helgeson, V. (2004). Is it beneficial to involve a family member? A meta-analysis of psychosocial interventions for chronic illness. *Health Psychology, 23*, 599–611.

Masters, W., & Johnson, V. (1970). *Human sexual inadequacy*. Boston, MA: Little-Brown.

Meston, C. (2006). Female orgasmic disorder: Treatment strategies and outcome results. In I. Goldstein, C. Meston, S. Davis, & A. Traish (Eds.), *Women's sexual function and dysfunction: Study, diagnosis, and treatment* (pp. 449–461). London, England: Taylor & Francis.

Miller, W., Wilbourne, P., & Hettema, J. (2003). What works? A summary of alcohol treatment outcome research. In R. Hester & W. Miller (Eds.), *Handbook of alcoholism treatment approaches: Effective alternatives* (3rd ed., pp. 13–63). Boston, MA: Allyn & Bacon.

Mousavi, R., Moradi, A., & Mahdavi, H. E. (2008). A study of effectiveness of structural family therapy approach in treatment of 6–12 years old children with separation anxiety disorder. *International Journal of Psychology, 43*, 3–4.

O'Farrell, T., & Fals-Stewart, W. (2003). Alcohol abuse. *Journal of Marital and Family Therapy, 29*, 121–146.

Patterson, G. (1976). *Living with children*. Champaign, IL: Research Press.

Pfammatter, M., Junghan, U., & Brenner, H. (2006). Efficacy of psychological therapy in schizophrenia: Conclusions from meta-analyses. *Schizophrenia Bulletin, 32*(1), 64–80.

Pitschel-Walz, G., Leucht, S., Bauml, J., Kissling, W., & Engel, R. R. (2001). The effect of family interventions on relapse and rehospitalization in schizophrenia: A meta-analysis. *Schizophrenia Bulletin, 27*(1), 73–92.

Renshaw, K., Steketee, G., & Chambless, D. (2005). Involving family members in the treatment of OCD. *Cognitive Behaviour Therapy, 34*, 164–175.

Reyno, S., & McGrath, P. (2006). Predictors of parent training efficacy for child externalizing behavior problems–A meta-analytic review. *Journal of Child Psychology and Psychiatry, 47*, 99–111.

Sanford, M., Boyle, M., McCleary, L., Miller, J., Steele, M., Duku, E., & Offord, D. (2006). A pilot study of adjunctive family psychoeducation in adolescent major depression: Feasibility and treatment effect. *Journal of the American Academy of Child and Adolescent Psychiatry, 45*, 386–395.

Schmidt, U., Lee, S., Beecham, J., Perkins, S., Treasure, J., Yi, I., . . . Eisler, I. (2007). A randomized controlled trial of family therapy and cognitive behavior therapy guided self-care for adolescents with bulimia nervosa and related disorders. *American Journal of Psychiatry, 164*, 591–598.

Smith, J., & Meyers, R. (2004). *Motivating substance abusers to enter treatment: Working with family members*. New York, NY: Guilford Press.

Snyder, D., Wills, R., & Grady-Fletcher, F. (1991). Long-term effectiveness of behavioral versus insight-oriented marital therapy: A 4-year follow-up study. *Journal of Consulting and Clinical Psychology, 59*, 138–141.

Stith, S. M., Rosen, K. H., & McCollum, E. E. (2003). Effectiveness of couples treatment for spouse abuse. *Journal of Marital and Family Therapy, 29*(3), 407–426.

Storch, E., Geffken, G., Merio, L., Mann, G., Kuke, D., Munson, M., . . . Goodman, W. (2007). Family-based cognitive-behavioral therapy for pediatric obsessive-compulsive disorder: Comparison of intensive and weekly approaches. *Journal of the American Academy of Child and Adolescent Psychiatry, 46*, 469–478.

Trowell, R., Joffe, I., Campbell, J., Clemente, C., Almqvist, F., Soininen, M., . . . Tsiantis, J. (2007). Childhood depression: A place for psychotherapy: An outcome study comparing individual psychodynamic psychotherapy and family therapy. *European Child and Adolescent Psychiatry, 16*, 157–167.

Weersing, V., & Brent, D. (2003). Cognitive behavioral therapy for adolescent depression. In A. Kazdin & J. Weisz (Eds.), *Evidence based psychotherapies for children and adolescents* (pp. 135–147). New York, NY: Guilford Press.

Wood, N., Crane, D., Schaalje, B., & Law, D. (2005). What works for whom: A meta-analytic review of marital and couples therapy in reference to marital distress. *American Journal of Family Therapy, 33*, 273–287.

Zagar, R. J., Busch, K. G., & Hughes, J. R. (2009). Empirical risk factors for delinquency and best treatments: Where do we go from here? *Psychological Reports, 104*, 279–308.

APPENDIX B
PROBLEMS AND PAGE NUMBERS

This is a list of some common presenting family problems, and problems in a family session, tied to page references in this book. These should help to narrow your search for something useful. Page numbers are in parentheses; terms in ***bold italic*** are techniques.

Problems	References in This Book
1. Parents have a problem teenager	Three Worlds of the Adolescent (73); Adolescent Problem Checklist (172); Managing Adolescents in Sessions (74); Young Person Problem (49–50); ***Strategic Predictions*** (139); ***Safe Rebellion*** (134); ***Guardrail*** (120); Substance-Abusing Adolescent (165, 171)
2. Parent(s) have an out-of-control young child	The Powerless Parent (65); Themes by Family Type (60–61); Single Parent Families (63); Parental Denial (69); Children Raise Adults (25)
3. Chemical dependency (CD) of a parent	CD Section (149–178); Two-Parent, CD Parent (164); CD Single Parent (167); Tips for CD Families (176)
4. Strong family resistance	Family Resistance (80–82)
5. Parental denial	Parental Denial (69); Adolescent Checklist (172); ***Strategic Predictions*** (139)
6. Disruptive child(ren) during family session	Managing Adolescents in Sessions (74); The Powerless Parent (65); Child or Young Person Problem (49–50); Children Raise Adults (25)
7. Absent family members	Recruitment (37); Missing Members (38–39)
8. Enmeshed parent/child	Parent-Child Enmeshment (67); ***Relabeling*** (133)
9. Family just sits there, waiting for you to do something. (So do something.)	***Alter Ego*** (108); ***Chair Work*** (111); ***Drawings*** (115–116); ***New Talk*** (126); ***Sculpting*** (135–136); ***Reflecting Team*** (129); ***Toybox*** (140); Techniques Section (106–142)
10. Parents have open (or hidden) conflict	***Guardrail*** (120); ***Parents' Childhood*** (128); ***Reflecting Team*** (129); ***Worried Child*** (141); "Split" Parenting (68)
11. Child custody disputes	Don't do it. Custody is a legal issue and must be settled by a judge in a courtroom, with metal detectors, bailiffs, and armed guards.

GLOSSARY FOR FAMILY COUNSELING

Alliance: Two or more persons in a family joined together by common endeavor, experience, interests, attitudes, or values. A natural alliance is formed, for example, between the two teenagers on the swim team, the two most academic children, or the mother and son who have similar temperaments.

Boundary: The psychological demarcation between individuals or subsystems in a family. Examples: the boundary separating parents from children, mother from daughter, father from children, older siblings from younger children, etc.

Centrality: A communication process during a family session in which the counselor is the communication switchboard; everyone talks to the counselor rather than to each other.

Chemical Dependency (CD): CD exists in a person who continues to use legal or illegal mood-altering substances in spite of repeated problems caused by their use.

Coalition: Two or more family members joined together *against* one or more other members; it usually results in splits and alienation in the family. (Compare **Alliance**)

Complementarity: A repetitive pattern between two or more people whose behaviors fit together in a dynamic balance. Examples: A spouse becomes passive when his or her mate becomes aggressive; a child becomes silent to the degree that he or she is quizzed by a parent or to the degree that one parent is lenient toward the child and the other is strict.

Disengaged family: A type of family in which members fail to form and maintain enduring relationships with each other. The opposite extreme is **Enmeshed.**

Enabling: Protecting the using member from the consequences of his or her substance use.

Enactment: A real-life conversation or interaction between two or more family members during a family session. It may be prompted by the counselor for a particular purpose such as facilitating the parents talking to each other to make decisions or prompting one member to express feelings or thoughts directly to another member.

Enmeshed: A type of relationship characterized by smothering closeness, where two or more members are so involved in each other's business and emotional life that the individuals don't have room to develop and grow. For example, one or both parents may be so protective and involved in their child's life that the child cannot develop autonomy.

Family: An interdependent group or pair of significant others who are important to one another because of blood relationships, emotional involvements, legal ties, common goals, or financial security and who have enough of a past together to suggest a future. A broader, systems-based definition would include the group from which a person draws support and may include anyone who could be helpful in solving problems.

Family Hierarchy: The top-down power structure in a family. Parents are usually more powerful (and responsible) than children, and older children are more powerful than younger children. Grandparents and other extended family members can occupy different places in the hierarchy.

Family Mapping: The technique of using symbols to draw the counselor's impressions of the family structure: which members are close or distant with each other, who is aligned with whom, who has the apparent power and influence, and who is in conflict with whom. A family map differs from a genogram in that it is not historical or factual; it represents the current clinical opinions of the counselor.

Focus: The counselor's task of keeping the family on the subject, without becoming intrusive or rigid. Focus is sometimes difficult because of the many feelings and issues present at any given time.

Hypothesis: A guess, or ''hunch,'' about what is occurring in a family or between certain members that may be contributing to the problems. Forming a hypothesis usually precedes making a therapeutic intervention.

Induction: The counselor's loss of objectivity; being ''sucked in.'' Largely outside the counselor's awareness, the counselor is ''boxed in and neutralized'' by the strong pull of the family system.

Intervention: Any professional action taken to improve behavior in an individual or group.

Joining: Establishing rapport and connection with the family to form a working relationship. The counselor gains admittance into the family by acknowledging and promoting the family's strengths, by respecting their hierarchy and values, and by confirming each member's feelings of self-worth.

Network: The influential people in a person's life, including professional service providers.

Power: The amount of influence a family member has; the ability to get others in the family to do what the empowered person wants him or her to do.

Recovery: A program of personal growth and abstinence from addictive substances.

Relapse: A temporary return to the use of substances by an individual who is in recovery.

Segmenting: The counselor divides the family into smaller groups for a particular purpose. Example: getting the parents' permission to have their children leave the session so the parents can make a private decision together about their parenting. It has several purposes, in this case to delineate a clearer boundary between the parents and children.

Strategic Family Therapy: A model of therapy that has several similarities to the Structural approach (see next item) but that differs by focusing more on the specific interactions in the family that maintain the symptomatic behavior. The goals of strategic therapy are to eliminate the presenting problem by changing the sequences, the rules, and the meaning of family interactions.

Structural Family Therapy: A model of therapy, developed by Salvadore Minuchin and his associates, that attempts to change the power, boundaries, and alliances in a family in ways that make the presenting problems less necessary.

Subsystem: A smaller component of a system. For example, the parents' relationship is a subsystem; the siblings' relationship; mother-son, father-daughter, and so forth.

System: A group of elements and the way they function together to create a unified whole. In family terms, it's the unit created by the behavior of family members as they strive to maintain organization, stability, and balance. The systems orientation assumes that an individual's behavior is the result, and cause, of relationship patterns within the family or within larger systems such as school, workplace, or community.

Task: Between-session homework for the family or for one or more members. Tasks can begin a change in a family's home environment; homework also keeps the family connected to the counselor between visits.

Therapeutic Theme: The counselor's broad goal, plan, or roadmap, which guides his or her interventions in a family. Example: interrupting the father-son enmeshment by strengthening the bond and teamwork between the parents.

Unbalancing: Interrupting established patterns in a family by a strategic use of the counselor's power and influence. Examples: temporarily joining with the more silent, passive member in an argument; encouraging the more detached parent to speak directly to the children while the more involved parent ''listens.''

Use of Self: The ways in which the counselor uses his or her personality and communication style to impact the family.

RECOMMENDED READINGS

Anderson, C., & Stewart, S. (1983). *Mastering resistance: A practical guide to family therapy.* New York, NY: Guilford Press.

Andersen, T. (Ed.) (1991). *The reflecting team.* New York, NY: W. W. Norton.

Beavers, W. (1985). *Successful marriage: A family systems approach to couples therapy.* New York, NY: W. W. Norton.

Bepko, C. (1985). *The responsibility trap: A blueprint for treating the alcoholic family.* New York, NY: Free Press.

Bowlby, J. (1988). *A secure base: Clinical application of attachment theory.* London, England: Routledge.

Boyd-Franklin, N., & Bry, B. (2000). *Reaching out in family therapy: Home-based, school, and community interventions.* New York, NY: Guilford Press.

Carter, E., & McGoldrick, M. (1999). *The expanded family life cycle: A framework for family therapy* (3rd ed.). Boston, MA: Allyn & Bacon.

Coleman, D. (Ed.). (1985). *Failures in family therapy.* New York, NY: Guilford Press.

Dattilio, F. M. (1998). *Case studies in couple and family therapy. Systemic and cognitive perspectives.* New York, NY: Guilford Press.

Dattilio, F. M., & Reinecke, M. (1996). *Casebook of cognitive-behavior therapy with children and adolescents.* New York, NY: Guilford Press.

de Shazer, S. (1988). *Clues: Investigating solutions in brief therapy.* New York, NY: Norton.

de Shazer, S. (1991). *Putting differences to work.* New York, NY: Norton.

de Shazer, S., Dolan, Y., Korman, H., Trepper, T., Berg, I. K., & McCollum, E. (2007). *More than miracles: The state of the art of solution-focused brief therapy.* Binghamton, NY: Hayworth Press.

Diamond, J. (2000). *Narrative means to sober ends: Treating addiction and its aftermath.* New York, NY: Guilford Press.

Edwards, J. T. (1990). *Treating chemically dependent families: A practical systems approach for professionals.* Center City, MN: Hazelden.

Fishman, H. C. (1988). *Treating troubled adolescents: A family therapy approach.* New York, NY: Basic Books.

Fontes, L. A. (2008). *Interviewing clients across cultures.* New York, NY: Guilford Press.

Gil, E. (1994). *Play in family therapy.* New York, NY: Guilford Press.

Goldenberg, I., & Goldenberg, H. (1980). *Family therapy: An overview.* Monterey, CA: Brooks/Cole.

Goldner, V. (1985). Feminism and family therapy. *Family Process, 24,* 31–47.

Greenan, D. E., & Tunnell, G. (2002). *Couples therapy with gay men: A family systems model for healing relationships.* New York, NY: Guilford Press.

Haley, J. (1980). *Leaving home: The therapy of disturbed young people.* New York, NY: McGraw-Hill.

Haley, J. (1987) *Problem solving therapy* (2nd ed.). San Francisco, CA: Jossey-Bass.

Haley, J., & Hoffman, L. (1968). *Techniques of family therapy.* New York, NY: Basic Books.

Hays, P. (2001). *Addressing cultural complexities in practice: A framework for clinicians and counselors.* Washington, DC: American Psychological Association.

Hoffman, L. (1981). *Foundations of family therapy.* New York, NY: Basic Books.

Johnson, V. (1990). *Everything you need to know about chemical dependence.* Center City, MN: Hazelden.

Kaufman, E. (1985). *Substance abuse and family therapy.* New York, NY: Grune & Stratton.

Krestan, J., & Bepko, C. (1980). The problem of fusion in the lesbian relationship. *Family Process, 19,* 277–289.

Laird, J., & Green, R. J. (1996). *Lesbians and gays in couples and families: A handbook for therapists.* San Francisco, CA: Jossey-Bass.

Lemieux, C. M. (2009). *Offenders and substance abuse: Bringing the family into focus.* Alexandria, VA: American Correctional Association.

Linesch, D. (1993). *Art therapy with families in crisis: Overcoming resistance through nonverbal expression.* New York, NY: Brunner/Mazel.

Lipchik, E. (2002). *Beyond technique in solution-focused therapy.* New York, NY: Guilford Press.

Madanes, C. (1981). *Strategic family therapy.* San Francisco, CA: Jossey-Bass.

McGoldrick, M., Pearce, J., & Giordano, J. (2007). *Ethnicity and family therapy* (3rd ed.). New York, NY: Guilford Press.

Minuchin, S. (1974). *Families and family therapy.* Cambridge, MA: Harvard University Press.

Minuchin, S., & Fishman, H. C. (1981). *Family therapy techniques.* Cambridge, MA: Harvard University Press.

Minuchin, S., Nichols, M. P., & Lee, W. Y. (2006). *Assessing families and couples: From symptom to system.* Boston, MA: Allyn & Bacon.

Morawetz, A., & Walker, G. (1984). *Brief therapy with single-parent families.* New York, NY, Brunner/Mazel.

Nichols, M. P. (2010). *Family therapy concepts and methods* (9th ed.). Boston, MA: Allyn & Bacon.

Rawson, R. A., Obert, J. L., McCann, M. J. (1991). Critical Issues in Cocaine Recovery. *Addiction and Recovery, 11,* 29–33.

Satir, V. (1964). *Conjoint family therapy.* Palo Alto, CA: Science and Behavior Books.

Satir, V. M., & Baldwin, M. (1983). *Satir step by step: A guide to creating change in families.* Palo Alto, CA: Science and Behavior Books.

Sells, S. (1998). *Treating the tough adolescent: A family-based, step-by-step guide.* New York, NY: Guilford Press.

Sexton, T. L., Kinser, J. C., & Hanes, C. W. (2008). Beyond a single standard: Levels of evidence approach for evaluating marriage and family therapy research and practice. *Journal of Family Therapy, 30,* 386–398.

Stanton, M., & Todd, T. (1982). *The family therapy of drug abuse and addiction.* New York, NY: Guilford Press.

Stith, S., & Rosen, K. (2003). Effectiveness of couples treatment for spouse abuse. *Journal of Marital and Family Therapy, 29*(3), 407–426.

Taibbi, R. (2007). *Doing family therapy* (2nd ed.). New York, NY: Guilford Press.

Weeks, G., & LAbate, L. (1982). *Paradoxical psychotherapy.* New York, NY: Brunner/Mazel.

Wegscheider, S. (1981). *Another chance: Hope and health for the alcoholic family.* Palo Alto, CA: Science and Behavior Books.

Whitaker, C. A., & Bumberry, W. M. (1988). *Dancing with the family: A symbolic experiential approach.* New York, NY: Brunner/Mazel.

White, M., & Epston, D. (1990). *Narrative means to therapeutic ends.* New York, NY: Norton.

Worden, M. (2003). *Family therapy basics* (3rd ed.). Pacific Grove, CA: Brooks/Cole Publishing Co.

ABOUT THE AUTHOR

John T. Edwards, PhD, an Approved Supervisor in the American Association for Marriage and Family Therapy (AAMFT), has conducted and supervised family therapy for over 30 years. He has served as director of counseling in a family health center, clinical director of an inpatient family care program, private practitioner in marriage and family therapy, and co-founder of a learning center for family therapy. John has conducted over a thousand family therapy training events in the United States and Canada. He is author of *Treating Chemically Dependent Families: A Practical Systems Approach for Professionals*, published by Hazelden (1990), and is currently a private trainer and consultant living in Durham, North Carolina. In his spare time, John enjoys nature and studying Eastern philosophies and practices and wholistic approaches to wellness.

Index

Adolescents
  managing in sessions (75)
  substance abuse (175)
  Substance Abuse Checklist (176)
  Three Worlds of the (74)
Alliance, definition (191)
Alter Ego (111)
Assumptions of the systems
  approach (5)

Basic tools (45)
Bedrock Beliefs (23)
Blended families (63)
Blended families (scenarios) (65)
Boundary, definition (191)
Brief Network Intervention
  (112–113)

Cause and Effect in Systems (11)
Centrality (99, 100, 191)
Chair Work (114)
Chemical Dependency
  Adolescent (175)
  Adolescent Checklist (176)
  Assumptions (157)
  CD Single Parent (171)
  Co-Dependency (177)
  Common Patterns (167–172)
  Couples Work (178–179)
  Definition (155)
  Drugs of abuse (156)
  Disease concept (158)
  Early recovery (165)
  Family Assessment (160)
  Golden Years Trap (173–174)
  Good Kid/Bad Kid (170)
  Identification of (160)
  Indirect signs of (159)
  Recovery (162)
  Recovery, stages of (163)
  Recovery Plan (164)
  Relapse (166)
  Single Parent–CD Teen (172)
  Summary (182)
  21 Guidelines (180–181)
  Treatment of (161)
  Two-Parent–CD Parent (168)
  Two-Parent–CD Teen (169)
  Working with Chemical
    Dependency in Families
    (154–182)
Child care, residential (18, 20)
Child Diagnosis (72–73)
Child identified patient (50–51)
Children Raise Adults (25)
Circle Method (118)
Circular Questions (115)
Clinical Suggestions (54–56)
Closed Families (79)
Coalition, definition (191)

Cocaine Addiction (163)
Code of Ethics (13)
Colleague Consultation (101)
Colleague Teamwork (116–117)
Complementarity, definition (191)
Conducting the Initial Interview
  (41–43)
Counseling Style (91–93)
Counselor Mistakes (94)
Counselor Successes (95)
Counselor Self-Disclosure (96)
Counselors
  Centrality (100)
  Inexperienced/Experienced (88)
  Mistakes (94)
  Review Lists for (103–106)
  Self-Disclosure (96)
  Session Checklist (58)
  Style (91–93)
  Successes (95)
  Use of Self (99)
  Whose Family Stuff Is It? (98)
Couples counseling (52–53)
Couples Work (76–77)
Couples Work–CD (178–179)
Cultural Sensitivity (14–15)

Department of Social Services
  (18, 20)
Difficult Parents (71)
Disengaged, definition (191)
Divorced Parents (62)
Draw-a-Dream (119)
Drawings (118–119)

Enactment (45, 191)
Enmeshed family, definition (191)
Ethics, Code of (13)
Experience Is Primary (28)
Experienced Counselors (88)
Expert Colleague (117)

Family, definition (192)
Family Counseling
  Blended (63, 65)
  in different settings (18–21)
  Family types (61–62)
  Fear of (87)
  Forms of (17)
  General Guidelines (47–49)
  Initial Interview (41–43)
  Learning family work (3)
  Recruiting families (38–40)
  Research (32–36)
  Resistance (81–83)
  Session-by-Session (57)
  Session Checklist (58)
  Style (91–93)
  Suggestions by Setting (20–21)
  Supervising (102)

  Too Brief Family Counseling (30)
  Uses of Family Counseling (16)
  Why Family Work? (4)
Family Drawings (118–119)
Family Mapping (120–121)
Family Questions (122)
Family Resistance (81–83)
First Interview Tips (44)
Fishbowling (151)
Focus (48, 192)
Forms of Family Work (17)
Four Basic Tools (45–46)
Friends as Family (80)

General Clinical Suggestions
  (54–56)
General Guidelines (47–49)
Getting a Grip on the Obvious (27)
Glossary (191–193)
Golden Years Trap (173–174)
Guardrail (123)
Guidelines, couples (76–77)

Hospitals (19)
Hypothesis (192)

Induction
  Explanation of (106, 192)
  Worksheet (97)
Inexperienced Counselors (88)
In-Home Services (19)
Initial Interview (41–43)
Inner/Outer Circle (151–152)

Joining (48, 192)

Learning Family Counseling (3)
Levels of Systems (9–10)
Lists for Family Counselors
  (103–106)

Managing Adolescents (75)
Mapping (120–121)
Marital issues (52–53)
Mental health agencies (18, 21)
MIGS Sheet (124–126)
MIGS Sheet, blank (127–128)
Missing members (39–40)
Mistakes (94)
Multiple Family Groups (148–152)

Neglected Relationships (26)
New Talk (129)
Novice's First Interview (89–90)

Paradox (130)
Parent-Child Enmeshment (68)
Parental Denial (70)

Parental Mindset (67)
Parenting, "Split" (69)
Parent's Childhood (131)
Positive Reframing (134–135)
Power, definition (192)
Powerless Parent (66)
Private Practice (19)
Problem Reframing (133)
Problems and Page Numbers
    (190)

Questions and Answers (107)

Rationales (22)
Recommended Reading
    (195–197)
Recruiting Families (38–40)
Reflecting Colleague (116–117)
Reflecting Team (132)
Reframing (133–135)
Relabeling (136)
Research on Family Work
    (32–36)
Research References (184–187)
Resistance, family (81–83)
ReSPECT Sequence (41–43)
Rule of 20/20 (27, 99)

Safe Rebellion (137)
Schools (19)
Sculpting and Movement
    (138–139)
Segmenting (45–46, 193)
Self, Use of (99)
Self-Disclosure, counselor (96)
Separated/divorced parents (62)
Session-by-Session (57)
Session Checklist (58)
Sexual Assessment (53)
Sibling Talk (140)
Single Parent Family (61)
Skills, summary of (145)
Strategic Child Assessment (141)
Strategic Family Therapy (193)
Strategic Predictions (142)
Strengths, search for (49)
Structural Family Therapy (193)
Student Colleague (117)
Style, counseling (91–93)
Suggestions by Setting (20–21)
Summary of Techniques (145)
Supervising Family Work (102)
Systems Orientation
    in Concepts (8)
    in Practice (7)
    in Theory (6)
    Levels of Systems (9–10)
    System, definition of (6, 193)
    Systems-Oriented Program (12)

Task (46, 193)
Techniques (110–145)
Temporary Co-Therapist (116)
Termination (56)
Theory of Change (24)
Therapeutic Themes (61–62, 193)
Three Worlds of Adolescents (74)
Too Brief Family Counseling (30)
Too Many Variables (29)
Toybox (143)
Traveling Pairs of Concepts (31)
Trust Exercise (152)

Unbalancing (46, 193)
Use of Self (99, 193)
Uses of Family Counseling (16)
Using Techniques (110)

Who's Missing? (152)
Whose Family Stuff Is It? (98)
Why Family Work? (4)
Worried Child (144)